# *Thinking About Web Accessibility*

# Thinking About Web Accessibility

Stumbling Blocks and Stepping Stones

to Global Use

H ROBERT KING

ISBN 978-1-79478-396-6

Printed in the USA

For my wife and daughter, who help me every day to take courage and be kind.

# Preface

When I started working with web accessibility, it felt like a virtual wasteland – few recognized the need and even fewer knew how to achieve it. In those days, the *World Wide Web* was still in its infancy, and "web developers", as we called ourselves, were frequently confused by, or dismissive of, the idea that those living with impairments were using the web – some even made outrageous claims like "blind people don't use the web". I would like to say those days are long gone, and they are going away for more and more people every day, but they are not gone.

Today web accessibility is not as foreign a concept to as many as it once was. That's not to say every product person, designer, content writer, and engineer knows it exists, why it's important, or how to design or code for it – but it's at least on the radar of a few more people. Even so, there are few resources that combine the various aspects of web accessibility in a single resource, which is, in part, why this book exists.

Compared to all those years ago, the amount of information available now is massive, but in some ways there is still a dearth of information about the topic. In most cases, each writer approaches it from their angle – offering specific design tips or development advice, and in most cases that advice contains bias introduced by industry trends like tools used or styles of the day. In many cases, the bias introduced, even though unintentional, is counterproductive and harms the very thing people are trying to create.

Not only is the advice those in our industry receive, or give, a mix of approaches, trends, and bias, but it also seldom comes from affected users. Seldom do designers responsible for designing interfaces live with impairments they must accommodate, or even talk to users with impairments, and the number of engineers building interfaces that live with the impairments their code must address or talk to users who benefit from the accessibility or suffer from the lack of it, is more limited still. Engineering is not only predominately white and male, it's predominately unimpaired – and therefore ableist – as well.

This book will, hopefully, introduce a few new ways of looking at accessibility in general, and accessibility in design and development in particular, as well as give some solid patterns – stepping stones – that can be adapted to meet the needs of your organization when creating accessible interfaces. The advice here is intended to cover the greatest possible range of users in its focus on inclusion, because the web is for *everyone*, *everywhere*, regardless of how fast or reliable their network connection is, regardless of how powerful their device is, regardless of what platform they use, and regardless of what impairment they bring to bear on the interface.

Finally, although this work is authored by one person, it did not happen in a vacuum. Along the way, I have had the benefit of working with amazing designers and engineers nearly as passionate as I am about providing accessible user interfaces, each at a different point in their own journey. There are, of course, several friends, each deserving of my gratitude, who helped immensely with the creation of this work, reading the original manuscript and offering their critique of my writing style, offering their perspectives on topics within the subject based on their years of experience in developing interfaces, and offering encouragement that helped me fight the monsters under the bed that I live with every day. The perspectives of *Jason*, *Steve*, *Starr*, *Prem*, and *Eric* were especially helpful.

Finally, those familiar with my writing know I usually sign off with the simple sentence "happy coding." As we'll learn, accessibility is about so much more than coding – it's about creating interfaces that everyone can use, so I'll instead end this foreword with this word of encouragement as you begin your exploration of web accessibility –

Happy exploring.

*H Robert King*
*September 2019*

# Introduction

Many of the topics in web accessibility can be made highly technical and complex; however, the intention in this work is to challenge that pattern and make the work itself understandable. To accomplish this, there are practices that have been followed.

First, specific language has been used to identify the fundamental pieces of user interaction, specifically, the words *interface* and *component*. In this work, a component is the smallest coherent interactive part of a web page or application. An interface, on the other hand, is a coherent interaction point in a web page or application. It is quite possible, for an interface to be composed of multiple components; however, a component may only be composed of HTML, CSS, and JavaScript.

Second, there are several symbols used throughout this book to highlight specific textual elements. The guide below gives an explanation of what the symbols indicate.

☞       A point of interest

⁎⁎      A stepping stone

☠       A stumbling block


▢       Container interface

★       Informational interface

✎       Input interface

⚓       Navigational interface

☝  The component uses JavaScript to *enhance* the experience.

⚠  The component *requires* JavaScript to function properly.

Finally, while creating an accessible interface is not impossible using tools other than the tools common across nearly all user-agents, it can be made considerably more difficult when certain tools, such as JavaScript frameworks like *Angular* or *React*, are used. To simplify what is an often complex process, the code for the design pattern samples will employ only the minimum HTML, CSS, and native JavaScript and will use Progressive Enhancement. In cases where customized code is required, such as ReST API integration to retrieve data, no code is provided.

# Table of Contents

# 1
# Understanding Accessibility

In order to understand what accessibility is and why it is important, it is first necessary to understand its opposite, disability. There are several models that might be used to understand disability, for example, in an *economic* model, disability can be understood as an economic problem tied to the degree to which a person is productive and the economic consequences for the individual and the greater community. In a *community* model, disability might be understood within the context of a community that derives a portion of its identity from the shared experience, an understanding that is particularly common in communities where the shared experience shapes the individual's daily reality, such as in the deaf community where the shared sign language shapes their reality. Disability might also be understood using a *medical* model, a perspective that considers only solutions or remedies, seeing individuals to be cured. Disability can also be understood, and often is understood, using a *charity* model, a perspective that regards people as unfortunate and in need of assistance. It should be noted that this last approach, one that often confuses sympathy for empathy, is particularly disliked by many who are identified as unfortunate and in need of assistance.

The approach taken in this resource combines multiple perspectives, regarding disability as a function of impairment *and environment*, often created by inadequacy in society, and something for which there are functional solutions. Although this perspective can downplay the embodied aspects of disability or encourage innovation that primarily benefits the innovator rather than those it is intended to help, it need not lead directly there, and in fact is unlikely to if our understanding is firmly grounded in the difference between *disability* and *impairment*.

## Accessibility, Impairment, and Disability

It is often difficult to identify what someone means when they use the word disability, because even though it is used frequently in conversation, how it is defined varies from one context to another. For example, in Australia and the UK, a person is considered to have a disability under the relevant statute if they have a physical or mental impairment that has a "substantial" and "long-term" negative effect on their ability to complete normal daily activities, while in the US a person is considered to have a disability under the relevant statute if they have a record of a physical or mental impairment that substantially limits one or more major life activities *or they are regarded as having such an impairment*.

The World Health Organization, or WHO, identifies a person as suffering from a disability when they have a problem in bodily function or structure, otherwise known as an impairment, difficulty completing a task due to an impairment, or a problem in involvement in life situations due to an impairment. Under this definition, disability is a "complex phenomenon" that reflects the *interaction* between a person's body, or mind, and the environment.

☞ Neither the severity of the impairment, activity limitation, or participation restriction nor its duration is important in the WHO definition.

Hidden in all definitions is the idea that in order for an impairment to be a disability is the interaction with the environment, even when that environment is defined differently, be it "normal daily activities", "major life activities", or "life situations". Hypothetically, a deaf person wouldn't be considered to have a disability if their normal daily activities did not involve sound, as the loss of hearing would not have a negative or limiting effect, and the same holds true of other impairments.

Here is the crux of web accessibility, *it is the creation or alteration of an environment in such a way that the limitations and negative effects that might come about due to impairment are eliminated.* When we talk about web accessibility we must not consider it something to be added, but rather the choice to not add obstacles, either through design or the technologies and techniques used in construction.

## Accessibility Myths

Over the years, when people have talked about web accessibility, several arguments against it have come up. Although it might be the case that these arguments come from well-intentioned people, that belief is becoming less and less tenable. What follows is a list of myths and the reality with which they are confronted. While this list is not nearly exhaustive, it does contain the most common myths heard.

## Accessibility is a cost with no benefit

This general myth comes in a few different flavors, and like the preceding myths, this is a serious misunderstanding of the data. Sometimes the myth takes the form that there is some benefit, but only to those users who are blind; however, neither of these forms is accurate.

First, there are demonstrable benefits to Search Engine Optimization, or SEO, that come about as part of resolving accessibility issues. Two of the most significant accessibility practices, providing text alternatives for media, like audio, images, and video, and providing a structure, specifically through the use of headings, have significant benefits to SEO.

Second, accessibility practices are also good usability practices and improve overall experience, benefitting all users and often lead to increases in revenue and reductions in costs, especially costs associated with customer support.

## An accessible website is boring or ugly

This myth was once reality-adjacent. In the early days of the World Wide Web, there were a number of technological limitations. The lingua franca of the web, HTML, was not as semantic as it now is and there were few realistic layout options, leaving many UI engineers to lay out a page using a table and forever altering the hierarchy, and scripting was almost always written to run in a single user-agent. The technological situation today, decades later, is significantly improved.

Historically, there has been a tendency to abandon hope that a good solution exists, one that is both accessible and beautiful or exciting, and instead offer a text-only or "accessible site" as an option. This idea seemed to offer the perfect solution; however, as found in many other instances, "separate but equal" is not really equal. Pursing this course of action, relegating accessibility to a secondary web page or website, will not only be likely to offend a number of users, it is likely to be illegal in more than one jurisdiction.

☞ In November of 2018, the US Department of Transportation assessed the Scandinavian Airlines System $200,000, two hundred thousand US dollars, in civil penalties for using the "separate but equal" approach to accessibility. The agency also directed the Scandinavian Airlines System to "cease and desist" in the consent order.

Still, the reality is that accessibility does place constraints on design. There can be issues raised with typography, color, and contrast that may leave an artist without their first choice in a few areas; however, designers can easily work within those constraints to create beautiful, interactive interfaces, as we have seen a number of times.

## Accessibility is not a requirement for my role or my organization

In this myth, the thought typically goes along the line that accessibility is not *my* concern because accessibility is the concern of someone else, someone in another role, usually either the designer or developer. Some argue that accessibility is not a concern for *my organization* because it only applies to other types of organizations, like government agencies.

First, as will be shown in following, similarly themed myths, accessibility is the concern of everyone in an organization, across all roles, including designer and developer. Second, not only should everyone in an organization share responsibility for accessibility, the idea that accessibility is not required for *all* organizations, from private industry to government agencies, is increasingly being abandoned. In the US alone, legal responsibility for providing accessible interfaces is being assigned to private organizations, not just public sector bodies and those organizations that receive or have received funds from the federal government where it has been a requirement for more than two decades under Section 508 and Section 504. Further, cases to demonstrate that an organization cannot shield itself behind a vendor who provides a web page or website are beginning to make their way through the courts.

# Web accessibility is necessarily expensive and time-consuming

Web accessibility is often seen as expensive and time-consuming because in the past, testing and evaluating for accessibility was performed either immediately before release or shortly after release, after all design, content, and coding had been completed. While there are good reasons for this approach, the primary one being that each piece can be accessible and the resulting mixture still have issues if each does not also consider the interplay between the constituent parts, this approach has been abandoned in general software development as cost estimates for fixing defects are one-tenth *if the resolution occurs in the previous step.* The test-at-the-end approach takes the position that waiting for problems and fixing them when they appear is easier than, or just as easy as, analyzing and predicting failures or risk points, but the industry has long known that waiting to fix defects is extremely costly.

Making the argument that accessibility is expensive and time-consuming also ignores the understanding that the associated costs are often not entirely recurring expenses but rather investments in staff who learn to design and build accessible interfaces through practice. Once the good habits associated with Introspective Design and writing Semantic HTML are established, the future costs associated with using those habits to build accessible interfaces is significantly reduced as defects that aren't identified until the end of the process are reduced or eliminated entirely, and the good news is that the cost associated with the initial training needed, the investment required to gain those good habits, is also negligible.

## Accessibility is about adding alt text

This myth has several companion myths, each proposing what accessibility is about. Other myths declare accessibility to be about closed captioning, WAI-ARIA, web standards, CSS styling, or removing a list of problem technology like tables, JavaScript, Flash, image maps, or frames. Another myth like it says that accessibility is about following the *Web Content Accessibility Guidelines* and that compliance fixes all the major issues.

Web accessibility, however, is not about any of the items on the lists and fixing all the big issues does not mean a web page or website is accessible. For example, even if there is an audio component on the page that does not mean the page is accessible when a screen reader is used. Even if an alternative is provided for the media, there still may be issues with the accuracy of the alternative or even discoverability, and there is no way to play an audio clip or read its alternative if the user does not know it is there or has no way to access it.

## Automated evaluation tools are enough

One of the biggest myths, especially amongst engineers, is that automated testing and evaluation tools are enough, or at least enough to ensure compliance with the *Web Content Accessibility Guidelines*.

As is revealed in the Testing section, automated testing can cover approximately twenty-five percent of the Success Criteria of the *Web Content Accessibility Guidelines*. Nearly three in four items in the guidelines cannot be tested using automated means, those items require human evaluation. Further, there are a number of potential issues for which no Success Criterion has been written, issues which a human will be likely to identify such as if the styling rules create a strobe effect when hover styles interact with other styles.

## We already fixed our site for accessibility, so we're finished

Once all design, development, and testing is completed and a web page or website has been released, even if accessibility has been included as part of the process, it is tempting to believe the job to be completed and fall victim to the myth that we fixed the accessibility.

Unfortunately, pages and sites change, and assistive technology changes, and user behavior changes. Each of these, from enhancements to behavior, can impact the accessibility of a page or website. The only way accessibility for a page or site has been solved is if it no longer exists.

## The disabled don't use computers

This is probably the oldest myth, but it is simply not true, and in fact becomes less true every day as computers are increasingly injected in everyday life. In fact, if we simply consider the computers in smartphones, we can easily dismiss this myth, as nearly half of all people over the age of 15 use smartphones.

## The disabled are not my customers

This is an updated version of "we don't sell to people with disabilities" or "that's not our demographic". With the rate of self-reported, permanent impairment that results in a disability at around twenty percent of the population, it is inevitable that a significant proportion of users will have impairments.

Even if an organization's users are not in the self-reported permanent disability category, many are likely to be in the unreported permanent disability category, or the temporary disability category, or even the situational disability category...because as the data below clearly shows, the group of individuals *without an impairment* is small.

# Impairment and Disability Data

When gathering and discussing data about *impairment* and *disability* there are a few factors to keep in mind. First, although this resource uses a definition of disability and impairment similar to the World Health Organization (or WHO), that is not the understanding held by most people. For the average person, impairment and disability are synonymous and when a disability is reported, the impairment either is, or is believed to be, permanent. Few, if any, people report temporary impairments like broken limbs or temporary illness, and even fewer report situational impairment as a disability even though for accessibility purposes they are.

The data about disability and impairments, gathered from the WHO, government agencies in first world countries where they're tracked, and NGOs (non-governmental organizations) involved in advocacy and support for specific impairments, is often staggering. The belief, used to justify not addressing, or considering, accessibility issues, that not many users are impaired is false. If your users are not complaining even though your website has accessibility issues, the conclusion should be that there is a vast number of people who either abandon tasks or suffer through them without complaint; it should not be that no many users are not affected.

☞ Disability is used to identify the negative aspects of the interaction between a health condition (or impairment) and the environment.

☞ Data presented here is not intended to guide an accessibility plan by demonstrating which features should be implemented first. The data presented here is intended to demonstrate that impairment is far more prevalent than is commonly thought. Further, the data presented here describes the prevalence of permanent impairment, rather than temporary or situational impairment.

# Prevalence of Reported Disability

The percentage of people who report living with a disability varies widely by area. For example, the percentage of people in Ireland who report living with a disability is approximately 9 percent, whereas nearly 13 percent of the US population reports living with a disability. Worldwide, approximately 15 percent of the population reports living with a disability.

We also know disability is affected by age. In the US, more than 10 percent of individuals between the age of 21 and 64 report living with a disability. For individuals between the age of 65 and 74 years, the number increases to over 25 percent, and nearly 50 percent of individuals over the age of 75 years report living with a disability.

# Categorization of Disability by Impairment

Typically, in discussions about web accessibility, features are implemented according to disability categories:

| Category | Prevalence of Reported Disability (percent) |
|---|---|
| Cognitive, learning, or neurological disability (CLN) | 20 |
| Visual disability | 20 |
| Auditory disability | 07 |
| Motor disability | 07 |
| Speech disability | 06 |

☞ One risk of shifting focus to disability categories is that it can fail to address those impairments which do not neatly fall into one of these categories, such as vestibular dysfunction (which affects roughly 35 percent of adults 40 years of age or older). This pattern can also encourage us to ignore comorbidity and strengthen accessibility for one category at the expense of another, or lead us into a false sense of security that says we've address accessibility because we addressed one type of accessibility.

## Permanent Impairment Prevalence by Category

Another approach often used in discussions about web accessibility is to implement features to address different types of impairment. One risk associated with this approach is the difficulties associated with determining the threshold that will trigger effort. The prevalence of a specific permanent impairment may not be very high in a target audience, and answering the "when does it become *high enough*" question is difficult. Also, although we can gather some data regarding the prevalence of a specific impairment, that data is related to permanent impairment, rather than temporary or situation impairment. This approach also relies heavily on the reliability of the data, because there is no way to verify which impairment(s) a user has(and I should point out that it would be extremely unethical, and potentially illegal in some jurisdictions, to invade someone's privacy by determining for which impairment(s) they seemed to be making adjustments).

☠ Because not all individuals experience an impairment in the same way, implementing features to address an impairment is likely to fail. This is especially relevant to impairments that are cognitive or neurological as outside comorbidity they seldom have well-defined physical attributes that can be accommodated. A well-documented example of this is dyslexia and the use of specific font families in an attempt to address the impairment. Individuals report success with different font families, some preferring fonts that resemble cursive, and some preferring standard fonts such as Helvetica, Arial, or Verdana.

| Category | Disorder | Individuals Affected per mille (‰) | Primary Group |
|---|---|---|---|
| **Vision** | Cataracts | 170 | Over 40 years |
| **Vision** | Colorblindness | 80 | Men |
| **Vision** | Colorblindness | 5 | Women |
| **Vision** | Glaucoma | 70 | Over 40 years |
| **Vision** | Low/no vision | 70 | |
| **Vision** | Macular Degeneration | 30 | Over 40 years |
| **CLN** | Attention Deficit/Hyperactivity Disorder (ADHD)† | 50 | |
| **CLN** | Dyscalculia | 60 | |
| **CLN** | Dysgraphia | 200 | |
| **CLN** | Dyslexia | 200 | |
| **CLN** | Memory | 130 | |
| **Auditory** | Hard of hearing/deafness | 80 | Under 40 years |
| **Auditory** | Hard of hearing/deafness | 150 | 40 to 60 years |
| **Auditory** | Hard of hearing/deafness | 300 | Over 60 years |
| **Motor** | Arthritis | 180 | Women |
| **Motor** | Arthritis | 100 | Men |
| **Motor** | Cerebral palsy† | 3 | |
| **Motor** | Essential Tremor | 20 | |
| **Motor** | Lost or damaged limbs† | 5 | |
| **Motor** | Paralysis | 20 | |
| **Speech** | Stuttering | 30 | Boys |
| **Speech** | Stuttering | 20 | Girls |

† Data about the prevalence of this impairment is suspect as the screening criteria has changed or is incomplete, or the prevalence varies widely between populations (e.g., first world countries compared to developing areas).

☞ It should be noted that as a comparison of the amounts for categories in the Prevalence of Reported Disability and the data in the Permanent Impairment Prevalence by Category table demonstrates, reporting a disability is significantly different than living with a disability or impairment. Many people who do not consider themselves to be living with a disability are living with an impairment, an impairment that may affect how, or even if, they interact with your website, and many people who are living with a disability do not report it. This knowledge must inform your accessibility plan.

## Costs of Accessibility Failures Related to Impairment

The hard costs of accessibility failures are difficult to measure across jurisdictions, because they tend to vary widely. Punitive costs associated with non-compliance are just one measure of the costs associated with accessibility failures. The soft costs, the cost of business lost, often to a competitor, is a little easier to estimate.

Business reputation firms have been telling us for some time that ninety percent of customers who experience a problem will not complain. Some organizations estimate the number of "silent sufferers" is higher, possibly ninety-six percent. We also know, given the disparity between self-reporting and the numbers gained through other means that for whatever unknown reason, or reasons, reporting of disability among impaired populations is low. The strong likelihood is that the number of reported versus experienced issues is significantly lower than ten of one hundred and is likely even lower than four of one hundred. An organization cannot assume that the lack of complaints about accessibility difficulties indicates that the difficulties do not exist or are not impacting customers.

Whether the interaction between impairment and environment is considered by the impaired person to be a disability is based almost entirely upon expectations. For example, if someone expects a concert to be loud, they might not consider the inability to hold a conversation to be an accessibility failure; however, if a person expects a business to have a ramp to provide physical access, the lack of a ramp is likely to be considered an *accessibility failure*. Whether or not a website, page, or application is *difficult to use* falls into a similar category, and that qualification is important.

On average, nearly three of four impaired users who consider a website, page, or application to be *difficult to use* will leave and go elsewhere. Nearly eight in ten impaired users will spend more on a website, page, or application that accommodates their needs. The data above gives a small indication of the size of the *impaired users* market in terms of the number of people, but the abandonment, users who leave a website, page, or application, in monetary terms is nearly ten percent of the total market. Although that number will vary somewhat between markets where expectations are different, it is a very accurate estimate in the UK, where accessibility-based abandonment is around £12 billion each year.

## The Impact of Impairment on Interfaces

For most categories of impairment even though we may not often consider the impact of the impairment on the interface, we typically *understand* the impact. In other words, we can often imagine what obstacles we might have injected into an interface for those living with an auditory impairment or visual impairment. That understanding is frequently missing when considering cognitive and neurological impairments as they manifest in ways that often share common features but are not the same across individuals in the way visual and auditory impairments are. For example, two people living with dyslexia will share some symptoms but others will be unique. This lack of commonality will persist because the definitions of specific cognitive and neurological impairments are necessarily broad. However, not only are definitions of impairments necessarily broad to accommodate individuals, the number of subcategories of impairment is greater than with other categories. For example, impairments in attention, memory, reasoning, math and language processing, and speed with which information is processed, all fall into the "cognitive and neurological impairment" category. The lack of commonality and the breadth of impairment types renders cognitive and neurological accessibility in a web application an order of magnitude more difficult than other types such as visual or auditory web accessibility.

How might impairment in these areas impact typical web accessibility? Consider the hypothetical purchase of tickets to an event. In this process the user would have to (a) keep their attention on the task at hand, not only through interruptions such as telephone calls and text messages, but also through minor interruptions such as in-page animations, (b) have to remember information about the event that may be out of view, (c) use reasoning to determine which optional features, such as parking or treatment packages to add, (d) ensure the price charged is what is anticipated and understand any legal verbiage regarding transferability and refunds, (e) all before the time limit provided for sale completion expires.

Additionally, the potential stumbling blocks in cognitive and neurological accessibility are often compounded by stumbling blocks typically associated with other types of accessibility, as many users facing language processing impairments, such as dyslexia will use assistive technology that is common for users with visual impairments because it will *read* content to the user.[1]

---

[1] Surveys of users of the class of assistive technology commonly called "screen readers" consistently find that only one-third of those users report a visual impairment.

# The Business Case for Accessibility

A business case is an often-necessary tool for organizations to use when determining how, or if, resources should be allocated. Generally, the thought around the business case falls into one of several different categories.

## Accessibility drives innovation

Accessibility is closely related to general usability, both aim to define and deliver a more intuitive user experience. As such, accessible design thinking provides varied and flexible ways for users to interact with websites and applications, options that are useful for people with and without impairment, ensuring an impairment doesn't become a disability. Typically, for example, a part of accessible design thinking considers experiences other than screens, and the result is interaction that is more human-centered, natural, and contextual.

We know that often those living with an impairment are *early adopters*, and in the past, innovations like the telephone, text to speech, and voice controls were initially meant to address environmental issues that turned impairments into a disability. Previous innovations driven by accessibility have found a much broader application, and the same will be true for driverless cars and artificial retinas. The usability increases seen from accessibility innovation seldom stops with the impairment it is intended to address.

## Accessibility increases market reach

The market of people with impairments is large and growing as the global population ages. In the UK, where the demographic of impaired individuals is known as the Purple Pound, people with impairment and their families spend at least £249 billion every year. In the US, the annual discretionary spending of people reporting an impairment is over $200 billion. Globally, the extended market is estimated at 2.3 billion people who control an incremental $6.9 trillion in annual disposable income.

☞ You can find more information about the prevalence of impairment in the Data section.

## Accessibility is good for legal concerns

Of course, the topic most organizations attend to is that accessibility addresses legal concerns, because lawyers and court cases come with a cost, both in hard dollars and soft.

In the US, the rate for private web accessibility cases, those known to be regarding web accessibility in which private enterprise was the defendant, which were filed in Federal Court, rose 400 percent annually between 2015 and 2018. These cases typically attempt to address the public interfaces of private enterprise, those entities in the US not covered by Section 508, which applies to US federal government entities, or Section 504, which applies to those entities that receive US federal government funds, however, they are not limited to that. It is important to note that Section 504 is far-reaching, covering not only airports and libraries, but also reaches into local schools, their extra-curricular activities, and even their after-school care programs in most cases. The private web accessibility cases also typically do not address employees of private enterprises who must be enabled to perform the duties for which they are hired, as those cases would be covered under the *Americans with Disabilities Act (1990)*.

Typically, in the US there has been a significant hurdle to finding web accessibility as necessary for the public facing website of a private enterprise, specifically whether or not the website is a "place of public accommodation". If the website is a "place of public accommodation," US courts have often held that the *Americans with Disabilities Act (1990)* applies. With increasing frequency, courts are finding websites to be a place of public accommodation, and in 2019, the US saw its first appellate court decision upholding the necessity of accessibility when the United States Court of Appeals for the Ninth Circuit reversed a lower court's decision to dismiss in *Robles v. Domino's Pizza*[2].

Although in *Robles v. Domino's Pizza* the parties specifically discussed the *Web Content Accessibility Guidelines*, other US courts have held that merely demonstrating compliance with those

---

[2] The decision from the US Court of Appeals for the Ninth Circuit in *Robles v Domino's Pizza* can be found at http://cdn.ca9.uscourts.gov/datastore/opinions/2019/01/15/17-55504.pdf

guidelines is not sufficient to ensure an organization has an accessible website.

Outside the US, the legal landscape is less clear. Some jurisdictions, Norway, for example, have specific statutory requirements and penalties to ensure accessibility is at least a consideration, if not a priority, while in other jurisdictions there may be no local statutory requirement or the local statutory requirement may not use the *Web Content Accessibility Guidelines Recommendation*. Many countries not covered by a local statutory requirement adhere to the United Nations' *Convention on the Rights of Persons with Disabilities*. Further, as is common with other topics, just as there is a difference between countries with regard to statutes, there are also differences in enforcement and penalties. World-wide, websites that prove a challenge to individuals with impairment are a significant legal risk.

## Accessibility is good for karma

Accessibility is, at its core, about inclusion and fairness. A clear commitment to accessibility can demonstrate that a business has a genuine sense of Corporate Social Responsibility. Increasingly, in the US and abroad, younger generations see inclusion as a necessity and are trending away from organizations that do not demonstrate their sense of social responsibility.

Additionally, employing people with disabilities is an essential aspect of creating a diverse workforce. Increasingly we see that a diverse workforce is a key contributor to success. In order for employees to be successful and satisfied, the technology that employees use, including websites and applications, must be accessible.

## Accessibility is a moral obligation

Beyond just giving an outward good impression and potentially generating goodwill toward the organization, improving our business, or protecting us from legal consequences, the case ought also be made to consider accessibility a moral obligation. There are three common arguments against considering accessibility a moral obligation, what we might call an argument from moral relativity, an argument from special obligations, and an argument from teleology.

### *My moral code does not necessarily apply to everyone else*

Much has been said about the relativity of moral statements after it was revived in a significant way in the 19th century. Most people today have embraced this concept of relativity so thoroughly that the common understanding is that every statement is relative except the premise that all statements are relative.

There are issues about which much of the world agrees, however, even if they can see acts such as stealing in a relative manner. After all, while stealing to simply improve your position in life might be worthy of admonition, stealing to avoid death by starvation would often be overlooked.

Consider, for example, a builder who builds homes. The choices each builder makes in materials and workmanship will, without doubt, affect the profit each makes, but those choices also affect others. If the choices the builder makes mean the one of every five collapses or stands as long as the other four, most would consider the builder who makes the choice to build a house at risk of collapsing an unethical builder.

Websites without accessibility can easily end up like a house that has collapsed, completely unusable for individuals with an impairment. Because one in five people report impairment of some type, the failure rate of a website without accessibility matches the failure rate of the homes built by the unethical builder in our analogy.

### Individuals with impairments bear some responsibility to manage their condition

Those of us who have worked on the web have often heard how it is the responsibility of the user to report problems, after all, they are experts regarding whether or not the website has "collapsed" for them. Even if it were true that the home owner bears some responsibility for reporting a failure, that does not absolve the builder of wrongdoing. Whatever moral duty the user has does not negate the moral duty we have to build accessible websites.

A further reality is that people are often conditioned to not complain or report failures but instead to seek satisfaction elsewhere. In fact, the ability to seek satisfaction elsewhere is one of the basic tenets of the free-market capitalism on which modern society is grounded. Some would even go so far to say dissatisfied customers in a free market have an obligation to seek satisfaction elsewhere to "let the market speak for itself". This is most certainly a different obligation than one to report failures.

## *Accessibility adds friction in an environment that was designed to be frictionless*

Building a website is not the same as building homes, we lack a jurisdictional building code, the "best practices" sometimes vary widely, and the tools used to build something are relatively easy to learn, even if they may be difficult to master. For example, the primary language used to identify the different parts of a website uses natural language, a paragraph is identified by a paragraph tag and an list that is shown in order is identified by an ordered list tag. The more basic elements of style, such as font family and size are identified by the properties `font-family` and `font-size`, in style sheets. The grammar rule books for the language are free and open on the Internet along with numerous tutorials and examples that even cover more arcane subjects within each area. The Internet, at least in this regard, has a significantly lower bar to entry than other avenues, but, the argument goes, accessibility is different because it adds significant barriers.

Just as we would not tolerate a builder who justified their collapsing homes by saying building was too complicated, we should not tolerate an web engineer justifying a collapsing website by saying building one that would stand every time is too complicated. Further exasperating the problem, the languages used to build a website are all accessible by default. Websites never suffer from poor-quality languages, unlike a builder who might have unknowingly been sold poor-quality construction materials. No, if accessibility is lacking in a website it is always in the work, never in the tools. Granted, just as a faithful builder can build a structurally unsound house when using a structurally unsound design, a web engineer can build an inaccessible website using an inaccessible design, but again, it is not the tools that are at fault. If a website is inaccessible, we have broken it.

If we have broken a resource that we share with everyone the way we share the web, we have an obligation, a moral obligation, to fix it, for everyone, because as Tim Berners-Lee said, "the power of the Web is in its universality. Access by everyone regardless of disability is an essential aspect."

# Designing Accessibility

Design enables the understanding of people, technology, business, and culture; however, design gone awry can end up disabling more interaction than it enables. As such, design is considerably more than what is identified in the idiomatic expression "beauty is in the eye of the beholder", and whether or not a design is visually appealing often has little impact on its accessibility or usability.

## Beyond the Visual

There is a temptation, especially among non-designers, to think web design is only about the visual aspect of an interface. This temptation is the trap Apple fell into in recent years and it has led to a decline in the usability of their devices. Because Apple is seen as a design leader, other companies have followed, leading design experts Don Norman and Bruce Tognazzini to write, in 2015,

*...companies have followed in Apple's path, equating design with appearance while forgetting the fundamental principles of good design. As a result, programmers rush to code without understanding the people who use the product.*

*...*

*The new generation of software has made gigantic leaps forward in attractiveness and conceptual power while simultaneously getting harder for people to use.*

Norman, Don and Bruce Tognazzini, "<u>How Apple Is Giving Design A Bad Name</u>", Fast Company, November 10, 2015. https://www.fastcompany.com/3053406/how-apple-is-giving-design-a-bad-name

The question before designers today then is how to build an interface that is a return to earlier times, to the key principles of design, key principles that instill the idea that design is more than just making something look good, to build an interface that is for *all* users.

# Considering Education, Experience, and Usability

A significant portion of whether or not a design is fully accessible is whether or not it is understandable. For many categories in accessibility, the tests are relatively easy, for example, tests often include instructions to turn off the display and interact with a page using a screen reader, or interact with a page using only speech recognition software, without a keyboard or mouse; however, easily-executed tests for cognitive accessibility and whether or not an interface is understandable are rare. One reason for the rarity of cognitive accessibility tests is that whether or not a design is understandable is often difficult to measure, as tests such as those for readability are bound to specific languages and cultures. Even though testing and assessment for cognitive accessibility is often difficult it is nevertheless important as we know, and have known for more than a decade, that the complexity of an interface has a significant impact. Even in otherwise accessible interfaces, even those with seemingly adequate cognitive accessibility, how complex an interface is becomes a critical consideration.

In addition to cultural differences, a user's prior knowledge and experience, their *technology proficiency*, affects their understanding of an interface, resulting in differences in cognitive accessibility between otherwise similar users. Technology proficiency is often difficult to predict, therefore, those responsible for designing and building interfaces should pursue all available avenues to ascertain the technology proficiency of their users. This is especially critical for those designing and building interfaces regularly as the introduction of *technology proficiency bias* is frequent.

## Organization for Economic Cooperation and Development Technology Proficiency Levels

Research conducted by the Organization for Economic Cooperation and Development (OECD) between 2011 and 2015 that collected data from thirty-three countries, testing more than two hundred thousand individuals between the ages of sixteen and sixty-five, revealed technology proficiency is lower than often believed[3]. The data revealed that approximately twenty-five percent of the population has no computer experience and cannot use a computer to complete even the simplest of tasks and only about forty-five percent of those with some computer experience can complete tasks that are relatively complex. *Fifty-five percent of those with computer experience cannot complete tasks that have any of the following characteristics*:

- navigation is required to access information or commands required to complete the task
- more than a few steps are required to complete the task
- the task involves implicit tasks or subtasks

---

[3] OECD (2015), *Adults, Computers and Problem Solving: What's the Problem?*, OECD Skills Studies, OECD Publishing, Paris, https://doi.org/10.1787/9789264236844-en.

- the goal cannot be readily inferred from the problem
- there are more than a few monitoring demands, like having to check progress toward a goal
- content and operations cannot be matched simply
- contrasting or integrating information is required

In the wide-ranging data, the technology proficiency of individuals in the testing group was assessed into five distinct categories using sample activities similar to those below.

### *Does not use a computer*

Individuals in this category might have failed the core competency tests, opted out, or have no experience with computer use. These individuals are not placed in one of the computer skill level categories below.

### *Below Level One*

Individuals in this category can perform a well-defined task involving the use of only one function, such as deleting an identified email in an email app.

### *Level 1*

Individuals in this category can perform tasks that require the use of widely available and familiar applications, such as using the reply-all feature to reply to an email.

## *Level 2*

Individuals in this category can perform a task that requires use of both generic and more specific applications and functions, such as locating an email with a particular subject from a specific individual.

## *Level 3*

Individuals in this category can perform tasks that require the use of both generic and more specific applications and functions, as well as a reasoning component that may imply navigation across page or applications or multiple steps and operations, such as scheduling a meeting room for a meeting based on information provided in several emails.

## *Summary*

Although the data shows significant differences between the countries reporting, it indicates that on average, nearly seventy-six percent of the population in the nineteen responding countries has some level of computer experience. It also indicates that approximately fifty-five percent of those with some level of computer experience are only able to complete the simplest of tasks, with approximately sixteen percent identified as being "Below Level 1" and nearly thirty-nine percent as "Level 1". The group of most advanced users, those identified as "Level 3" account for less than eight percent of the respondents.

# OECD Data – Adults, Computers and Problem Solving, Table A2.2 Percentage of Adults Scoring at Each Proficiency Level

| Country | Below Level 1 | Level 1 | Level 2 | Level 3 | No Experience | Failed Core | Opted Out | No Data |
|---|---|---|---|---|---|---|---|---|
| Australia | 9.2 | 28.9 | 31.8 | 6.2 | 4.0 | 2.5 | 13.7 | 2.7 |
| Austria | 9.9 | 30.9 | 28.1 | 4.3 | 9.6 | 4.0 | 11.3 | 1.8 |
| Belgium | 14.8 | 29.8 | 28.7 | 5.8 | 7.4 | 3.5 | 4.7 | 5.2 |
| Canada | 14.8 | 30.0 | 29.4 | 7.1 | 4.5 | 5.9 | 6.3 | 1.9 |
| Czech | 12.9 | 28.8 | 26.5 | 6.6 | 10.3 | 2.2 | 12.1 | 0.6 |
| Denmark | 13.9 | 32.9 | 32.3 | 6.3 | 2.4 | 5.3 | 6.4 | 0.4 |
| England | 15.1 | 33.8 | 29.3 | 5.7 | 4.1 | 5.8 | 4.6 | 1.6 |
| England/NI | 15.1 | 33.9 | 29.1 | 5.6 | 4.3 | 5.8 | 4.5 | 1.6 |
| Estonia | 13.8 | 29.0 | 23.2 | 4.3 | 9.9 | 3.4 | 15.8 | 0.5 |
| Finland | 11.0 | 28.9 | 33.2 | 8.3 | 3.5 | 5.2 | 9.7 | 0.1 |
| France | | | | | 10.5 | 6.0 | 11.6 | 1.5 |
| Germany | 1.4 | 30.5 | 29.2 | 6.8 | 7.9 | 3.7 | 6.1 | 1.5 |
| Ireland | 12.6 | 29.5 | 22.1 | 3.1 | 10.1 | 4.7 | 17.4 | 0.6 |
| Italy | | | | | 24.4 | 2.5 | 14.6 | |
| Japan | 7.6 | 19.7 | 26.3 | 8.3 | 10.2 | 10.7 | 15.9 | 1.3 |
| Korea | 9.8 | 29.6 | 26.8 | 3.6 | 15.5 | 9.1 | 5.4 | 0.3 |
| Netherlands | 12.5 | 32.6 | 34.3 | 7.3 | 3.0 | 3.7 | 4.5 | 2.3 |
| Northern Ireland | 16.4 | 34.5 | 25.0 | 3.7 | 10.0 | 5.8 | 2.3 | 2.2 |
| Norway | 11.4 | 31.8 | 34.9 | 6.1 | 1.6 | 5.2 | 6.7 | 2.2 |
| Poland | 12.0 | 19.0 | 15.4 | 3.8 | 19.5 | 6.5 | 23.8 | 0.0 |
| Slovak Republic | 8.9 | 28.8 | 22.8 | 2.9 | 22.0 | 2.2 | 12.2 | 0.3 |
| Spain | | | | | 17.0 | 6.2 | 10.7 | |
| Sweden | 13.1 | 30.8 | 35.2 | 8.8 | 1.6 | 4.8 | 5.7 | 0.1 |
| US | 15.8 | 33.1 | 26.0 | 5.1 | 5.2 | 4.1 | 6.3 | 4.3 |
| Avg | 12.3 | 29.4 | 28.2 | 5.8 | 8.0 | 4.9 | 9.9 | 1.5 |

# Special Considerations in Internationalization

In addition to considerations of design being more than a visual medium and the overall complexity of an interface, there are multiple areas in which internationalization and accessibility interact. First and foremost, accessibility becomes critical when a product moves into international markets, as different jurisdictions have different requirements around accessibility and the impact of design and development becomes greater, highlighting even the slightest flaw. Additionally, the effort expended during internationalization can be one of the greatest influencers of cognitive accessibility. Such effort ought to include the areas where cultures are similar but not the same, as they are prime candidates for cognitive accessibility issues as well as general confusion[4]. Two such areas that deserve special attention are the use of color and special data types, as they are especially prone to cause issues.

## Color

Frequently, color theory tells us that people respond to colors in much the same way; however, that is only partly true. *People from the same culture respond to colors in much the same way.* Often the

---

[4] The more closely similar cultures are, the more likely there are to be misunderstanding. As Oscar Wilde said, "we have really everything in common with American nowadays, except, of course, language" (*The Canterville Ghost*, 1887), which may explain why confusion about the format of dates between England and the United States has caused several incidents as data is identified as false simply because the month and day are switched.

connotations a culture holds about color work their way into idiomatic expressions, such as "true blue" or "green thumb" or even "jealousy is a green-eyed monster". However, it is important that such idiomatic expressions are seen for what they are, rather than as generalizations about color.

In various cultures, the color red can represent luck or good fortune, represent a ward against evil, represent danger or attention, or even represent happiness. White, in some cultures is the color of mourning, while in other cultures the color of mourning is black. Although purple is often used to represent those in the LGBT community in the US, in Russia the same group is represented by blue. The different connotations held by red, white, and purple is only a partial list, there are many more differences in connotation and adjustments that have been made by various groups over the centuries as they have established relationships and attempted to convey their message.

## Language

Language is one of the more subtle aspects of internationalization, even though it seems it should be the most obvious.

For instance, there are differences between languages that govern how they are to be read, left-to-right or right-to-left, and even if it should be read top-to-bottom as part of the left-to-right or right-to-left. Because of the way user-agents work, most languages now have restricted top-to-bottom for special cases, with the general cases of either left-to-right or right-to-left as the primary use.

In addition to language direction, the *size* of words used can have a significant impact on more than the overall style of a web page or site. Although average word size hovers around six characters across several languages, the use of long words, which is more common in some languages than others, may alter how a design looks. To counteract the alterations that would otherwise naturally occur due to word wrapping, a design that will be translated into multiple languages should allow thirty percent more space than the content uses in English, in other words, the English content should use no more than seventy-seven percent of the available space.

Aside from word size affecting the layout of a page, word size often also reflects the complexity of content. Rather than measuring complexity as the *Flesch-Kincaid Grade Level* does, by counting the number of syllables in a word, a simpler, cross-language measure uses word size. Evaluating content in this way is what the *Roking-A11y Readability Tool*[5] is designed to do. Using such a tool enables the evaluation of content across languages to ensure, not that translations are correct, but that translations are less likely to be a source of additional complexity, allowing content writers and developers to quickly monitor the likelihood of cognitive

---

[5] The *Roking-A11y Readability Tool* is available in the collection of accessibility tools at https://hrobertking.github.io/roking-a11y/

accessibility being affected when content has been translated into a different language.

Finally, special care must be taken to evaluate designs regarding what data is collected when presenting an international version of a web page, site, or application. Not only are there jurisdictional restrictions regarding what data can or cannot be collected or shown, there are cultural differences regarding what information is more sensitive and the language surrounding the collection of that information. For example, one payment processing company discovered that while customers in the US would never reveal their bank account information to another person or company, the same was not true for other cultures. As a result of this cultural difference, it was found that in cultures where more information was shared, the average user was more knowledgeable about the process for sharing and the language used was more technical in tone than corresponding language in more restrictive cultures. As a result, rather than simply translating existing content, new content had to be written in order to reduce confusion by over-simplifying a process.

## Special Data Types

Another area that requires special attention is special data types, such as dates, numbers, phone numbers, names, and addresses; in fact, for most organizations the first three items on that list, dates, numbers, and phone numbers, create the most issues that require additional intervention to resolve, which means they are the data points it costs the most to collect and maintain and the data points that are most likely to affect conversion.

## Dates

As was mentioned earlier, designers and developers who deal with international markets often understand there are different formats used for date values, both collecting them and displaying them, in use across the world. These formats are generally well-documented and information about different collection techniques can be found in the information about the Date Input component in the *Patterns* section.

☞ The differences in how dates are collected can have significant impact to accessibility and might also have disastrous consequences, including denial of services for a number of reasons, especially when collected in a manner that enables confusion regarding the month and date.

## Numbers

There are several different formats that can be used internationally when collecting and displaying numbers; however, issues surrounding the collection and display of numeric data are relatively simple to resolve, in part because there are a limited number of formats that different languages and cultures use. As a result of the cultural constraints around numbers, developing a plan for the collection and use of numbers is straightforward. For more information about the collection and display of numbers, see the information in the Number Input component in the *Patterns* section.

## Addresses

Address formats vary widely, in fact, almost as widely as names. In most cases, formats are tied to postal services, and attempts have been made to create an international standard to identify address parts. Most such attempts have failed, because of the vast difference in address parts. For instance, in two very similar countries, the US and Great Britain, the way addresses appear is very similar, however, the constituent address parts are very different.

In the US, each address has a house or building number, followed by a street direction, street name, and street type. If the area is limited, the street direction and the street type may be omitted. In addition to the street information, the US implemented a Zone Improvement Plan in 1963, adding a non-regional postal code, called a "ZIP code", to the formal address. In the US in order to find a location, a package will likely need all these components of an address, the house number, street name, and postal code, whereas in Great Britain you might only need the postal code, or perhaps the postal code and house number.

There have been multiple attempts to create a standard list of address parts. In terms of the web, this first came about as microformats and then as microdata. Although there are minor differences between these two specifications, the general format is street-address, extended-address, locality, region, and postal-code. By using this standard, and the general display format, it is possible to normalize the data collected, which is often critical, especially in those multilingual markets where the language used determines how the address is displayed.

☞ Although many consider postal codes to be easily paired to a region, this is not always the case. For example, although it's common in Great Britain for a postal code to refer to a single building, in the US a postal code can refer to multiple cities, towns, or even states. Because of these important differences, care should be taken to ensure those designing and building an address interface understand the relation of postal codes to other portions of the address, as building an interface with a tightly-bound postal code will negatively impact accessibility.

### Names

Years of building interfaces has resulted in learning few *absolute* truths, but there are a few, especially in regard to names, the first being that names are particularly troublesome, and not just in *Romeo and Juliet*. For those in the financial industry, however, names are seen as critical information and designing for their collection and use is equally so. In order to design collection and use, we must identify some common practices, and this is where we run into the first problem.

Over the years, several facts about names have emerged, including:

- people do not always have exactly one "full name", not even at any single point in time, let alone over time
- sometimes names change, and not necessarily at specific events like marriage or the achievement of some goal
- names may have important prefixes or suffixes
- names may contain numbers
- names can be written in any script and in either uppercase or lowercase
- a person can have any number of names, including zero
- names can be written in any order
- the ultimate authority for a person's name is the person

This short list of facts, which is by no means exhaustive, poses a number of problems for designers. How might we design an interface that can accept any data in any format and make it even mildly accessible by clearly labeling it and giving accurate feedback? The most common way to collect name information is to separate a name into name parts, but even then, what do we call the name parts? Standards typically identify the following name parts: *given name*, which in most western countries is the name given to an individual; *family name*, or surname, is the name given to members of a specific family unit; and *additional names*, which in some western countries is a middle name. Even this approach is overly simplistic, as cultures may include groups other than families as an additional name or may include family names of all parents.

However, as any employee of a financial firm in most any western country understands, the need to collect a name that is also a relatively unique identifier is important. In those cases, the content that describes the collection *must* make it clear the name referred to is the name as listed on the appropriate legal document, such as a passport or other formal identification. As a design is internationalized, it must expand to accommodate patterns in the international markets.

☞ How the name parts are labeled, the order in which they are collected, and the feedback given to the user when they are collected all impact the accessibility of the data collection form; many of the same factors affect the accessibility of pages and applications that display a name as well.

## Phone Numbers

Collection and display of telephone numbers can be especially troublesome. Not only are there culturally-based differences in privacy concerns, the format of telephone numbers is also frequently an issue. Few people in the US make international calls or offer their telephone number to international contacts. However, if an organization is international, the organization may have a need for international access. The affordance and signifiers used when collecting telephone numbers internationally must be carefully considered in order to keep the accessibility of a page or application in the forefront.

☞ Keep in mind that even if a *click-to-call* link is used to display a telephone number, the telephone number should be displayed in a localized format rather than its international format as not all devices provide the same functionality and not all users will understand an international telephone number format.

## The Need for a New Approach to Design

Empathy is frequently seen as the key to accessibility in interfaces, often to the extent that designers and engineers who make accessibility a priority claim that the first step to building an accessible product is to build our sense of empathy to instill an inclusive design mentality in or our organization. However much the need for empathy in technology is emphasized, there is seldom any discussion of what is meant when we talk about *empathy*, so we are left with trying to find a common understanding. Those who would claim empathy is needed are neither referencing *Cognitive Empathy*, the ability to put oneself in another's place but absent the need for engaging their emotions, nor referencing *Emotional Empathy*, or the ability to feel another's emotions alongside them, but *Compassionate Empathy*, or the feeling of someone's pain and taking action to help[6].

In web design, there are currently two approaches that are typically referenced when the topic of accessible design is discussed, *Human Centered Design* and *Universal Design*. Although the two approaches are different in many ways, both approaches are built on a foundation that claims *Compassionate Empathy* as a primary aspect, a fact only partially hidden in the first principle of both systems, which is to "focus on the people" in *Human Centered Design*, and promote "equitable use" in *Universal Design*.

When the state of accessibility is measured against the tools that have been employed, however, the vast divide between the tools used and the desired end is laid bare. One must question whether the tools have always been wielded by inadequate hands or whether the tools themselves are inadequate. While it is true that everyone involved has room to learn and grow, and it is true that there are a host of issues affecting accessibility, such as the prevalence and variety of user impairment, the technological proficiency of users, cross-cultural and international issues, and the need for design to be more than a visual medium, the resulting

---

[6] Dr. Paul Ekman described these three very different ways to sense another person's feelings to Dr. Daniel Goleman, who described them in greater detail on http://www.danielgoleman.info/three-kinds-of-empathy-cognitive-emotional-compassionate/.

decreasingly-accessible web pages and applications show the current approaches are insufficient.

We might posit that *Compassionate Empathy*, although a lofty goal for our everyday lives, is not an appropriate tool for the development of accessible products, as it is frequently impeded by our conscious and unconscious bias and easily migrates into *Cognitive Empathy* when employed in product development where the constraints are more likely to be monetarily rather than emotionally driven.

Further, beyond the long-term, maintained emotional connection necessary for continuous development built on a foundation of *Compassionate Empathy*, even the initial emotional connection required is difficult when experiences are similar, and impossible when experiences are so vastly different, and even slight, common misunderstandings often result in serious error. As many involved in cultural studies might tell us, it is nearly impossible to enter another person's perspective, to imagine ourselves in another's situation, enough to feel empathy in any consistent manner, and many attempts to do so go horribly awry. That development of Compassionate Empathy is a nearly impossible difficulty is especially true for those heavily steeped in what are often called the "hard sciences" as the engineers building interfaces are.

The inability of current tools to produce useful results has led to the place where we must acknowledge empathy, not as the foundational building block of an

> *...if we are uncritical we shall always find what we want: we shall look for, and find, confirmations, and we shall look away from and not see, whatever might be dangerous to our pet theories.*
>
> Karl Popper
>
> The Poverty of Historicism

accessibility practice, but as a nearly insurmountable stumbling block that impedes our progress. It is not *empathy* we need so much as the critical insight *introspection* brings. Examining our own mental and emotional processes to uncover the bias inherent in our design, all those unconscious assumptions we make about how each *persona* will use the interfaces, features, and products we design and build, and in doing so, begin to reduce the detrimental effects of that bias. Introspection also encourages us to see the privilege in our designs, whether that privilege is based in race, gender, nation of residence, socio-economic class, or abilities, in an examination that is part of the key to creating a design that is usable regardless of culture or ability.

Seeing the role we play in creating environments that hinder effective interaction is the area we have greatest control over. Introspection is the key to creating a design that meets the goal of the internet, to reach all people. Realizing how little we know, and what we can and cannot do, it becomes our responsibility to constantly push ourselves to be introspective, to polish the lens with which we view the world. Empathy-based design systems, like *Human Centered Design* and *Universal Design* are not enough, we must make a shift.

Through introspection, thoughtfully considering how our own experiences and patterns shape our designs, we begin to see points in which we can improve the design, eliminating those things that are likely to become obstacles to others who have different experiences and patterns. Seeing our own *normal* for what it is, *our own*, we can begin to look past colors, animations, input patterns, and the myriad other layers added to an interface to the simplicity beneath, a simplicity that once found and nourished eliminates obstacles and truly makes our interfaces accessible.

Through this new paradigm, *Introspection Centered Design,* we are encouraged to see the bias in our attitudes about color and content and culture and will more easily see the need for design features like simple colors and a simple, consistent layout, an interface that someone under stress, or someone who is on the spectrum, is better able to use, and it is often simply a matter of asking the question "where is my bias in this design", because it is there.

# Key Principles of Accessible Introspection Centered Design

As we move to a new paradigm, it remains tempting to rely on the principles of *Universal Design* or *Human Centered Design* we learned before. Equitable Use, Flexibility in Use, Simple and Intuitive Use, Perceptible Information, Tolerance for Error, Low Physical Effort, and Size and Space for Approach and Use are all good principles, just as Focus on the People, Find the Right Problem, Think of Everything as a System, and Always Test Your Design Decisions are.

Each of these principles is good advice that might lead down a productive path. However, the goal of accessible design is much like the first principle of *Universal Design*, an interface that is "useful and marketable to people with diverse abilities". Without introspection a "focus on the people" and what constitutes "equitable use" will be very different.

To continue the paradigm shift, join the principles of accessibility, perceivability, operability, understandability, and robustness, with introspection to determine where your bias lies and how others might understand those principles in a different way.

## Perceivable in All Ways

How simple or flexible a design is, or any of the other qualities good designs have, will be meaningless if the user cannot perceive the interface. This simple fact is why *perceivable* is the first of the four principles of accessibility.

Being perceivable also speaks to the trend to treat design as a purely visual medium. In order for an interface to be considered perceivable, it cannot rely on one sensory ability alone, it must be noticeable to the user *regardless of the user's surroundings or the user's sensory abilities.*

In practical terms, although there are some senses which have not been included in traditional interfaces to date, such as smell and taste, there are still numerous ways in which we perceive an interface. Sight qualities such as the brightness and contrast of images and text, auditory qualities such as the tone and volume of sound, and even touch and vestibular qualities such as the frequency and duration of any movements such as vibration and animation have to be managed in a way that increases the perceptibility of an interface.

⁑ *Have you introduced bias by treating design as a visual media, as Don Norman and Bruce Tognazzini decried, or does it communicate with the user through as many senses as possible?*

## Operable Ubiquity

There are many factors that make an interface operable, and while we often consider an interface operable if a user can navigate to the interface and interact with it, those are generally details of the construction of the interface rather than the design. However, there are design concepts that affect operability, concepts such as simplicity, flexibility, and maneuverability.

## Simplicity

There are several different aspects that affect a design's ease of use. For example, the *Universal Design* principle "Low Physical Effort" certainly applies here, even though for electronic interfaces we might be tempted to think anyone could sit down and use an app "efficiently and comfortably with a minimum of fatigue". However, motor and dexterity impairment can significantly affect fatigue when tasks are repeated or when specific gestures are required, and in the past, the difficulty of repeated clicking and gesturing has influenced the development of things like "one-click checkout" where payment for an item is as simple as a single pointer click.

Even if a design follows the Low Physical Effort principle, it might still fail to be fully accessible, which is why this principle is simplicity rather than low physical effort. Although physical fatigue can be a significant problem, what nearly every ecommerce and payment processing service has discovered is that mental fatigue is much more significant than physical fatigue, both in terms of the prevalence and its effect. While physical fatigue *might* reduce conversion, we know mental fatigue *will* reduce conversion.

Before adding features or content, ask yourself "does the user need this to complete their task?" because if the answer is *no*, you're increasing cognitive load and mental fatigue. For some, cognitive load is extremely important, as their tolerance for complexity may be very low. Don't assume that their use of your web page or application indicates that they automatically understand how your web page or application works and are accepting of complexity.

⁑ *Have you introduced bias by adding unnecessary complexity to the design, like animation or a heavy use of icons, or does your design minimize the user's effort, both physically and mentally?*

### Flexibility

One of the first lessons designers and engineers must learn is that there are chasms between the way something is designed, the way it is built, and the way it is used. We have recognized this for a long time in building trades, where we recognize that every client has a different perspective. Some clients want smaller, separate areas that offer cozy accommodations while others want larger, open spaces that accommodate everyone. These differences are even carried into the appliances we install and use in our homes every day. Of course this is not apparent to only those in building trades, even in psychology we are beginning to realize the difficulty variance imposes. While we can often identify behaviors that are harmful, we are recognizing that it is becoming rare to identify behaviors that are normal. Some psychologists have even discarded the notion of normality entirely, separating behavior instead into harmful and not harmful.

Because of these vast differences, the likelihood that an interface will be used in a way the designer did not intend when it was designed and the engineer did not intend when it was built is very high. Experienced engineers have long recognized this gap and have long recommended manual (human) testing of interfaces alongside any automated testing to ensure human behavior is accounted for during development. Experienced designers also often recognize that the interface they struggled to create will not be used in the way they intended and have sought to minimize the impact of the gap between design and use through focus groups and variant, or A/B, testing. Although not all recognize these chasms between the design, the construction, and the use, it is imperative they be not only recognized but accommodated through a measure of flexibility built into the design and construction of the interface.

In practical terms, this flexibility often takes the shape of design and development to accommodate different device types such as keyboards, displays, and pointer devices; however, even this amount of flexibility of device types is insufficient, as there are a range of interaction styles. For example, users who have used a screen reader might navigate within a page using the keyboard and shortcuts built into the assistive technology, like a list of all links on a page, or users may use a speech-to-text interface to accomplish their task. There simply is no one way of interacting and designs and construction methods used must be flexible.

⁂ *Have you introduced bias by using terms like **click** and **hover**, or have you anticipated and accommodated a wide range of interaction styles?*

## Maneuverability

Even the simplest of designs are not operable if the interface is too small to activate or if there is not adequate empty space in which to operate. This is one area in which the *Web Content Accessibility Guidelines* are less than clear. While touch targets are identified as having a specific minimum size of forty-four CSS pixels or 44/96 inches, the guideline is less clear about whether both the height and width are to conform to the guidance presented or if an appropriate minimum size for only one direction is acceptable. Further, the empty or inactive space around those touch targets is generally not covered by test criteria. Here, maintaining maneuverability provides solutions for the lack of specificity in the guidance offered by requiring sufficient space to use an interface without accidentally activating another.

While ideally the empty space would be sufficient to allow for the relative isolation of an interface regardless of the user's body size, posture, or mobility, there is simply no way to create a design in the limited real estate of an electronic world that is so flexible. Because of this practical limitation, the empty, maneuverable space around an interface should be the same as the touch target itself, forty-four CSS pixels.

⁂ *Have you introduced bias by emphasizing the scarcity of viewport real estate, or have you provided sufficient empty space to increase ease of comprehension and navigation?*

## Understandable with Ease

The sole purpose of the user interface is to facilitate user interaction with your system. If users can't figure out how to do this, quickly and easily, they will abandon their interaction[7]. A well-designed interface is understandable without access to a specific user experience, language, skill, or education level, even if certain aspects of the interface are not. For example, a well-designed interface to collect a number will not rely on specialized knowledge, like only accepting values in scientific notation, or be limited to one type of user experience such as always including a decimal character as would be the case in input masking, or be limited to a specific language, like requiring a specific decimal character. Of course many of these details are implementation details covered during the construction of the interface, but these implementation details *should be* specified as part of the design in a way that increases understandability.

A large part of understandability is the readability of content used in a design. It is important in this endeavor that readability and legibility are not confused. While both are important, they are

---

[7] Data from large ecommerce and payment processing firms shows a roughly two percent reduction in conversion for every second a user spends on a page.

important for different reasons. Legibility is an issue for *perceivability* and readability is an important factor for *understandability* in a user interface. One of the greatest factors in understandability is the presence of clear, concise content in labels and navigational interfaces. However, even though readability is important, one must not sacrifice simplicity for clarity, in other words, avoid cluttering your interface up with unnecessary or lengthy explanations.

✲✲ *Have you introduced bias by emphasizing brevity, or specific cultural norms, that prevents or hinders simple and understandable interactions, or does your design communicate in a clear manner?*

## Consistency

Consistency, both internally, within the features of your interface, and externally, with patterns that frequently appear on the internet, enables users to develop usage patterns that fit them. These usage patterns, the habits that accompany familiarity, reduce cognitive load, and reduced cognitive load will result in increased interaction, including conversion.

✲✲ *Have you introduced bias by emphasizing your patterns or your organization's patterns of interaction, or is your design consistent, both within the ecosystem and with external patterns, both online and offline?*

## *Familiarity*

One way some describe good design is by use of the word intuitive; however, *intuitive* generally describes the user's *familiarity* with the components of a design or the design itself rather than being a quality of the design. Familiarity is promoted by consistency internally and externally but is one of the key measures of whether or not an interface is successful. Ask yourself if your interfaces are familiar to your users.

⁂ *Have you introduced bias by emphasizing the differences between interaction patterns or is there a recognizable repetition?*

## *Organization*

One of the often overlooked aspects of design is the visual hierarchy. How features, content, or interactions are identified as being important is, well, important. Poor visual hierarchy, a visual hierarchy that does not match the structure of the content, for example, increases cognitive load and reduces the quality of the user experience. The differences in size, color, and placement of elements should allow users to quickly understand your interface and what the call-to-action or calls-to-action might be. Additionally, good organization can increase the perceived simplicity, even in cases where the actual complexity cannot be reduced.

⁂ *Have you introduced bias by applying visual styles rather than organizational structure or applying visual styles that compete with the structure, or does the visual hierarchy match the organizational structure?*

## Robustness and Resilience

There are many ways in which a design can be robust. Typically we think about designs being robust if they are understandable in multiple ways or by multiple types of users. Again, the description borders on the defined goal being one of the principles we use to build the interface, which is a little like suggesting that if we want the right answer we should simply stop getting the wrong answer. Rather than look at robustness as a measure of the breadth of understanding, let's take a look at how machines are considered robust, which is through their *efficiency* and *reliability*.

### *Efficiency*

A good interface is one which is efficient, in other words, it completes the task by taking the shortest possible path. This principle is closely related to the design concept of simplicity discussed earlier, but where the consideration of *simplicity* is the effort associated with the steps a path takes, *efficiency* is concerned with the number of steps taken.

In real-world terms, ask how many clicks or keystrokes a process takes. If you're collecting a date, for instance, can the user type the date in or do they pick it from a list or calendar? If the user can enter a date using the keyboard, does the input accept the format the user is used to, or must they enter the date in an unfamiliar format? In many ways selecting a date from a list or a calendar is simpler, because the variance between date formats and which date part is entered in which order is entirely avoided. On the other hand, if the user is selecting a value from a list, how many items do they have to read through? If the list is long or the calendar starts on a distant date, it may be more efficient to type the date into an input.

Often the time required to complete a form depends, not on the amount of information collected on the form, but the manner in which that information is collected, and the time required to complete a form is inversely proportional to the rate of conversion.

⁂ *Have you introduced bias by applying your own patterns of interaction to the design, or are there multiple ways to accomplish a task, allowing the user to find their own efficient patterns?*

### Reliability

There are several factors that affect the overall reliability of an interface; however, a good measure of reliability is how, or even if, different states are handled. When we look at how different states are handled in a design, we are addressing feedback provided to the user.

Does your design accommodate the user by providing feedback when there are hidden processes, like when additional content is requested, or when the user has done something correctly or incorrectly? Providing such feedback so will improve the user's perception of the reliability and robustness of your interface.

Of course, feedback is another aspect of interface design where there is typically a significant difference between the real-world performance and the perception of that performance. In some ways, masking the responsiveness by giving the user immediate feedback about what is expected can be as important as improving the actual system responsiveness, just be careful that the feedback is accurate. Slow, accurate feedback is better than fast, inaccurate feedback[8].

⁂ *Have you introduced bias in the complexity or frequency of feedback, or does the design give the user ample, accurate, and understandable feedback?*

---

[8] The presence of feedback regarding requesting content or submitting information is especially important, as such feedback will often give otherwise missing insight to the user, improving the *perceived* performance of an application even if the actual time taken is not reduced.

# Doing Accessibility

When designing and creating interfaces, there are a number of best practices, practices known to result in increased usability and improved conversion rates, as well as a number of anti-patterns, practices known to result in decreased usability and conversion rates, and a number of frequently repeated errors.

## Stepping Stones and Best Practices

It is often difficult to see a way clear to claim that there is a standard way of creating accessible designs or even a standard way of developing them. However, there are points of overlap, areas in which all, or nearly all, those who have been working with accessibility for some time agree. The practices related to these areas are identified here because the results produced are superior to the results produced otherwise.

### Animation

Animation is frequently used to make a site or application appear more dynamic and engaging; however, animation can cause a wide range of ailments, including headaches, dizziness, and nausea, especially in individuals with vestibular disorders. Flickering or flashing animations can also trigger seizures in those with photosensitive epilepsy.

While it is important to note that animations can pose accessibility issues, that does not mean animations should never be used. With attention to details it is possible to create animations that are merely distractions. While distractions may potentially increase the cognitive load of a page, they may also increase engagement or the clarity of an interaction. With care, these competing concerns may be balanced in a way that creates an engaging interface without significant loses in conversion.

Two of the issues you will want to keep in mind when creating animations, duration and size, are discussed below; however, one of the most important things you can do with animations, is give the user control over the duration of those animations, i.e., the ability to turn them off. One way this can be done for animations created using CSS is with the use of the prefers-reduced-motion media query.

CSS
```
@media (prefers-reduced-motion: reduce) {
  * {
    animation-duration: 0s !important;
    animation-iteration-count: 0 !important;
    transition: none !important;
    -webkit-animation: none !important;
  }
}
```

It is important, when turning off animations using prefers-reduced-motion, that the animation-duration be set to 0 rather than setting the animation to "none" so the end result is rendered correctly even without the transitional frames. Failure to set the animation-duration to 0 is likely to result in errors related to the animation, which will likcly lead to more confusion than the original animation.

This same approach, adding style rules to prevent animation, can be used in conjunction with a checkbox input for users without support for prefers-reduced-motion by pairing the universal selector with a checked checkbox.

⁂ *Provide a mechanism for preventing animation entirely.*

## Duration

Animations that happen too quickly or that run too long can be troublesome. If an animation happens too quickly, the result will likely be surprising or even jarring. Surprising animations can be especially troublesome for those who suffer from vestibular disorders, leaving them feeling off-balance. If an animation takes too long to run, it may block user interaction, and lower conversion or create other risks.

In addition to the duration of animations, you ought also consider the number of times an animation will loop, but note that this applies only to animations and not CSS transitions, which run only once. If animation is to loop, set a limit on the number of times will loop, or better yet, give the user control over the number of times the animation will loop.

⁂ *Specify duration and speed of all animations, as well as the number of times it will loop.*

### *Size*

One of the larger issues to consider when creating animations is the *size* of the elements that are animated. In general, the animation of smaller elements, like a button for which the border or background change, is seldom significant enough to cause an issue. The larger the size, however, the greater the number of people who will be affected by the animation.

One general exception to the proportional relationship between size and the number of people affected is a parallax animation, when the foreground and background move at different speeds. Parallax animations are especially problematic, often even affecting individuals when the areas animated are significantly smaller than the size of the viewport. Because this category of animation negatively affects a disproportionate part of the population, it should be avoided whenever possible.

✲ *Animate smaller elements rather than larger elements whenever possible, and avoid parallax animation.*

## ARIA: The Accessible Rich Internet Applications Recommendation from the Web Accessibility Initiative (WAI)

ARIA, or more formally, *WAI-ARIA* or the *Accessible Rich Internet Applications Recommendation*, is a specification from the *Web Accessibility Initiative*, or WAI, is a collection of items that are intended to *extend* the accessibility of HTML by enabling the creation of custom interfaces.

☞ Although the argument may be made to include WAI-ARIA in markup before JavaScript is loaded, the various parts of WAI-ARIA are effectively useless *without* JavaScript; therefore, placing WAI-ARIA in markup without using JavaScript adds page weight that serves no purpose.

The *Recommendation*, currently at version 1.1, groups the collection of items into two primary categories: (a) *roles* and (b) *states* and *properties*.

☠ Although there is often significant encouragement among the development community to use the roles and states and properties provided in the *WAI-ARIA Recommendation*[9], it should not be used without a *thorough* understanding of how it affects the *Accessibility Tree* in various platforms. As the stated purpose of the WAI-ARIA roles, states, and properties is to *expand* or *enhance* the accessibility information of an interface, and are not intended to replace existing semantic information that can be provided using HTML, *if there is an existing HTML element that has the desired role, it must be used*. Poorly thought-out use will undoubtedly lead to unintended

---

[9] The *WAI-ARIA Recommendation* can be found at https://www.w3.org/TR/wai-aria-1.1/

consequences, some of which can render your page or application unusable[10].

⁑ *When Semantic HTML is used, the need for WAI-ARIA roles, states, and properties, will be **reduced** or **eliminated**, and the resulting interface will also be significantly more robust.*

WAI-ARIA *roles* are separated into six categories: *Abstract, Document Structure, Landmark, Live Region, Widget*, and *Window*, with the most commonly used roles being in the *Landmark, Live Region*, and *Widget* categories. Each category is often associated with specific issues, some of them minor; however, *all roles* must be used with extreme care as, unlike states and properties, each WAI-ARIA role will modify the semantic meaning of the elements, and using them and will, as a result, directly modify the *Accessibility Tree*.

There are a number of explicit restrictions on the use of WAI-ARIA roles in the *Recommendation*, such as rules against an author using an *Abstract* role, and a number of more practical, less frequently documented issues each engineer should consider, such as not updating the aural portion of a *Live Region* more frequently than fifteen second intervals to give screen readers adequate time to announce the updated content even with the slowest speech rates

---

[10] Analysis of the data from the *WebAIM Million* indicates there are sixty-five percent more discoverable accessibility errors on a website using WAI-ARIA compared to those that do not use WAI-ARIA.

in any language, the segregation of Widget roles on some platforms[11], and specific interaction requirements that may accompany roles[12].

☠ It is important to note that although a single *Landmark* role, "main", is *required*, many user-agents will act differently dependent on whether the native HTML `main` element is used or a WAI-ARIA `role` of "main" is used. In some user-agents, use of the HTML element will modify the tab order in the window significantly, effectively creating a *focus trap* that isolates the portion of a page outside the `main` element after navigating into the `main` element, making it nearly unreachable.

Although the WAI-ARIA states and properties seldom modify the *Accessibility Tree* as roles do, they are remarkably powerful, and as with roles, extreme care should be used whenever they are added. Fortunately, even though there are numerous states and properties, with each being allowed within specific roles, the number

---

[11] *Widget* roles may cause assistive technology to virtually move interfaces to a dedicated section in the assistive interface. This segregation is likely to cause confusion for users who have difficulty discovering the relocated interface.
[12] *Window* roles such as "dialog" and "alertdialog" often have specific interaction requirements, such as including an accessible name that is announced when the content is displayed, as well as a means to dismiss the content and return focus where it was immediately before the "dialog" or "alertdialog" was opened.

commonly needed are relatively limited and include `aria-describedby`[13], `aria-expanded`[14], and `aria-live`.

Of these three properties and states, the "aria-live" property deserves special attention as it is used to announce content or visibility changes within an element that may be outside a user's focus, making it an important piece of accessibility for the visually impaired, and it is *critical* for a *Single Page Application*, or SPA.

Although there is some debate about whether "aria-live" should or should not be used along with the WAI-ARIA roles alert or status, as those roles have a specific implied live value, because of the inconsistent nature of WAI-ARIA support an approach that uses both aria-live and a role of either "alert" or "status" is more robust. Be consistent in its use, however, always using "polite" with a status role and "assertive" with an alert role.

Be aware that by default, only the updated content inside the element will be announced; however, this behavior can be changed with the aria-atomic property. Setting the aria-atomic property to "true" will cause assistive technologies to present the entire

---

[13] Used to provide additional detail about an interface through the Accessible Description, the "aria-describedby" property would not be used to provide a label, but something longer and more verbose. A common example would be differentiating between types of addresses on a page, e.g., a billing address versus a shipping address.

[14] The "aria-expanded" state identifies whether the element, or the element it controls, is currently expanded. This is typically used for interface components such as an *Accordion*, and it may only contain one of two values: "true" or "false".

contents of the element, including the live region label, rather than just the changed node. Also, because of potential timing issues associated with when and how content is announced, a live region should not be updated more frequently than every fifteen seconds, and no two live regions should be updated within fifteen seconds of each other. Failure to maintain this time delay may lead to overlapping announcements or announcements not being made at all.

☠ Because of the way aria-live works, with the assistive technology tracking changes to monitored regions, the aria-live attribute must be added in the markup when the region is loaded, not after. While failure is not assured if live regions are added dynamically, success is likewise not assured.

There are two other powerful properties not mentioned earlier, `aria-label` and `aria-labelledby`. Although these two properties are frequently used in an attempt to make a design lacking accessibility accessible, they directly assign an Accessible Name and are, therefore, exceedingly dangerous. These two properties should only be used in very special circumstances and, because the potential for misuse is significant, should not be used for input elements or buttons.

☠ Because "aria-label" is always non-visual, it will cause accessibility issues for any users who are using speech-to-text assistive technology without also using a text-to-speech assistive technology, as those users will be unaware what the Accessible Name for the interface is.

⁂ *Because the use of WAI-ARIA role, states, and properties is one of the leading indicators of the existence of accessibility issues in a web page or application, no ARIA is better than bad ARIA.*

## Breakpoints

Breakpoints are, traditionally, expressed in absolute values known as pixels, or `px`. Most of the time, screen sizes established by breakpoints are considered to fall into one of three, or perhaps four, categories based on the size of the device display, in CSS pixels. While there are some accessibility issues isolated to mobile devices, most of those issues can be resolved by simply following Mobile First principles. In fact, many general accessibility issues can be resolved by simply following Mobile First principles; however, one issue with breakpoints cannot.

If a design uses breakpoints expressed in CSS pixels, it is likely to fail, probably significantly. This probability rises if the user has increased the default font size of the user-agent, because most breakpoints are evenly divisible by sixteen, the default font size in most user-agents. If the user increases their font size to *large*, or around twenty pixels, they have increased the size of the content by twenty-five percent, and increased the likelihood that at least some of your content is no longer displayed on the screen.

⁂ *Specify breakpoints in relative units (rem).*

## Color

Color is frequently misused. First, although a cross-cultural evaluation of color is beyond the scope of this work, it should be noted that there are strong, often unspoken, cultural understandings about color that should inform your decisions about how to convey meaning with color, or what meaning might be conveyed. Beyond cultural understandings and the potential for cognitive accessibility issues those understandings expose, however, there are additional accessibility concerns surrounding color choice. For example, individuals susceptible to migraines as well as individuals on the autism spectrum often find bright hues troublesome and rarely seen hues can be troublesome for those on the spectrum as well.

Often, organizations overlook their own cultural understanding about color as well as how others, be they from a different culture or someone who has difficulties with specific hues, understand colors and then go further to make a complex or troublesome palette a significant part of brand identity. Some organizations even refer to specific shades of a color as *their color*, like "John Deere Green" or "PayPal Blue". After being so named, the organization will often make every effort to create a strong association between the specific hue and the organization, establishing specific branding guidelines about how and when to use the color. This is one way in which Introspection Centered

Design will help, with Introspection Centered Design we are less likely to overlook such issues.

Finally, color alone should never be used to convey meaning. A significant portion of the population has reported colorblindness, and any meaning conveyed by color alone, rather than a mixture of color, shape, and text, is likely to be missed.

⁂ *A simple color palette should be used, along with a mixture of shapes and text for a more widely accessible interface.*

## Luminance Contrast

In addition to cross-cultural and sensitivity issues there are other potential issues associated with color. For example, some hues are, by their nature, lighter than others and pose *Luminance Contrast Ratio* problems.

☞ The contrast between foreground and background is identified as *color contrast* in the *Web Content Accessibility Guidelines*; however, the test is not related to color, but the comparative brightness, or lightness, of a color.

While cultural issues surrounding color may be difficult to anticipate without significant market research, *Luminance Contrast Ratio* issues are not, as there are many tools that quickly perform calculations that identify potential problems, and many of those tools are available as plugins to browsers, giving designers the opportunity to assess contrast in all aspects of their design, including images[15].

🕸️ There is a potential accessibility issue with a *Luminance Contrast Ratio* that is too high. A *Luminance Contrast Ratio* that is too high is known to trigger migraines as well as lowering the ability of those with some forms of ADHD to focus.

⁂ *Maintain at least a 4.5 to 1 Luminance Contrast Ratio for text and at least a 3.0 to 1 Luminance Contrast Ratio for adjacent colors, and offer users a mechanism to change the Luminance Contrast Ratio whenever possible.*

### Simplifying Development

Often designers will want to use values for light, medium, and dark in the same hue. Although the calculations to get these values can be difficult for colors the way they have been traditionally defined in technology, as values of red, green, and blue, all modern user-agents give the option to define colors using the hue, saturation, and lightness, or HSL, model, a model designers have used for quite a long time.

⁂ *To aid the development of a color palette that maintains a sufficient Luminance Contrast Ratio, it is recommended that colors be specified*

---

[15] One such tool, the *Roking-A11y Color Tuner*, available at https://hrobertking.github.io/roking-a11y/, will even calculate the nearest compliant match for the given test, whether it be for large or normal-sized text or adjacent colors, and its companion tool, the *Roking-A11y Color Matrix* will allow the evaluation of an entire color palette at once.

*using HSL rather than RGB or their hexadecimal value. Although all the values are functionally equivalent, specifying the values as HSL allows the lightness and saturation to be adjusted easily without affecting the hue.*

## Content

Content is the most important aspect of any interface. It is enormously important for content to be clear and concise, and without jargon or slang. Content that does not meet this description will be nearly unusable for a vast number of people using your interface. This rule holds true regardless of whether the content is consumed visually or aurally.

### *Readability*

There are two important measures of content that is consumed visually: legibility and readability. The legibility of content refers to its typographical features, such as font size and alignment. The readability of content refers to how easy, or difficult, it is to read.

### *Flesch*

In the US, readability is often measured using an algorithm developed by Dr. Flesch and Dr. Kincaid, the *Flesch-Kincaid Grade Level*, with measurements given in "grade level". There is a secondary algorithm, the *Flesch Readability Ease*, developed by Dr. Flesch that is not tied directly to a US school grade level. The *Readability Ease* can be calculated as

*Readability Ease*

$$= 206.835 - (1.015 * Average\ Sentence\ Length)$$
$$- (84.6 * Average\ Syllables\ per\ Word)$$

1. Count the number of words in the text
2. Count the number of syllables in the text
3. Count the number of sentences in the text
4. Divide the number of words by the number of sentences (Step 1 / Step 3) to get the Average Sentence Length
5. Divide the number of syllables by the number of words (Step 2 / Step 1) to get the Average Syllables per Word
6. Multiply the Average Sentence Length by 1.015 and multiply the Average Syllables per Word by 84.6
7. Subtract the two numbers from Step 6 from 206.835

Because both algorithms, the *Flesch-Kincaid Grade Level* and the *Flesch Readability Ease*, use the number of syllables to determine word complexity, they are language-dependent, being limited to English. Additionally, grade-level assessment relies on standards used in US primary and secondary schools in the mid-to-late 20th century.

If you are evaluating the readability of US English, the *Flesch Readability Ease* score might be sufficient; however, if you are evaluating non-English content, neither of the aforementioned algorithms will be sufficient.

## Läsbarhetsindex

Rather than using the *Flesch-Kincaid Grade Level* or the *Flesch Readability Ease*, a more reliable scoring method that works across languages, is the Läsbarhetsindex. The Läsbarhetsindex, or LIX, can be calculated as

$$LIX = Average\ Sentence\ Length + (Percentage\ of\ Long\ Words * 100)$$

1. Count the number of words in the text
2. Count the number of words longer than average, or long words in the text
3. Count the number of sentences in the text
4. Divide the number of words by the number of sentences (Step 1 / Step 3) to get the Average Sentence Length
5. Divide the number of long words by the number of words (Step 2 / Step 1) to get the Percentage of Long Words
6. Multiply the Percentage of Long Words by 100 (Step 5 * 100)
7. Add the Average Sentence Length to the result from Step 6

☞ Additionally, although the default measure of a "long" word is six characters, that number can be adjusted to represent the number of characters based on a specific language and the Läsbarhetsindex can be calculated accordingly. It is also important to note that because this algorithm uses character length rather than syllables, this algorithm allows for a greater range of automated testing and verification.

## Readability Scores

The Flesch models and the Läsbarhetsindex are only two methods that can be used to assess the readability of content. Additionally, a third method, Ordvariationsindex, or OVIX, measures the uniqueness of the words used as follows:

$$OVIX = \log(number\ of\ words)\ /\log\ (2 - \frac{\log(number\ of\ unique\ words)}{\log(number\ of\ words)})$$

1. Find the natural logarithm of the number of words in the sample.
2. Find the natural logarithm of the number of unique words in the sample.
3. Divide the value found in Step 2 by the value found in Step 1.
4. Subtract the value found in Step 3 from 2.
5. Find the natural logarithm of the value found in Step 4.
6. Divide the value found in Step 1 by the value found in Step 5.

Generally, a high Läsbarhetsindex or Ordvariationsindex indicates a text is more difficult to read.

☞ All readability scores, whether a Flesch model or the Läsbarhetsindex, might yield incorrect results for extremely short portions of text, such as a label for an input in a form. Therefore, it is very important to review content to ensure that it has been written uses plain language, is without jargon, is "clear and concise", and is well-structured, e.g., has appropriate headings and white space.

⁂ *Content should be clear and concise and well-structured, preferably with a Läsbarhetsindex between forty and sixty.*

### Hiding content

Content can be hidden from either visual presentation or assistive technology, however, each such case should be considered individually to ensure other forms of accessibility, such as cognitive accessibility, are not impacted.

### Hiding content from visual presentation

There are many ways in which content can be hidden from visual presentation, such as by setting the display property, moving the content off screen, or even making the color transparent; however, a good number of the methods commonly used affect other aspects of a page, such as Search Engine Optimization (SEO) or even the *Accessibility Tree*[16]. For example, in most cases, changing the value of the `display` property will change the *semantics* of an element, including not only changing whether or not an element is hidden

---

[16] Search engine bots are typically designed in a way that renders pages in much the same browsers do, meaning they receive the same content users see. This practice increases the likelihood that searches return the best matches possible. Of course this also means that if content is not available in the browser or *Accessibility Tree*, the content is likely to be ignored by the search bot, removing its effect(s) from any optimization.

from visual presentation but also whether or not it is available to assistive technology, and how the element is rendered in the *Accessibility Tree*.

⁂ *Although there are many techniques that can be used to purely hide content, a modified clip method (using the following style rules) should be used, because this method works across the greatest range of user-agents, without affecting the presentation of the content in assistive technology and without affecting search ranking.*

```
.clipped {
  border: 0 !important;
  clip: rect(0, 0, 0, 0);
  clip-path: polygon(0 0, 0 0, 0 0, 0 0);
  left: -200% !important;
  overflow: hidden;
  position: absolute !important;
}
```

This method maintains the semantics of the element, by not changing the display, and maintains the height, visibility, and width of the element, which keeps the element, including an overflow, available to assistive technology[17] and visually *clips* the content, somewhat like cropping an image. Finally, the element is absolutely positioned but sets only the left property. This approach avoids some focus issues that can occur when the left and top coordinates are provided together. In most user-agents, the left property is relatively meaningless; however, not all user-agents

---

[17] A height of "0", a width of "0", or "hidden" visibility will often prevent an element of rendering in the *Accessibility Tree*.

calculate a clipped region correctly, and as a result, alignment will be an issue[18].

## Hiding content from assistive technology

In some cases, we will want to hide content from assistive technology, either temporarily or permanently. If the content is to be hidden temporarily, such as images in a Carousel that are outside the viewport, use the `aria-hidden` attribute. However, if the content is to be hidden permanently, such as an image that is purely decorative, use "`role="none"`". It is important to note that if a *presentation* or *none* role is used, the item will not be added to the *Accessibility Tree*.

## Hiding content from visual presentation and assistive technology.

In some cases, we will hide content from visual presentation *and* assistive technology, such as an inactive Tab. In this case, using the display style property with a value of "none", is the simplest way to completely hide content.

## Data Visualizations

Data visualizations can be a significant accessibility issue. Often the visualization is used in place of the data, the visualization is not adequately described, and the visualization does not meet accessibility requirements regarding color. Each of these issues

---

[18] A overly-large negative value for the left can also cause this issue; therefore, the use of 200% is highly recommended.

alone is significant and will render your page inaccessible by failing several of the Web Content Accessibility Guidelines tests. While the relationships between data elements are complex, they still be must be described as completely and accurately as possible, all elements that use color must be described in visible text, and all adjacent colors and text must pass *Luminance Contrast Ratio* guidelines.

⁂ *It is highly recommended the data used to generate a visualization be represented in a table in the document, even if the table is not visually present but only available to accessibility technology. If the data is not visually present, a mechanism that enables the visual presentation of data should be present in the page. Additionally, all references using color should be clearly labeled to avoid instances where color alone is conveying meaning.*

## Floating Buttons and Sticky Elements

One design trend is to float a button, typically on the left or right side of the screen, as the user scrolls vertically. These buttons are always present in the user's view and often offer navigation features such as the ability to jump to the top of a page through a scroll-to-top button, or additional interaction options, such as click-to-chat button that opens a window to a customer representative.

It is best that you avoid *all* sticky elements, floating buttons included, whenever possible. While the interactions provided by buttons is likely not at issue, the placement of sticky elements frequently proves to be an issue. When sticky or floating, a button or other content is at risk of obscuring other content. Additionally, these elements create a movement difference between the foreground and background. This movement difference is the same movement difference that makes parallax animations work, and it frequently triggers vestibular impairment and illness in users. Cognitive issues may come into play with sticky elements as they're taken out of the visual hierarchy and seem to be taken out of the tab order as they are prominently visually present even though they are not in focus.

## Forms

Forms can be one of the most difficult interfaces to design. Each data element to be collected must be matched to the appropriate input type and labeled, keeping simplicity and clarity in mind. Luckily, there are a number of different types of input, both native to HTML and common interfaces, each meeting a particular need.

☞ After almost a quarter of a century of research, we know a number of things about how users interact with forms. We know, for instance, which types of data, like dates and numbers, are likely to pose problems, as well as how the overall style of a page, style features such as backgrounds and borders, will perform. Several of the hard-won conclusions based on the data collected over years of research is presented here.

Although a number of accessibility issues can be resolved by simply selecting the correct input type, some input types are not accessible in their native HTML format; for example, a date type, i.e., "`<input type="date" />`", exposes the different date parts as unlabeled lists. However, accessibility issues may be resolved or at least reduced through the use of the best practices in development and use of specific design patterns.

## Input Types

The basis of any form is the collection of data. This is done in a web page or application through the use of various input types which may be specified through the use of an HTML `input`, `select`, or `textarea` as well as a number of other combinations. A partial list of input types, some of which can be specified using native HTML, includes the following. Each of these types can be found in the *Design Patterns* section.

- *Checkbox*: Allows a user to select and unselect. When it is in a group, zero or more can be selected.
- *Combobox*: Allows the user to select from a list of options or provide a value not on the list.
- *Date*: Allows the user to enter a value that is a valid date.
- *Password*: Typically hides what the user is typing, keeping the value hidden from a *Passerby Attack*.
- *Radio*: Must be used in a group in which only one item can be selected.
- *Slider*: Allows selection of a value within a range, e.g., a value between 1 and 10.

- *Switch*: A two-state button-like input, typically representing an on or off state.

⁂ *Forms should only ask for information necessary for the completion of a task, clearly labeled, and using the appropriate input type.*

## Backgrounds

Although there are significant differences between cultures regard color in general, the visual cues given by a lighter background inside an editable field than is used in the background color of the form indicates the value is empty and needs to be filled. Using a darker background color for the form strengthens this visual cue. Additionally, providing empty space around fields to be updated not only strengthens visual cues associated with the fields, but may also improve the accessibility for individuals with motor impairments by separating touch targets.

⁂ *Use a light background for inputs and a darker background for the overall form.*

## Borders

Borders can, importantly, give a visual cue to important features such as where the user should enter information, and borders are a special case where there exists a strong, globally-shared understanding that directly affects a form's accessibility. Sharp, square corners are seen as aggressive and unfriendly whereas rounded corners are not interpreted as aggressive or unfriendly. Interestingly, the degree used when rounding the corner, or rather the size of the `border-radius`, does not seem to significantly influence this impression, as long as the border is visibly rounded.

Missing borders, thin borders, and borders on only one side, such as a bottom-only border, pose accessibility issues, especially for those facing cognitive impairment as the affordance they give is often unclear. Aside from the lack of clarity single side borders pose, thicker, higher-contrast borders are more difficult to miss visually and can offer significant clickability cues.

⁂ *Keep in mind that if someone has difficulty seeing a sixteen pixel font, they'll likely have difficulty seeing a two pixel border, so it will be to your advantage to specify the border width relative to the font size. Use high-contrast borders that are approximately one-sixteenth (0.0625) to one-eighth (0.125) the size of the font.*

### Fonts

Although much can be said about typography in general, fonts used within a form deserve special attention, because in many user-agents, fonts used in input interfaces in forms are *different* than that specified for the remainder of the web page or application. In most cases, the font size is smaller and in many cases, a different font family is used[19]. These browser defaults can, and should, be overridden for the best experience.

---

[19] At the time of this writing, the *Google Chrome* browser uses a font within an input that is less than seventy percent the font size used in the remainder of the page, as the default font size for an HTML input in a page with an unmodified root font size of sixteen pixels is a mere eleven pixels.

*⁂ Specify the font details to be used in input interfaces. If the style rules recommended in the Summary section are not used, it is highly recommended that `font: inherit`, `letter-spacing: inherit`, and `word-spacing: inherit` be added to your stylesheet.*

## *Focus Styles*

A very common practice in many designs is to remove the *outline* that appears around an item. This practice is so common, in fact, that it makes nearly every accessibility expert's top ten list of don'ts. Removal of focus indicators will result in a decrease in the accessibility of your webpage or application and may result in a failure to pass Web Content Accessibility Guidelines tests. While your page does not necessarily need the default focus indicator provided by the CSS outline property, if the outline is removed, it must be replaced by other style changes that indicate focus.

Another common practice is to remove focus indicators for device interactions that are not through the keyboard, such as a mouse or other pointer device. While this does not technically result in an error according to the *Web Content Accessibility Guidelines*, it still reduces accessibility, especially cognitive accessibility.

*⁂ Focus indicators must always be present. Also, consider adding a hover interaction that corresponds, but does not duplicate, the focus styles applied.*

## *Labels*

With the decreased real estate of mobile environments, designers are often encouraged to either remove or hide the label that goes along with an input. Hiding and removing labels has become even more common practice despite the use of eye-tracking technology clearly demonstrating the greater performance of left-aligned labels displayed above the input to which they are tied. Even though removing or hiding input labels has become increasingly common, we must acknowledge that removing or hiding a label reduces the accessibility of inputs and should not, under any circumstances, be allowed.

⁑ *Every input must have a visible label, created using a label tag that is paired with the input using the for and id attributes as shown below. Additionally, the label and input should be stacked.*

```
<label for="myinput">A visual label for the associated input</label>
<input id="myinput" type="text" />
```

Further, the label and input should be grouped together with either a semantic tag, e.g., `p` or `li`, or a non-semantic tag, e.g., `div` or `span`.

⁑ *The label should not wrap the input. The accessible name of the label is determined by content, and including an HTML tag within a label results in text fragmentation on some platforms, resulting in an incorrect, and sometimes missing, accessible name. If the label must wrap the input, as in some implementations of the Switch, extra steps* *must be taken to mitigate the risk of an incorrect calculation, namely, the **aria-labelledby** attribute must be set correctly.*

Finally, the label provided to assistive technology should be the same as that provided visually. The exception to this rule is needlelike, as a difference between the visual label and the assistive label is only allowable when there is only one so labeled item. For example, an *add to cart* button might have the label "add to cart" for assistive technology and a different visual label, one that does not say "add to cart"[20]. In this example, the difference between the visual label and the accessible label is acceptable only if there are not multiple "add to cart" buttons. Having different visual and assistive labels in other situations will cause difficulties for those using speech recognition technology as they are likely to struggle to select the correct item.

⁂ *All inputs should have a visible label, and the visisble label and the assistive label should be the same.*

### Placeholders

A placeholder, sometimes called "ghost text", is special text displayed within an input. It is not a default value, but rather may be an entry format hint, like *mm/dd/yyyy* inside a date input, or perhaps a field label.

---

[20] Even though the name does not have to match exactly when there is a single labeled item, the visual text must be a part of the accessible name, e.g., our single "add to cart" button could have visible text that simply says "add".

☠ Although the placeholder has been added back into the accessible name calculation in the latest version, it should *never* be used as a field label as the support for placeholders as a label is nearly non-existent.

There are a number of well-documented usability issues and accessibility issues associated with the use of a placeholder, including *Luminance Contrast Ratio* errors, and the content being ignored by assistive technology, which may leave fields without a label or users without key formatting information. Placeholders can also cause confusion in other ways. Consider the following markup.

```
<label for="ccnum">Card Number</label>
<input id="ccnum" maxlength="16" placeholder="1234 5678 9012 3456"
type="text" />
```

In this markup, the card number is restricted to sixteen digits and the example provided is sixteen digits in four groups, each group separated from the others by a single space. If the user understands the hint from the placeholder, they are likely to attempt to enter the card number with the spaces, however, that behavior will be blocked by the character limit imposed by the `maxlength`, leaving the user confused.

⁂ *Because of the myriad accessibility and usability issues, placeholders should never be used.*

## *Validation*

Validation within an input is very useful. Although it often requires the addition of JavaScript, it can be an important part of accessibility. Displaying the results of validation and information that indicates how the input can be corrected is an important part of accessibility, and is a requirement if the validation is done in real-time. It is important to point out that validity of input may be determined by a number of rules. For example, a credit card number that can be fifteen or sixteen digits may be required, valid only if the length of the account is greater than a minimum number and less than a maximum number, and internally valid as ensured by the Luhn algorithm. These rules represent *missing, too short, too long*, and *invalid account* errors. Each of these errors must be correctly identified by text that accompanies the invalid status that specifically identifies the error and gives an indication how to resolve the error. Regardless of which error occurs, however, the validity of the contents of an input with one or more validation rules can either be valid, invalid, or unknown. It is common to represent these states by either a checkmark icon, a warning icon, or no icon, respectively. In the markup, these three states are generally identified using "aria-invalid="false"", "aria-invalid="true"", or either "aria-invalid=""" or the lack of the aria-invalid attribute.

Although it is possible to use background images to convey this status, there are occasionally problems with the display of background images. For this reason, the use of UTF-8 content is recommended. This approach requires the addition of a container for the content as the HTML input tag does not allow a before or after pseudo-element. The markup and CSS in the *Summary* section below assumes the label and input are wrapped in a containing element, as is suggested above and facilitates the identification of different states using the `aria-invalid` attribute. Because an empty `aria-invalid` state defaults to false, including an empty `aria-invalid` attribute allows for consistent styling with accurate reporting.

Additionally, the validation status is tied directly to the input using the `aria-describedby` attribute for those cases in which the status role is not used by the assistive technology in use.

⁂ *Validation is an important part of responsiveness and significantly reduces cognitive load in forms; however, it should not be restricted to assistive technology alone, there should be a visual indicator paired with the **aria-invalid** attribute.*

### Summary

As noted above, each editable field should have a light background, rounded borders, a focus indicator, a validity indicator, and a descriptive hint. For that reason, the recommended pattern[21] for declaring fields shown in the image below follows the image.

Tax ID Number (required)   Date of Birth (required)   Telephone (optional)

```
123-45-6789        ✔   i        [                 ⚠ ]        [                 ]
999-99-9999                     mm/dd/yyyy
```

## HTML

```
<span class="field">
  <label for="tid">Tax ID Number (required)</label>
  <input
    aria-describedby="tid-descr tid-status" aria-invalid="false"
    id="tid" type="text" />
  <span id="tid-status" role="status"></span>
  <span role="tooltip" tabindex="0">
    <span role="alert">
      We are required by law to collect this information.
    </span>
  </span>
  <span class="hint" id="tid-descr">999-99-9999</span>
</span>
<span class="field">
  <label for="dob">Date of Birth (required)</label>
  <input
    aria-describedby="dob-descr dob-status" aria-invalid="true"
    id="dob" type="text" />
  <span for="dob-status" role="status"></span>
  <span class="hint" id="dob-descr">mm/dd/yyyy</span>
</span>
<span class="field">
  <label for="tel">Telephone (optional)</label>
  <input
    aria-describedby="tel-descr tel-status" aria-invalid=""
    id="tel" type="tel" />
  <span for="tel-status" role="status"></span>
  <span class="hint" id="tel-descr"> </span>
</span>
```

## CSS

```
/* general formatting */
fieldset {
  border: 0;
  padding: 0;
}
```

---

[21] The recommended pattern includes both the HTML pattern and the CSS that applies to that pattern.

```
.clipped {
  border: 0;
  clip: rect(0, 0, 0, 0);
  clip-path: polygon(0 0, 0 0, 0 0, 0 0);
  left: -200%;
  outline: none;
  position: absolute;
}
.clipped :focus {
  outline: none;
}

.field {
  display: block;
  margin: 0.25rem 0.25em 1em 0.25em;
  position: relative;
}
.field label {
  display: block;
  margin: 0;
  padding: 0;
}
.field button,
.field input,
.field select,
.field textarea,
.field [role="listbox"] {
  border: 0.0625em solid hsl(204, 100%, 30%);
  border-radius: 0.25em;
  font-size: 1em;
  min-height: 1.2em;
  padding: 0.25em 1.2em 0.25em 0.25em;
  -webkit-appearance: none;
}
.field button {
  text-align: center;
  padding: 0.25em;
}

/* status indicators and hints */
input[aria-invalid] + [role="status"],
select[aria-invalid] + [role="status"] {
  clip-path: polygon(0 0, 0 1em, 1em 1em, 1em 0);
  display: inline-block;
  font-style: normal;
  height: 1em;
  line-height: 1.2em;
  margin: 0 0.5em 0 -1.5em;
  overflow: hidden;
  position: relative;
  top: 0.125em;
  width: 1em;
}
textarea[aria-invalid] + [role="status"]::before {
  margin-left: -1.2em;
  position: absolute;
  top: 1.1em;
}
```

```css
input[aria-invalid] + [role="status"]::before,
select[aria-invalid] + [role="status"]::before,
textarea[aria-invalid] + [role="status"]::before {
  content: '\2007';
  display: inline-block;
}
input[aria-invalid="false"] + [role="status"]::before,
select[aria-invalid="false"] + [role="status"]::before,
textarea[aria-invalid="false"] + [role="status"]::before {
  color: hsl(120, 60%, 35%);
  content: '✓';
}
input[aria-invalid="true"] + [role="status"]::before,
select[aria-invalid="true"] + [role="status"]::before,
textarea[aria-invalid="true"] + [role="status"]::before {
  color: hsl(0, 100%, 35%);
  content: '⚠';
}
input ~ label,
input ~ .hint,
select ~ label,
select ~ .hint,
textarea ~ label,
textarea ~ .hint {
  color: hsl(0, 0%, 45%);
  display: block;
  font-size: 0.8em;
}

/* group formatting */
.field [role="group"],
fieldset [role="group"] {
  align-items: center;
  display: flex;
  margin: 0;
  padding: 0;
}
.field [role="group"] > .field:first-of-type,
fieldset [role="group"] > .field:first-of-type {
  margin-left: 0;
}
.field [role="group"] > .field:last-of-type,
fieldset [role="group"] > .field:last-of-type {
  margin-right: 0;
}
```

## Graphics and Media

Graphics and other forms of media can pose a number of problems.
*All media* requires alternative or descriptive text. For all audio
present, a transcript must be provided, and descriptive text should
be provided for both moving and still visual content, i.e., images
and video. The exception to this general rule is when an images is

inside a link, as is shown the code samples, Image as a link and Image with a link, below.

☠ A transcript alone does not meet level AA of the Web Content Accessibility Guidelines, descriptions *must* be present.

### Image as a link

```
HTML
<a href="resource.htm">
  <img alt="Alternative text" src="resource.svg">
</a>
```

### Image inside a link

```
HTML
<a href="resource.htm">
  <img alt="" src="resource.svg">
  Alternative text
</a>
```

⁂ *When an image is a link, the alternative text should be a description of the link, not the image.*

### Text in Graphics and Media

Additionally, text content that is not also present within the content of the page should not ever appear in a visual resource, moving or still, unless it is purely decorative. While it has generally been suggested that images be placed in the background when they are decorative to improve performance, this can pose a problem if the image conveys meaning, even as a background. A background image that conveys meaning, such as an icon used in a button, poses a special problem as background images are removed in some platforms. Also consider whether or not the image could be served as a traditional SVG with path elements that define the image. If it can be included as an SVG, it will be available offline and the compression for an inline SVG, compressed as part of the HTML, will render it as small as, or in some cases smaller, than a comparable external file in another format.

The reverse of this practice is also recommended. As much as possible, text should be paired with an image. This is especially true as complexity increases, in equations, for example, or as data is summarized, such as in a visualization.

*⁎* *Images and text should have a complementary relationship, each reliant on the other. Additionally, inline images should be used when possible to avoid difficulties that come from presenting graphics as background images; however, they must always have an **alt** attribute provided, even if it is empty. If the image is decorative only, consider removing it from the Accessibility Tree by using the **role** attribute along with an empty **alt** attribute.*

## Icons

Although there are icons that are nearly universal in a channel, the hamburger menu icon for example, no icon should stand on its own. All icons *must* be accompanied by a label that identifies the icon. Even in cases where UTF-8 symbols are used, there should not be a reliance on the platform announcing them. In some platforms UTF-8 symbols are announced, just as some emoticons are, without additional labeling, however, there is not nearly enough support across platforms to consider such behavior standard.

In those cases where an icon comes from a *font* and the label exists outside the icon, the icon should be hidden from assistive technology using the "aria-hidden" attribute to prevent the mapped character from being announced. Consider that the *best* method for ensuring correct labeling and use of icons may not be the current practice of providing an alternative font, but rather to use an SVG image that can easily scale and adapt to use font color and size, and providing the label as alternative text.

⁂ *Because of the variance in platforms, it is recommended that announcements of UTF-8 special characters be considered a fallback and that a practice of overriding announced values and labeling all icons be followed.*

## Infinite Scroll

It is tempting to add infinite scrolling to your page when there's a lot of data, and several large corporations employ this approach, but the number of well-documented accessibility issues with infinite scrolling should give a clue to just how bad it is. It's so bad, in fact, that it has made the anti-patterns list.

⁂ *Use a button to load more data rather than infinite scrolling.*

## JavaScript

Any discussion about JavaScript in relation to accessibility must include the approach taken when JavaScript is not available. There are three general reasons JavaScript is not available to a user and they are: the user, the source page or application, and what lies between the source and the user.

Although most methods used to track users require JavaScript and therefore cannot capture the number of visitors without JavaScript, the percentage of users reportedly visiting sites across the internet without JavaScript has consistently hovered around one percent for the past decade. It should also be noted that the use of JavaScript does not render a site or application inaccessible; however, *how* JavaScript is included may render a site or application inaccessible[22].

Of the three groups of "no js" users, the members of the first group either uses a device or user-agent that does not include JavaScript or have disabled JavaScript in their device or user-agent. This group are those typically identified by user tracking and represent the one percent of users reported as not having JavaScript. The other two groups, those without JavaScript due to the source and what lies between the source and the user, seldom are reported at all but generally contain more than twice the number of the first group.

The first of these two other groups, those without JavaScript due to the source, may have its members reduced by thorough testing and

---

[22] It should also be noted that with few exceptions, the use of JavaScript frameworks, such as React, Angular, or Vue, and the use of JavaScript libraries, such as Lodash, Moment, and jQuery, *dramatically* increase the likelihood of simple accessibility issues that can be discovered with automated testing.

control of the source. Frequently a small, undetected defect that is inappropriately handled will disable the use of JavaScript entirely, so thorough testing is imperative, as is control of the source. This group includes not only blatant errors that even the smallest amount of testing will identify, but also includes errors that find their way into a source because of browser support policies.

The second of these two other groups, those without JavaScript due to something between the source and the user is a much larger group than either of the others. For members of this group, the source has been thoroughly tested and is without error, and the user's device is capable of using the JavaScript that is to be included in the experience, but the JavaScript doesn't arrive. Because members of this group do not fall into either of the other two easily-identified and easily-accommodated groups, they are the least likely to be accommodated and at the greatest risk for accessibility issues, and they are also the reason many accessibility experts live by the maxim that "none of your users are using JavaScript while they're downloading your JavaScript". There are a number of reasons the experience may fail for members of this group, as delivery of the JavaScript may be delayed or prevented entirely.

If the entire user experience is governed by JavaScript, as it often is when a JavaScript framework is used, the entire user experience is at risk, accessibility included. However, the experience of all three groups can be addressed using the best practices for web development that were established nearly two decades ago when users were much more likely to fall into one of these three "no js" groups. Even though we have lost sight of the number of people in these groups over the years, the best practices of keeping JavaScript unobtrusive and using it to enhance functionality rather than building it entirely still applies.

※ There is a special word of warning about including CSS in JavaScript. While this practice is intended to keep stylesheets from becoming bloated, the dynamic nature of the class names creates special challenges to individuals with impairment who have adapted their behavior and environment to compensate for issues as the dynamic class names cannot be added to any of the usual tools users may employ.

⁑ *Development is best done using <u>Progressive Enhancement</u>, which provides that the content and functionality are available to the greatest number of people, which is what accessibility is all about.*

## Sizes

Designs, with borders and drop shadows, margins, and padding are all relative to the font. If a font is too thin or small to be read by a user with visual impairment, narrow borders and margins will also not be seen clearly. Although it is relatively common knowledge that fonts should not be specified in absolute values such as pixels (px) or points (pt), the same advice for other design elements, like margin, padding, and borders, is seldom followed.

If a user has visual impairment issues which would lead them to alter the default font size, they can still enjoy the design as the designer intends it if margins, padding, and borders are all also relative to the font size.

⁂ *All sizes, including borders, margins, padding, and breakpoints, should be specified as relative to the font size used, i.e., in* **em***.*

## Tooltips

Tooltips can be difficult to implement correctly; however, one thing the majority of accessibility experts agree on is that the "title" attribute should not be used. In short, using the title attribute excludes users with touch-sensitive devices, such as smartphones and tablets, and keyboard-only users on laptops and desktops, as well as anyone using assistive technology. Because it excludes keyboard-only users, it will fail the guidance given in the *Web Content Accessibility Guidelines* without modification.

Even when not using the title attribute, there are a number of good reasons to do away with dynamically-shown tooltips altogether in favor of a static option where content is always available; however, if your page or site simply must have a dynamic tooltip, take a look at the Tooltip component in the *Design Patterns* section.

## Touch Targets

As the use of mobile devices, both phone and tablet, has increased, so has the importance of the size of touch targets. The requirement regarding touch targets from the *Web Content Accessibility Guidelines* is that they must be a minimum of 44 *CSS pixels*. It is important to note that the specification uses CSS pixels rather than a calculation that uses pixel depth, because while resolution varies across devices, and therefore the number of actual pixels varies, a *CSS pixel* is a set width value that uses print resolution of 96 pixels per inch, making the touch target requirement approximately 12 millimeters[23].

☠ If two touch targets overlap, the area of overlap is not part of the calculation when determining whether or not the target size minimum is reached.

Of course, as important as touch targets are, the space surrounding the touch target, the non-reactive area, is equally important. The minimum size of space around a touch target is also 12 millimeters.

---

[23] Although the *Web Content Accessibility Guidelines* list target size under their most stringent of compliance levels and leave exceptions for inline controls, those controls rendered unmodified by the user-agent, and those controls whose present is essential to the information being conveyed, it is strongly recommended this guideline be followed closely as mobility issues are becoming increasingly prevalent as the population ages.

⁂ *All touch targets and surrounding non-reactive space must be at least forty-four CSS pixels, in height and width, or approximately 12 millimeters.*

## Typography

Although typography is often the first thing that comes to mind when we mention readability, it is important that those two terms not be confused. Typography is a part of legibility, but generally has nothing to do with readability, which was covered in the section above regarding content.

One of the more important aspects of typography is the font used. In considering the font family used, there are two general issues that should be considered: distinctiveness and stroke width. Although designers will often consider the distinctiveness offered by serif fonts as opposed to sans serif fonts, they less frequently consider that the thickness of the stroke is often more important. In recent years, many of the designs coming out of Apple used fonts with a thin stroke; however, they have moved away from the extraordinarily thin stroked fonts as they pose legibility problems, even when the *Luminance Contrast Ratio* is sufficient. As a design leader, Apple's shift away from thin strokes will hopefully bring along those who followed their initial design lead.

⁂ *Use a distinctive font with adequate stroke width.*

❀ Beyond the distinctiveness of the font and stroke width, there are issues specifically around font family for those with dyslexia. Certain fonts are significantly more difficult to read, and while it is not possible to identify a single font usable for all those with dyslexia, it is important to note that the use of the keyword `!important` to lock a font family into use is definitely a great enough threat to be considered more than a stumbling block and is certainly an anti-pattern.

A third consideration with typography is the size as some fonts are less legible even at the standard width of sixteen pixels. The difference in legibility at different sizes is the basis for the *Web Content Accessibility Guidelines* stipulating that users must be capable of resizing the font by two hundred percent, and designs must be able to accommodate such increases without suffering collapse. In addition to the design accommodating different font sizes, the ability to resize the font must be maintained technically. In order to maintain the ability to resize fonts, font sizes must be specified in *relative* units rather than in absolute units, such as pixels or points. Specifying font size in relative units is especially critical for users who have adjusted the default font size in their browser, because font sizes specified in absolute units will override the default browser font size, rendering the user's choice about what works best for them moot.

⁂ *Always design assuming font sizes will be increased and specify font size in relative units.*

Beyond the quirks about font, there are several little-known aspects of typography that can impact accessibility, such as words that appear in uppercase are sometimes spelled rather than read by assistive technology, and vice versa. While this may be desired behavior for some abbreviations, care should be used to ensure that words appearing in uppercase, including acronyms like NASA, be thoroughly tested and, if required, have an adequate label to correct for this behavior, as the behavior will vary between platforms.

☠ This behavior may also occur when the letter case is modified using CSS, not just when the text appears in uppercase in the markup.

In addition to how case affects word announcement by assistive technology, case also affects overall legibility for a number of impairments. Although there is a common misconception that word shape, especially the reduction in variance that accompanies words presented in all uppercase, reduces reading speed the evidence clearly indicates that it does not reduce reading speed for those with low or normal vision. In fact, the data demonstrates that reading speeds are faster for words presented in uppercase[24].

---

[24] Arditi, Aries & Jianna Cho. 2007. "Letter case and text legibility in normal and low vision." *Vision Research* 47, no. 19 (September): 2499-2505. https://dx.doi.org/10.1016%2Fj.visres.2007.06.010

Although the data is limited regarding reading speed for those with normal and low vision aside that have cognitive impairments, anecdotal evidence suggests the lower shape contrast for words in all uppercase might be problematic for those with cognitive impairments, such as autism or dyslexia, making *comprehension* more difficult.

⁂ *Uppercase and smallcaps should be used only for those abbreviations and acronyms that are common or should be spelled out rather than read.*

In addition to font size and stroke width, letter case, and variants, the justification used also affects accessibility. All paragraphs should be left justified in languages that read left-to-right. In languages that read right-to-left, paragraphs should be right justified. *At no time should full justification be used* as it causes difficulties for those with several different kinds of impairment.

⁂ *Use language-specific paragraph justification, never full justification.*

## Web Content Accessibility Guidelines

One of the primary resources used to measure conformity to an accessibility standard is the *Web Content Accessibility Guidelines*, or WCAG. The *Web Content Accessibility Guidelines* identifies not only recommendations in the form of guidelines, but tests a web page must pass in order to be considered compliant, called *Success Criteria*. In some places, the guidelines and tests contained in the

*Web Content Accessibility Guidelines* are used in statutes that order compliance and in others they're merely strongly recommended.

☞ While it is not possible for a resource to fail a test criterion in the *Web Content Accessibility Guidelines* and be considered accessible, the reverse is not necessarily true. It is possible for a resource to pass all tests listed in the *Web Content Accessibility Guidelines* and still not be accessible. Passing the test criteria is a necessary condition, but it not a sufficient condition, for accessibility.

⁂ *Basic evaluation of pages and processes, using the Web Content Accessibility Guidelines should occur at each stage of the development process; however, such testing should not be the sole evaluation method.*

## Stumbling Blocks and Anti-patterns

Anti-patterns are common solutions to common problems where the solution is both ineffective and may result in undesired consequences. An anti-pattern is different from bad practice, because while it is a common practice that initially looks like an appropriate solution, it frequently results in negative consequences that outweigh any benefits.

### Ambiguous Label

Perhaps the most common *Ambiguous Label* anti-pattern is the one known as "click here", but this anti-pattern includes any content that is overly concise, gaining a portion of its meaning from proximity or other context, such as a related noun. Other examples include verbs without nouns, like "select", "delete", or even short phrases such as "add to cart".

As one might expect, this anti-pattern primarily affects users relying on screen readers as screen readers fail to gather context from visual surroundings.

## Conveying Meaning with Hover

It is tempting, and is in fact a common practice, to use hover to convey meaning, displaying dynamic content like a tooltip for example. However, not only is the ability to hover limited by device type, for example, a user can't hover when using a mobile device, it is not a universal ability across all users as not all users employ a pointing device. The dual device dependence introduced as a part of this practice may lead to a poorer overall experience and is a direct violation of the *Web Content Accessibility Guidelines*.

## Disabled Resize

It is often tempting to disable the ability to resize an interface. This often is the result of difficulties associated with breakpoints and the use of an adaptive design that delivers one experience to a mobile device and a different experience to a laptop or desktop computer coupled with the desire to deliver a usable experience to everyone regardless of their device. However, users with low vision often depend on the ability to zoom content, especially when other methods of increasing the size fail, and as a result, a web page should never set the "user-scalable" property to no or set the "maximum-scale".

## Div-itis

When developing an interface, it is tempting to wrap every item in a container and adding containers whose sole purpose it is to alter the display by forcing content to another position, making the visual representation match the specified visual. This results in more content being read by the user-agent and, at the very least, delaying the experience for many using assistive technology, and may affect the *Accessibility Tree*.

## Important

It can easily be argued that in most cases[25] the use of the CSS keyword, `!important`, causes enough issues it qualifies as more than a mere stumbling block, becoming an anti-pattern. Properly understood, it is a specific instance of the *Usurping the User* anti-pattern. This anti-pattern deserves special attention because it directly overrides the user's experience and any custom settings they may have put in place to counteract the obstacles that exist in a web page or application. For example, colors and fonts that present difficulties for a user can often be altered by the user in a manner that allows them to continue unobstructed interaction;

---

[25] There are few instances where the use of `!important` should be accepted, such as when content should be hidden and overriding properties that might reveal hidden content is critical.

however, the presence of this keyword prevents that override ability.

## Infinite Scroll

The number of accessibility and usability problems with infinite scrolling are enough to earn it a place on the anti-patterns list, but it might also cross the *Usurping the User* anti-pattern with the context switching its automatic loading brings on. Even the most optimistic would be realistic in claiming that it is extremely difficult to construct an infinite scrolling component that even comes close to being accessible, it should be considered impossible.

## JavaScript Protocol

Although *JavaScript Protocol* sounds like it could be the latest thriller, it is when the word "javascript" appears in the href attribute of a link, e.g., `<a href="javascript:alert('Hello World')">say 'hi'</a>`, telling the link to execute a script rather than navigate to a resource. The list of accessibility issues this practice yields is too long to list here in its entirety. Anchors, or links, written in this way are almost never announced correctly and always blur the line between a link to a resource and a button that performs an action. They are often used because a designer wants something to appear like a link even though programmatically it is not a link, which in itself poses cognitive accessibility issues.

## Manipulated Focus

While there are cases in which setting focus is not an anti-pattern, such as when a "dialog" is opened, those situations are rare exceptions. Setting focus earns a place in the anti-pattern list because it not only creates inconsistency, which is critical for accessibility, it takes away the user's control.

Additionally, the few advantages offered by setting focus, such as mouse users being saved a click and sighted keyboard users being saved a few tabs, are only beneficial if the user understands where focus has been placed. It is for this reason that focus should never be manipulated unless the element receiving focus is not preceded by content, and more importantly, the element describes the purpose of the interface.

## Opening New Windows

Product teams are often reluctant to encourage, or allow, users to go somewhere outside their site in the middle of the current process as users are seen as unlikely to return. The teams spend a significant amount of effort and money to attract users and feel the need to convert users into profitable transactions. As such, links that provide additional content are likely to open in a new window to keep the user in the current process while also being able to review additional content.

Although there are some who consider forcing links to open in a new window an anti-pattern because the application is taking control away from the user, that opinion is not universally shared. However, while there is debate about whether or not a link opening in a new window is by itself an anti-pattern, there is no debate that *opening a new window without letting the user know beforehand is an anti-pattern*.

Not only does the lack of notification associated with opening a link in a new window take away the user's autonomy, it will almost certainly leave the user confused, lacking a clear understanding their location. It should be noted that notification must be given to both non-sighted and sighted users; the mere addition of clipped text that is only announced to those using a text-to-speech tool is not sufficient.

## The Placeholder

The *Placeholder* anti-pattern takes two forms, in one form there is an accompanying label for the input and in the other form the placeholder is used as the input label.

### Placeholder with a Label

There are several issues associated with the use of the placeholder attribute, the worst of these exist even when a label is used. For example, the placeholder content is a visual-only cue, as the content is unlikely to be announced reliably even though it *might* be announced on some platforms. As a visual-only cue, however, the *Luminance Contrast Ratio* is not sufficient for sighted users and the content can seldom be styled in a way that overcomes this inadequacy. On the other hand, if the content is styled to give a sufficient *Luminance Contrast Ratio*, placeholder content lacks other affordances that indicate it is not a pre-filled value, decreasing cognitive accessibility.

## Placeholder without a Label

If the placeholder *replaces* the label for an input, there are several additional issues that arise. For example, the touch target of the input becomes significantly smaller, leaving open the risk of violating one of the *Web Content Accessibility Guidelines*. Additionally, the placeholder content always disappears when content has been entered in the field, but often disappears when the field receives focus, leaving the user wondering what data should be entered or updated, making both filling the form and correcting errors more difficult.

## Scrolljacking

*Scrolljacking* is when the scrollbar is redesigned or manipulated to behave independently of the user's efforts and intents. In most cases, the intention is to manage animation or viewable content in a way that makes sense to the designer; however, therein lies the problem, as the user's experience is secondary to how the designer or developer believes the interface should work.

Because a scrollbar is native to nearly all user-agents, users expect the scrollbar to look and behave a certain way, a way that is consistent across all websites and web applications. When the scrollbar is hijacked, either in style or behavior, that consistency, a key concept of accessible design, is broken. When consistency is broken, cognitive accessibility is reduced, and along with cognitive accessibility, usability and conversion.

## Shiny New Thing

The *Shiny New Thing* anti-pattern is when a design or development trend takes precedence over accessibility and usability that comes as a result of good design and development practices. Although this anti-pattern usually includes claims of significant improvement, those claims are seldom well-tested or are fraught with bias. In this anti-pattern, teams lose sight of the needs of users when creating an interface, including design or development features that correspond to a specific fad or fashion, and it often occurs as the result of an imbalanced product team, heavily weighted toward designers or technologists.

## Tabindex Overload

Given that the *Web Content Accessibility Guidelines* speak specifically about the requirement for keyboard navigation, it is tempting to make certain that all users who are using a keyboard can get to any element on the page. To make certain users can reach any element, developers are tempted to add a "tabindex" attribute so an element can receive focus; however, developers should not apply the tabindex attribute to non-interactive elements like headings or paragraphs. Applying the tabindex will add additional, unnecessary tabstops that tend to overload the user. Additionally, tabindexes on non-interactive elements are likely to confuse users because attempts to interact with the element will fail to provide feedback to the user.

## Tables as Layout

In the early days of the web, it was relatively common to use a table to layout a page in a user-agent. However, use of a table as layout results in confusion for many users, especially when the tables used for layout compete with tables used for data. Additionally, a table used for layout is often announced incorrectly unless appropriate precautions are taken. Further, because of the availability of web technologies, like "grid" and "flexbox", developers no longer need a table for layout, and can easily leave tables to conveying data. It is because of these advances and the confusion that results from the misuse of tables that *Tables as Layout* makes the list of anti-patterns.

A table must only be used to represent relationships between data. The HTML table tags, "table", "tbody", "td", "thead", "tfoot", and "tr", have semantics that will cause confusion for screen reader users unless used properly. Additionally, on many platforms, these problems will also occur if the CSS display property is set to a table-like value, such as "table", "table-cell", "table-column", or "table-row", as many CSS properties transfer their semantics to the *Accessibility Tree*.

If your legacy code uses tables for layout, a quick method of bandaging this that will give you time to refactor your code is to set the role attribute of the layout table to *presentation*, i.e., "`role="presentation"`" or *none*. This will remove the semantics of the table in the *Accessibility Tree*.

## Titles

The "title" attribute is one of the most misunderstood and poorly implemented features that exists today. The title attribute is used to show a small amount of text when the user hovers over an item. As noted in the *Hover* anti-pattern, the ability to hover is not generally available to those using a touch device, such as a smartphone or tablet, and this requirement for a pointing device violates the *Web Content Accessibility Guidelines* requirement that interfaces be keyboard accessible.

Additionally, some incorrectly assume that text in a title attribute, especially in an image element, will be announced as alternative or as supplementary text, when in fact that is not correct. The title attribute should never be used in place of alternative text as most assistive technology will not announce it. Further, most SEO bots treat the title attribute with the same respect most assistive technology does, meaning there is no SEO benefit to be gained by using the title attribute either.

With so many opportunities for failure and such little perceivable advantage to be gained by use of the attribute, it is recommended that its use be abandoned entirely.

## Usurping the User

*Usurping the User* is an effort, whether in design or construction, to deceptively take final control away from the user. Most dark patterns are, at their core, instances of *Usurping the User* where the control being taken away is the user's freedom to choose. The most classic, forthright use of this anti-pattern appears during the construction of a web page, site, or application when it is decided that user input is be trapped or tracked without advanced warning or a user's ability to control elements or even choose which user-agent features to use to aid interactions is supplanted.

Many forms of *Usurping the User* would be blocked by various *Success Criteria* in the *Web Content Accessibility Guidelines*, such as controlling the size of fonts and preventing the use of high contrast modes; however, not all forms have corresponding tests to ensure user control is not usurped, so care must be taken, especially during the construction phase, that certain practices, such as the use of the "!important" keyword in CSS, are never engaged.

☞ Although it is impossible to foresee the variety of ways in which control can be wrested from the user, significant attempts have been made in this resource to identify points of greatest risk.

# Building Accessibility

One of the largest pieces of accessibility is in constructing the interfaces. A significant amount of effort will generally go into the planning and execution associated with the design and development of an accessible website. As designers and developers become more familiar with the topic and the various issues that might arise, their performance will improve and the investment made in education and practice will return significant results.

In addition to the constructed interface, there are hidden, behind-the-scenes factors that affect accessibility that are typically left out of the discussion, such as performance[26].

## Performance

Although not typically included in accessibility topics, performance is in fact an accessibility concern, because the *Accessibility Tree* is not typically built until after a page is *completely* loaded and painted. Further, although there are many aspects of performance, the most important aspect to how quickly the *Accessibility Tree* is built is *rendering*, which will be discussed in greater detail than the other aspects of performance that encompass how quickly a web page, or

---

[26] Other often ignored topics that are web accessibility adjacent are issues surrounding the cost associated with the amount of data transferred by a website and the effect web design and content has on battery life. These are increasingly important as more and more users adopt mobile devices, especially those traditionally perceived as "disabled".

the pages on a site, get from their starting point, the user's request, to their destination, the user being able to use them.

Due to its importance to how and how quickly the *Accessibility Tree* is built, an understanding of how a web page gets from the user's request to what the user sees in the user-agent is critical for a discussion about accessibility. To reach a thorough understanding of what happens and why it's important, we need to start at the beginning, understanding performance through the *Request-Response Model*.

### *A Brief Introduction to the Request-Response Model*

The web is built on what is called the *Request-Response Model*. When a user types an address into the address bar of a user-agent or navigates to an address by activating a link in a web page, the user-agent makes a *request* for a resource from a server. When the server receives the request, it locates the resource being requested, and performs any necessary actions, like validating that the person requesting the resource should have access to it, before returning the *response*, typically HTML, CSS, and JavaScript, to the user-agent. Once the user-agent receives the response, or perhaps a part of the response, the scripts are compiled and run to render any missing HTML and add it to the HTML rendered by the server and the CSS is compiled. On most platforms, once the user-agent has HTML that can be understood it begins to build a document. It is to this document that any HTML rendered by the scripting is added[27]. As the CSS is compiled, which often happens in parallel to the document creation, items that match the style rules in the CSS are painted. It is important to note that in creating what the user sees in the user-agent, HTML is *rendered*, scripts are *executed*, and CSS *paints* the interface. Although the CSS can modify the *Accessibility Tree*, it is the rendered HTML that builds the *Accessibility Tree*, and because of this difference, the rendering of HTML is vital to accessibility.

## Rendering

Over the years, the options engineers have had for rendering HTML have grown. When the web first started, *Static Rendering* was the only option. Unchangeable documents were placed on a web server and when they were requested by a user-agent, they were returned to the user-agent and shown to the user. It wasn't long before people saw the need for interfaces that were more dynamic and *Server Rendering* was born. Suddenly web developers could add code to the files that were stored on the web server and that code could do something on the server, like retrieve data from a database and insert it into the document that was returned to the user-agent and displayed to the user.

---

[27] It is important to note that scripting may or may not block other processes such as image retrieval. Even if, however, other process are not blocked, scripts are not compiled and executed until they are downloaded, meaning any additional HTML embedded in a script *cannot* be added to the document until after the script is downloaded and compiled.

With both *Static Rendering* and *Server Rendering* server speed is the primary factor in performance; however, as the server is not the only computer involved in the cycle, web engineers sought to expand their options in pursuit of the ever-elusive best performance goal. In addition to expanding the number of points at which performance can be affected, engineers and their management sought to increase the organizational ability to create applications that are easily maintained and will scale up well as customers, products, markets, and features are added. Although giants in the technology industry each have had different solutions, the meteoric rise of Google and Facebook resulted in two different but similar approaches, Angular and React respectively, and the era of *Client-Side Rendering*, where pages rendered for the user are generated by scripts that construct pages by executing instructions that add markup and style rules to the user-agent, began in earnest.

In the years since *Client-Side Rendering* was added, another rendering method, *Hydration*, a combination of a *Static Rendering*, *Server Rendering*, and *Client-Side Rendering* that passes the scripting used to generate the HTML as well as the HTML back to the user-agent, has been added to the list of possibilities. Other options that rely on some form of *Hydration*, such as *Streaming Rendering*, *Progressive Hydration*, and *Trisomorphic Rendering* may also be used, depending on the specific configuration of the web server and the content being delivered back to the user-agent.

Each of the different types of rendering have pros and cons, and more than a few points at which they interact with accessibility.

## The Importance of the Rendering Method

Ordinarily, the different rendering methods are compared along standard performance measures, such as how long it takes the web server to respond or *Time to First Byte*, how long before the user gets feedback in the screen or *Time to Paint*, how long before the user can interact or *Time to Interactive*, and how large the required files are or *Content Size*; however, when the

| Rendering Method | Time to First Byte | Time to Paint | Time to Interactive | Content Size | Flexibility |
|---|---|---|---|---|---|
| Static | *Best* | *Best* | *Best* | *Best* | Poor |
| Server | *Good* | *Best* | *Best* | *Best* | Average |
| Client-side | *Best* | Average | Poor | Average | *Good* |
| Hydration | Average | Average | Poor | Poor | *Best* |

different rendering methods are fully evaluated, how customizable the interface is or the *Flexibility* of the interface, must also be included, as the performance on the device can be a factor when the platform enables fully dynamic rendering of the *Accessibility Tree*[28].

For rendering methods that emphasize the client, both *Client-side Rendering* and *Hydration*, the *Time to Interactive* is often significantly beyond the painting of the screen, but the interfaces have greater *Flexibility*, being more dynamic than the less flexible server methods. The size of the content delivered by the client methods is also a potential problem as any additional markup not delivered as

---

[28] Not all platforms allow fully dynamic rendering of the *Accessibility Tree*, forcing the author to include such things as live regions in the markup before the live region updates will be announced.

pure markup must be included in the scripting, a method that always increases the size.

As is noted elsewhere in this resource, one of the underlying principles of accessibility, ubiquity, or the ability for anyone, anywhere to access a website, page, or application, is built on the web's universality. As a part of the ubiquity principle, the amount of content delivered to the user-agent becomes an important factor as it not only affects the time it takes for a resource to load, it also, in many cases, counts against bandwidth limits. The group of users for whom network speed, reliability, and bandwidth are *not* a concern is significantly smaller than those for whom it is. Beyond the issues associated with *delivering* the content, the amount of time required to parse and render the content is also an issue, and even more so for those who rely on the *Accessibility Tree*.

☠ Although some platforms start building the *Accessibility Tree* earlier than others or allow some interactivity before the tree is completed, engineers should expect the *Accessibility Tree* to be built only after everything else is completed, and interactivity to not be available until sometime after the document has completed loading. In real-world situations, failing to anticipate platforms that do not delay rendering the *Accessibility Tree* until all resources are available may mean that animations, videos, or audio elements may begin playing before content and functionality is available to assistive technology causing confusion that can easily be avoided.

An even more important factor in selecting a rendering method, however, is how the rendering is accomplished. For client rendering, whether using *Hydration* or *Client-side Rendering*, the authoring utilizes scripting as elements are added and remove dynamically.

The first issue related to this dynamic authoring is that the scripting must work. If scripting is not available in the user-agent, is turned off in the user-agent, or if the scripting delivered to the user-agent is broken, whether it is a resource you provide or one provided by someone else, or a portion of the scripting was not delivered because it was blocked in some way, if any of those are true, the best case is that only a part of your website, page, or application will be rendered and the worst case is that users will face what has come to be called the "white screen of death", named after the "blue screen of death" seen when Microsoft Windows crashes. Fortunately, user-agents and assistive devices have progressed in the years since those early days of the web and nearly all of them support scripting, which leaves only the risks that scripting is turned off, broken, or blocked.

The second, perhaps more significant issue for accessibility, is how assistive technology functions on the user's platform. Some platforms generate a relatively static *Accessibility Tree*, one with a set number of elements that can be altered by setting their contents or adjusting their attributes. For these platforms, the addition of elements is not notification that there is a problem, the elements are simply not added. If the user has one of these platforms, client rendering will leave them without an interface entirely[29].

## A Brief History of Measuring Performance

It wasn't too long before organizations began collecting data about visitors to their websites, including who spent money, what they did before and after spending money, and what went into their decision to spend money. It was shortly after the data collection began that the correlation between how long users waited and how much money, or even if they spent money, was identified. Shortly after the correlation was identified measuring the performance of a website or a process became one of the leading activities for web engineers.

Network speed, during those early days of the web, was abysmal. The documents were delivered to user-agents at the blinding speed of about 300 characters per second after the server found the file in the system and replaced all the code with text. In a relatively short time the delivery speed increased, jumping first to 1200 characters per second and then to 1950 characters per second before finally

---

[29] For those developing the code and performing the accessibility testing, platform that generate relatively static *Accessibility Trees* can be especially troublesome as defects will be difficult to reproduce and measures intended to accommodate the more static platforms may lead to doubled assistance on other platforms.

rocketing away. There was little that could be done regarding network speed, however, so attention quickly turned elsewhere.

As web professionals started seriously talking about performance they came up with several different time spans they could measure to figure out if their pages were performing adequately. On web servers we started measuring the amount of time between when a request came in, when the content was sent out, and finally received by the user-agent as part of the *Time to First Byte*. In those early days, the servers were doing the heavy lifting as the HTML was rendered before the response was returned. After more data collection than should have been necessary, we noticed a correlation between the size of the file and the code in it, the amount of work the web server was doing, and the distance between the web server and the end user to the *Time to First Byte*.

## Network Speed and Reliability

Because individual web professionals have more control over the server than over networks, they paid more attention to how they might improve server performance. However, the speed of the network, because it determines not only how quickly a response is transferred but how quickly the name lookup, or lookups, are completed and how quickly requests are sent to the server, is a major factor in the velocity of a page.

Much is made of network speed. Many mobile networks happily report when they make the jump from 3G to 4G or 4G LTE, and rightfully so, as 4G is, on average, ten times as fast as 3G, a whopping 15Mbit, or fifteen megabit or just under 2MB, per second transfer rate. The published network speed, however, is not the only measure, as network reliability is equally important. Taken together, the speed and reliability, make an effective rate that is often much lower. Poor reliability can make a 4G network seem like a much slower 3G or even 2G as the network struggles to compensate for packet loss.

## Time to First Paint and Time to Interactive

Ever eager to improve, we added more and more measures to identify areas where improvements could be made. As we looked at the measure *Time to First Byte*, we found it lacking and added a measure to give some insight into the amount of time required before the user begins to get a *visual* rendering of the page and the *Time to First Paint* was added[30]. The belief was that users were less impatient when the user-agent provided the feedback of an updated screen, even if they could not meaningfully interact with the screen Finally, late in the first decade of the 21st century, Twitter presented their take on performance measurement and introduced a measure they called "Time to First Tweet", a measure we now call *Time to Interactive*, which is the point at which the user-agent and the user can interact. For many platforms, the *Time to*

---

[30] Additional painting marks are typically tracked as part of page performance. The *Time to First Contentful Paint* and the *Time to First Meaningful Paint* measure various points at which the screen changes, however, they are not generally included in discussions about accessibility

*Interactive* marks the beginning of the creation of the *Accessibility Tree*.

## Content Size

In the early days, when network speeds were slower, *Content Size* was an important measure of how a page performs. As network speed grew, those who built web pages and processes became less concerned about the size of the content returned to the user. As a result, the average size of a web page has continually grown. However, even today one of the largest factors in web page speed is the size of a response, how much data is transferred. The size is important in two ways, first, in its interaction with network speed and the amount of time required to transfer all of the data to the user-agent, and second, in how long the user-agent takes to draw the page.

Even though the average size of a web page has grown consistently[31], the speed of networks, hardware, and software have also all seen growth. As a result, although the overall velocity has continued to slow, it has slowed at a much smaller rate than web page size has increased[32]. The unrelenting fact remains, however,

---

[31] The average size of a desktop website has grown from just over 500 kilobytes in July 2011 to nearly 2 megabytes in July 2019. The average size of mobile websites has grown even faster, from under 150 kilobytes to nearly 2 megabytes in the same period.
[32] Without the improvements in network speed, hardware, and software, velocity would be far slower than the 2017 average of around nine seconds.

that the size of the content returned in the response directly affects speed and user behavior[33].

# Patterns

Beyond performance, one of the biggest factors affecting accessibility in a user-agent is the design patterns used. Over time, several design patterns have emerged as different designers have built interfaces and those interfaces have been copied and refined. To aid in the understanding of the interplay between design patterns and accessibility, the patterns, which are commonly called components, listed in this resource are described along with their accessibility concerns and, in most cases, the relevant code is provided in the *Code Examples*.

## Basic Requirements

Each of the patterns described here, as with every accessible component, must meet a few basic, global requirements. These requirements are in addition to individual requirements about color or alternative text that might apply to a specific component. The most basic requirement is that every interactive control must be perceivable as an interactive control. For many designers being visually perceivable as an interactive control, with distinctive states, is enough; however, using visual perception as a baseline is

---

[33] One experiment performed by a large ecommerce platform determined the increase of a mere 160 kilobytes in content size resulted directly in a 12 percent increase in abandonment.

inadequate. Controls must be perceivable programmatically as well, which means all components must have a defined role and name. A component's role may be defined either through the HTML specification or using the WAI-ARIA role attribute. How a component acquires a defined name is more complex. In general, each role has a method associated with it that determines how a name is defined. In most cases the accessible name is the label provided either by the "label" tag, which is used for inputs only, or by using the WAI-ARIA attributes "aria-label" or "aria-labelledby".

❧ Although the elements with a defined role are added, if an element does not have a defined role, it will not be added to the Accessibility Tree. For example, a "div" containing an "input" will not be added to the Accessibility Tree; however, the "input" will.

In addition to being able to be perceived as an interactive control, the user must be able to activate the control using different activation methods, including but not limited to the keyboard, such as through a pointing device or speech-to-text software.

In order to ensure the patterns here meet these requirements and to follow the recommendation in the *Best Practices*, all components have been developed using *Progressive Enhancement* and, in many cases, will work without JavaScript, degrading gracefully. Graceful degradation is important, because as experienced user interface engineers are fond of saying, *all users are non-JavaScript users while the JavaScript is being downloaded.*

☞ It should be noted that code for the patterns, HTML, CSS, and JavaScript, provided in the *Code Examples* works with the CSS presented for form fields in *Best Practices*; however, the JavaScript present does not include the code required to perform real-time updates to list items or search results as that would require knowledge of specific APIs. Where relevant, sample list items are provided to demonstrate what markup is required.

In most cases the components described can be constructed using standard HTML; however, in some cases, WAI-ARIA widget roles are used. This should *not* be taken as encouragement to use WAI-ARIA roles to simulate existing elements such as buttons and checkboxes.

☠ WAI-ARIA roles serve to give the user as many clues about functionality of an interface as possible; however, an interface that uses a WAI-ARIA widget role may also suffer from discoverability issues as some platforms segregate widgets.

## Accordion ☐

An Accordion is a widget that expands and collapses when the control, commonly called a "twisty", is activated. In some browsers, this widget can be built using the `summary` and `details` elements; however, not all browsers implement the expand and collapse feature, notably, Microsoft's Internet Explorer and Edge browsers are in this category.

This element is one of the most basic, but requires JavaScript to function properly. If the content is clipped, and not hidden from assistive technology, there are no additional features needed; however, if content is hidden

> ▶ Copyright 2018

> ▼ Copyright 2018
>
> All content on this site is controlled, managed, and licensed by its author under Artistic-2.0.

or is not present in the document until the details are shown, the additional content should be identified by an WAI-ARIA live region so assistive technology is notified of the additional content.

It is recommended that the expanded and collapsed state be controlled using CSS associated with an attribute selector that checks the value of the `aria-expanded` attribute. Because this widget will not function correctly without the use of JavaScript to modify the value of the `aria-expanded` attribute, it is recommended that JavaScript be used to set the `aria-expanded` attribute when the component is loaded.

## Alert (Notice) ★

There are two types of *Alert* or *Notice*. One, a simple *Alert*, or *Notice*, is a message displayed and announced to the user within a browser window. The other, an *AlertDialog*, is a message displayed and announced to the user within a *Dialog*. Where an *Alert* is straightforward and requires little in the way of markup and no special styling, an *AlertDialog*, because it is an implementation of a *Dialog* pattern, requires more markup, special styling, and JavaScript as well to meet the specific requirements of a *Dialog*.

Although the markup required for an alert message is relatively simple, needing only the addition of the WAI-ARIA attribute `role` containing the value "alert", visual styles that draw attention to the content in the same way an assertive announcement would draw attention are necessary, especially for those not using assistive technology to identify alert events.

### *AlertDialog*

Because an *AlertDialog* is an application window that is designed to interrupt the current processing of an application in order to display an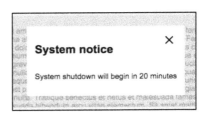

alert message, there is no viable HTML5 native option; therefore, it must be created as a widget and use the WAI-ARIA `role` attribute with "alertdialog" as its value.

In addition to the WAI-ARIA `role`, as with a *Dialog*, in order to be accessible, there are a few requirements the *AlertDialog* must meet.

- The *AlertDialog* has an accessible name, provided through either `aria-label` or `aria-labelledby`
- The *AlertDialog* is dismissed when the *Escape* key is pressed

- The *AlertDialog* traps focus by keyboard and a virtual cursor while it is open

- The *AlertDialog* receives focus when it is opened

- The *AlertDialog* returns focus to the last element that had focus when it is closed

- The *AlertDialog* has a button that closes the interface in the header

- The *AlertDialog* closes when the area outside the *AlertDialog*, the area typically called the underlay, is activated by a pointer device, e.g., receives a mouse click or tap

- The *AlertDialog* controls have an ample target area

- The *AlertDialog* uses either the content in the header or the contents of the body as its accessible name

## Autocomplete (Auto-suggest) ✎

An *Autocomplete*, or *auto-suggest*, is an input with a predictive feature in which the interface predicts the rest of a word a user is typing. Although there is an `autocomplete` attribute that has behavior similar to an *Autocomplete* component on some platforms, the native feature set is not nearly robust enough to warrant its use as a complete design pattern. It is highly recommended that an *autocomplete* widget be used instead.

☞ The `autocomplete` attribute may be used on an input as an enhancement to an existing input without causing an accessibility issue as that is an enhancement that aids in filling commonly used information stored by a user-agent, such as name or address, rather than a design pattern.

In practice, although the interface looks markedly different than a *Combobox*, it functions in much the same way, with only slight differences. For example, although a *Combobox* has a button that will expand the list of choices, the

Side item

Side item

a|

Apple
Apricot

*Autocomplete* does not. Much like the Combobox, however, in order to be accessible, there are a few requirements we must keep in mind.

- The input has `autocomplete` set to "off" to disable the interfering autocomplete HTML feature.
- The input has `aria-expanded` set accurately.
- The input has `aria-activedescendant` set accurately.
- The list has a unique id.
- The list uses the WAI-ARIA `role` of "listbox".
- The list items each use the WAI-ARIA `role` "option".
- The list items each have a unique id.
- The list items have `aria-selected` set accurately.
- The list can be opened, closed, and navigated using ArrowDown and ArrowUp.

- If the list has live updates, the list should be identified as a live region using the WAI-ARIA `role` "status".

## Breadcrumbs ⚓

*Breadcrumbs* are a navigational tool

Components ▸ Input ▸ **Breadcrumb**

that lets the user discover their current position in relation to the overall organization of a website or process. Although the term is used to refer to both categories: a site and a process, there are some slight differences between the two.

A breadcrumb used as a site navigation aid does not use a link in the last item, nor does it use the `aria-current` attribute as the process navigation instance does. The site navigation also typically uses a slightly different design as it is not a list of ordered steps.

☠ It is important to note that using breadcrumbs can mask cognitive accessibility issues your site might have. Ideally, a site is organized well enough that most used resources are within a few page transitions from the main page. It is recommended that if a breadcrumb component is used, additional analytics tracking be added to the links in the breadcrumb component so cognitive accessibility issues can be identified. This also applies to a breadcrumb-like component used for a process, like the *Progress Bar* used for a Non-linear Manual Journey.

It is recommended, unless the process is relatively simple, a *Breadcrumb* be used only to identify site navigation rather than process navigation, and a *Progress Bar* be used for process navigation.

## Button ✎

A *Button* should always be created using the HTML `button` or `input` tag. The content displayed inside the *button*, whether provided via content inside the `button` tag or the `value` attribute of the `input` tag, should never be ambiguous, which would make the button an instance of the *Ambiguous Label* anti-pattern. Buttons should also **never** open a page or navigate to another location, use a *Link* for those cases; however, a *Button* may update the hash portion of the URL, for example, when a single page application manages the History API, or may control another component, such as a *Dialog*.

☞ Although the use of unlabeled icon buttons is a common pattern, such components fall into the *Ambiguous Label* anti-pattern. If an icon is used as *button* content, the label should also be displayed to facilitate activation when the user is using speech recognition technology.

There is a common use for a *Button* that is worthy of further discussion, a *Request Button* or *Busy Button*, a button which starts a potentially long-running process such as submitting data in a form or component or generating a specific document type. This type of button will often show what is commonly known as a spinner while the associated process, such as a submission, is busy and will update a status when the request is complete.

### Request Button

The *Request Button* is multiple interfaces bundled together into a single component, a button, a presentational component to visually indicate the status changes, and a non-visual live region, that uses all three front-end languages, HTML, CSS, and JavaScript, as well as WAI-ARIA to create the interface with the Accessibility API.

Although there are many ways such an interface can be created, it must use the `button` tag in order to wrap the

presentational element. It is also recommended that CSS be used to manage the animation of the spinner in order that performance not be reduced as it would be if the animation were implemented using JavaScript. This also allows a separation of concerns that provides other benefits such as scalability and maintainability.

The WAI-ARIA states and properties include an `aria-busy` to indicate when a component is busy, however,

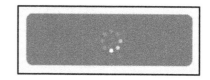

if the `aria-busy` state is used then the order of updates must be strictly managed as updates associated with the busy control will often not be carried throughout the platform.

For example, if the `aria-busy` state is set to "true" on a button that also contains the live region, the live region must be updated after the `aria-busy` state is removed, otherwise the update to the live region will not be passed through, even after the `aria-busy` state is removed.

☞ As all actions using HTTP request are different, the JavaScript provided in the *Code Examples* for this component is commented such that the necessary modifications should be easily identifiable. Also note that although the CSS is not wrapped in a way that allows the animation in the visual presentation to be turned off, the ability to stop animations, especially those that run longer than three seconds, *must* be part of the implementation.

## Carousel ⚓

A *Carousel* is a component used to show a series of content blocks and also commonly allows either animation of the transition or user control of the transition.

Product Two has all the features of Product One *plus* a large grin.

Like many components, the Carousel is related to another pattern, in this case its related to the *Tab* component.

Although there is plenty of debate about whether or not they are useful or desirable and whether or not they improve usability, they are relatively popular for a number of implementations. A large part of the reason many in the accessibility experts dislike them is because they are seldom built with accessibility in mind, but this need not be the case. In order to be accessible, there are a few requirements the *Carousel* must meet.

- The Carousel must be preceded by a heading
- The Carousel must be a list, either ordered or unordered
- The Carousel items outside the viewport are not in the tab order and are hidden using `aria-hidden`
- The Carousel animation is under user control, the user is able to start, stop, and pause the animation
- The Carousel controls are indicated both visually and programmatically
- The Carousel controls have text labels
- The Carousel controls have an ample target area

As a *Carousel* can only be implemented as a widget, one of the most important parts is the WAI-ARIA enhancement to the markup, in this case, the use of WAI-ARIA `role` to identify portions of the carousel that function as a "tablist" and "tabpanel" and the use of the `aria-labelledby` attribute given non-visual users additional information about how the interface performs.

☞ It should be noted that this approach, the code for which is

provided in the *Code Examples*, is a different approach than that

suggested by the WAI authoring practice guidelines.

In addition to an element that identifies the list position of the

currently-displayed panel, a Carousel should also have a *previous*,

or *back* button, and a *forward*, or *next* button. The *back* and *forward*

buttons are typically displayed alongside the panel.

If the Carousel can be animated, playing independent of user

action, a *play* button as well as a *stop* or *pause* button must be

provided. Additionally, the animation should not begin without

user action.

## Checkbox ✎

Whether a *Checkbox* is used alone or in a group, it is often difficult

to style in the desired manner. The solution providing an easily

styled interface is relatively simple, however, and, even better, it's a

solution native to HTML and CSS. With the approach provided

here, there are a few accessibility issues related to the input label

that should be managed.

☞ The accessible name for a `label` is generated from its contents,

which means pseudo-elements generated by CSS, both *before*

and *after*, will be included in the accessible name. If an element

generates its accessible name from *content* that also means it is

susceptible to the fragmentation bug that occurs on some

platforms when content tags have elements as content. In order to avoid both of these potential issues, the `label` is wrapped in a `span` and the `span` contains both the `label` and the pseudo-element used as the visual presentation.

In addition to the accessibility issues that accompany a styled checkbox, the label for a checkboxes is an exception to the practices that places the label before the input. Although the placement of a checkbox label before the input is not forbidden, it will generally reduce cognitive accessibility, especially in those instances where the checkbox is a member of a group.

Using CSS to hide the native input using a technique called "clipping", visually hides the element in place, which is important because moving an

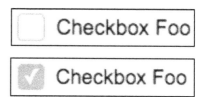

element outside the view box can cause a few focus issues in some instances. Once the native input is hidden, a styled element can be added that displays the state of the checkbox, either "checked" or "unchecked". This styled element should use the `height`, `line-height`, and `width` of the line-height of the font used to display the label, rendering a visual element that will align with the label appropriately.

Unlike radio inputs, checkboxes may be used alone; however, if there are multiple checkboxes representing the same information, they should be presented in a group. When checkboxes are combined in a group, there are additional accessibility concerns that might arise associated with labeling. For example, if users were given a list of fruits and asked to select those they like, an individual *Checkbox* may have the label "apple" or "pear" but without the context of the group label, the label associated with the Checkbox may lose nearly all its meaning. Although it is possible to use a "group" `role` to identify the checkbox group, the native `fieldset` tag is preferable as it is more robust. Additionally, it is recommended that the `legend` be given a unique identifier and the value of that identifier be used in the `aria-describedby` attribute of the individual checkboxes.

### Two-state and Three-state Checkboxes

Most checkboxes are traditional two-state checkboxes, they are either checked or not; however, there is another type, a three-state checkbox which has "checked", "unchecked", and "indeterminate" states. In a WAI-ARIA terms, the states are represented by `aria-checked` with the values "checked", "unchecked", and "mixed".

☞ Although there are two different ways to set the "indeterminate" or "mixed" state, the former being set using JavaScript, e.g., "`document.getElementById('mycheckbox').indeterminate = true`", and the latter being set using WAI-ARIA, "`<input aria-checked="mixed" id="mycheckbox"`

`type="checkbox">`", they mean virtually the same thing. The indeterminate state comes with a default visual style, one that varies greatly between browsers, whereas the mixed state does not.

The three-state checkbox is often used as a representative and control for a checkbox group, where "checked" and "unchecked" are used when all items in the group are either checked or unchecked, and "mixed" or "indeterminate" is used to represent a group containing both checked and unchecked items.

If we examine the five most commonly-used browsers, we would  see the default visual for them is fairly evenly divided. In two browsers, Chrome and Android, the indeterminate state is represented by a solid horizontal line in place of the checkmark and in two others, iOS Safari and Internet Explorer, there is no visual difference between an indeterminate checkbox and an unchecked checkbox. One browser, Edge, uses a box in the place of the checkmark to represent an indeterminate state.

❀ Although it is possible to set the WAI-ARIA `aria-checked` attribute directly in the markup, it is strongly recommended that the attribute *not be used* unless a three-state checkbox is being used and the `aria-checked` attribute is set via scripting. Additionally, style rules should be added to any stylesheet to normalize the visual style for aria-checked and the indeterminate state using an "`aria-checked="mixed"`" attribute selector and the "`:indeterminate`" pseudo-class selector.

## ComboBox ✎

A *ComboBox* is a widget made up of the combination of three distinct elements: a single-line text input, a button to control the open state of the list, and an associated list for helping users set the value of the text. The user may select an item from the list or enter a value directly.

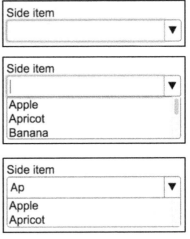

As there is no native HTML input that mimics a combobox, the only solution available is construction of a widget, and in order to be accessible, there are a few requirements we must keep in mind.

- The input has "`autocomplete="off"`" to disable the interfering autocomplete HTML feature.
- The input has "`role="combobox"`".
- The input has `aria-expanded` set accurately.
- The input has `aria-activedescendant` set accurately.
- The button will open or close the list, but does not change focus
- The list has a unique id.
- The list has "`role="listbox"`".

- The list items each have "`role="option"`".

- The list items each have a unique id.

- The list items have `aria-selected` set accurately.

- The list can be opened, closed, or navigated using *ArrowDown* and *ArrowUp*.

- The list length is updated in an off-screen element with "`role="status"`".

☞ As with many components, their basic structure comes from many years of designing and building interfaces, years that have framed user experience as well as the development of the interface. Although it is a common practice, to include a button that opens and closes the list, it is not mandatory. However, removal of the button is likely to cause confusion among users who understand the unusual *Combobox* as an *Autocomplete* instead.

## Date ✎

As mentioned earlier, one of the most difficult types of input to create is a *Date*. One of the reasons for this difficulty is the array of ways in which a date can be represented. A short list of ways a date can be represented include these common formats:

- numeric month, day of the month, and year with each value separated from the others by a variety of symbols, typically shown as "mm/dd/yyyy"

- numeric day of the month, month, and year with each value separated from the others by a variety of symbols, typically shown as "dd/mm/yyyy"

- numeric year, month, and day of the month with each value separated from the others by a variety of symbols, typically shown as "yyyy-mm-dd"

- numeric day of the month, a full or partial month name, and year, with each value typically separated by a space, typically shown as "dd mmm yyyy"

As a result, there are a number of ways one can collect a date value, including a native HTML date input type, and a number of those ways either enforce a particular format or run a significant risk of conversion error caused by misunderstanding the format used for input.

The methods of input can be separated into three distinct categories: single inputs, multiple inputs, and a "date picker". Of these, the least restrictive to users, the single input, is the most prone to error because of the different, similar formats used. For example, there is little difference between the first two formats, the only difference being the order in which the day of the month and the month come, and unless the day of the month is larger than 12, there are few clues that can be used to ensure the correct value has been entered.

☞ Of the three types, the multiple inputs type has the best

accessibility as it clearly labels each date part, day of the month,

month, and year, leaving the user with little-to-no confusion

regarding what input is required. If another method is used, it is

recommended that the computed value showing the day of the

month, a full or partial month name, and the year, be provided

to the user as a description of the input.

## Single Inputs

Single inputs, including the native
HTML date input, are generally
difficult to construct in a way that is
usable and contains data that can be

> Date of birth
> dd/mm/yyyy
> 31/12/2018
> Montag, 31. Dezember 2018

parsed effectively. Additionally, because of the difference in

formats, especially formats that are very similar, the input interface,

regardless of whether the type is date or text, needs descriptive text

that identifies how a value should be formatted. Additionally,

because of the potential for confusion a "long date" should display

the parsed value of the field.

🕸 The native HTML date input, shown below, does not allow for

different formats and gives an unnamed list for date, month,

and year values, neither of which improves accessibility, and it

should be noted that a select list without a label, which is the

interface for the date parts in a date input, would not be

considered accessible under the *Web Content Accessibility Guidelines.*

## Multiple Inputs

Multiple inputs, with each date part, date, month, and year, being fully

labeled, is arguably the most accessible interface. This pattern also allows for greater flexibility when internationalizing the interface as the various date parts can be re-ordered to match cultural norms. In this pattern, the label for the date as a whole, e.g., "date of birth", becomes a description and each date part, month, day, and year, will receive its own label. As a group, the label for the group comes before the individual inputs even though the label for the individual input comes after the input.

☞ It should be noted that this markup works with the CSS presented for form fields in *Best Practices*, and the JavaScript provided below adds validation to the fields. Additionally, it should be noted that the inputs need not be text inputs. The inputs for month and day could easily be a `select` or an input using the type number with a `min` attribute and `max` attribute restricting its value. It is recommended that the input interface for the year not be a `select` type as selecting a year from a list means a very long, often unmanageable, list and a better experience is either a text input using the `pattern` and `maxlength` attributes to restrict input or a number input using the `min` and `max` attributes.

## DatePicker

The third type of date input, a *DatePicker*, combines a date input, as described above, with a calendar

| Date of birth |
| mm/dd/yyyy |
| 12/31/2018     🕐 |
| Monday, December 31, 2018 |

inside a *Disclosure* component that controls it. This interface is one of the most difficult interfaces to make accessible because of the complexity involved with these three separate, complex interfaces that are combined into a single usable interface.

☞ Although a *DatePicker* and a *DateRange* are related, they are not the same interface. The relationship between the minimum and maximum values that can be selected in on or the other, for example, an event cannot end before it starts, and how that relationship is described or identified can become an accessibility issue. One should not assume that the inclusion of two *DatePicker* widgets, each labeled as either a starting or ending date is sufficient to address accessibility.

## Date Input and Disclosure

The first of the three complex interfaces is the *Date* input. Although much of this interface is typically as described in the Single Input section above, there are some notable differences, as the date input value is bound to the calendar displayed in the *Disclosure*.

In addition to the date input, a *DatePicker* has a *Disclosure* control that shows and hides a calendar that allows the user to select a specific cell in a table and have that selection action fill the input with the date value.

☞ It is possible to create a calendar interface for a radio button group that selects a date. Potential accessibility issues associated with this approach are discussed below.

## Calendar

The simplest calendar is an HTML table, with columns clearly identified. If there are specially identified days, like holidays, a legend must be added to the end of the table that clearly identifies any visual differences alongside the descriptive text. For example, if holidays are shown with a different background color or pattern, that visual style must be identified by descriptive text just as an image would be. In those cases, the date cells in the table should also be tied to the descriptive text in the legend using `aria-describedby` and the corresponding `id` attribute. Also, because of the accessibility issues associated with the use of color, the legend and identifiers within the calendar *must not* use color alone to identify the relationship. This is one instance in which the use of an icon may prove helpful.

| January 2018 | | | | | | |
|---|---|---|---|---|---|---|
| Sun | Mon | Tue | Wed | Thu | Fri | Sat |
| 31 | 1 | 2 | 3 | 4 | 5 | 6 |
| 7 | 8 | 9 | 10 | 11 | 12 | 13 |
| 14 | 15 | 16 | 17 | 18 | 19 | 20 |
| 21 | 22 | 23 | 24 | 25 | 26 | 27 |
| 28 | 29 | 30 | 31 | 1 | 2 | 3 |

Holiday

This pattern is shown in the HTML sample for the calendar in the *Code Examples*, which identifies January 15, 2018 as a holiday.

Beyond the general advice above, the calendar portion of a *DatePicker* must be navigable using the keyboard rather than just a pointer device that allows the user to click on a date to select it. This means each date cell must be in the tab order and have keyboard event handlers that mimic the click event on a button. Additionally, the arrow keys, left, right, up, and down, should move focus within the table by weeks or days, as should the *Home* and *End* keys.

In summary, in order to be accessible, there are a few requirements we must keep in mind.

- The different day categories cannot be identified by color alone.
- The interface elements must be clearly labeled.
- The days can be navigated using *ArrowLeft* to go to the previous day, *ArrowRight* to go to the next day, *End* to go to the end of the week, and *Home* to go to the beginning of the week.
- The weeks can be navigated using *ArrowDown* to go to the same day in the following week and *ArrowUp* to go to the same day in the previous week.
- If the table will be updated using JavaScript, the table body should be identified as a live region using `aria-live`.

☞ If the calendar is bound to an input, the day cells should update the input when the *Enter* or *Space* key is pressed or when the user clicks on the cell.

## Calendar as a Radio Button Group

As an alternative to creating an interaction and binding the calendar to a date input, it is possible to create a table that contains radio buttons and functions as a radio button group. If this pattern is used, all radio buttons within the calendar should be identified within a "group", the `table` should be enclosed inside a `fieldset` and each radio input, contained in a table cell, must have the same value for the `name` attribute. Additionally, the `tabindex` should be removed from the table cell and the navigational keys, left, right, up, down, *Home*, and *End*, should behave as previously described by moving focus to the corresponding radio button rather than table cell.

Although it would be tempting to follow a pattern similar to the above and substitute a checkbox to set a date range, there are difficulties that will arise from attempting to manage ranges that cross over month boundaries as a calendar typically only displays one month at a time.

# Dialog (Modal) ★

A *Dialog* is an application window that is designed to interrupt the flow of an application in order to prompt the user for a response. A generic *Dialog*

may be used for something as simple as a message the user must react to, something as complex as a nested form, or anything in between; however, typical cases allow for separate functional types of dialogs, namely the *Confirm*, *Detail*, and *Prompt*. The examples below are of the *Detail* type.

In order to be accessible, there are a few requirements all *Dialog* instances, no matter their type, must meet

- The Dialog has "`role="dialog"`".
- The Dialog has an accessible name, provided through the `aria-labelledby` attribute tied to either the heading, if one is present, or the body if no heading is present
- The Dialog is dismissed when the *Escape* key is pressed
- The Dialog traps focus by keyboard and a virtual cursor while it is open
- The Dialog receives focus when it is opened
- The Dialog returns focus to the last element that had focus when it is closed
- The Dialog has a button that closes the interface in the "header"

- The Dialog closes when the area outside the Dialog, the area typically called the underlay, is activated by a pointer device, e.g., receives a mouse click or tap
- The Dialog controls, all call-to-action buttons and closers, have an ample target area

☠ There is a native HTML5 `dialog`; however, support for the HTML5 element is currently limited in many user-agents, and even in the user-agents in which it is supported, the support is incomplete. For example, focus is not managed when the dialog is opened, there is no way to facilitate dismissing the dialog without the use of JavaScript, and the accessible name and accessible description are not calculated in a consistent manner. Because of the incomplete and inconsistent experience, it is strongly recommended that all dialogs be constructed as widgets rather than rely on the HTML `dialog` element.

## Confirm

The *Confirm* pattern provides not only content, but two choices as a call to action. Typically, the choices are to "confirm" or "cancel", even if the labels provided use different content. In this pattern, it is often recommended the cancel button in the heading be removed; however, that can only be done if there is another means of dismissing the dialog without affirming.

If the sample code provided in the *Code Examples* is used to generate a *Dialog*, the onCancel and onConfirm methods of the generated instance provided must be initialized as a JavaScript function or the click handler must be passed in directly via the onclick attribute of the "cancel" or "close" element as well as the "confirm" element, e.g., "`<button class="close"`

`onclick="alert('Hello world!');"`

`type="button">OK</button>`".

## Prompt

The *Prompt* pattern is an extension of the *Confirm* pattern, with one or more inputs that collect data from the user in addition to the call to action. In this pattern, the "save" action would equate to the "confirm" and the "discard" or "cancel" would be the "cancel" or "close" action. Additionally, any input fields contained in a dialog should also be identified as a group using a `fieldset`.

If the sample code provided in the *Code Examples* is used to generate a dialog, the "save" function should be assigned to the onConfirm method and the "discard" function to the onCancel method.

☠ Designs more complex than can be addressed with simple "cancel" and "confirm" buttons should not be placed in an overlay to minimize risks to cognitive load. This admonition against use also includes the pattern of opening a dialog of any type from within a dialog.

## Disclosure (Show and Hide) ☐

A *Disclosure* component hides or reveals content based on a user interaction. Although the *Disclosure* is similar to an *Accordion*, it is semantically and structurally different in that the controlling element is not a summary element, such as a heading, and the controlling element is likely separated from the shown or hidden content, identified by the `role` "region".

In this pattern, the use of the `aria-expanded` attribute is necessary to identify whether or not the content is available, and the use of the `aria-controls` attribute is strongly encouraged because of the separation between the controlling and the controlled elements, and because it also gives the user the ability, on some platforms, to jump to the associated content when it is expanded. Additionally, if the code sample provided in the *Code Examples* is used, the `aria-controls` attribute is used to pass information to JavaScript function that shows or hides the content.

☠ This pattern should be used with caution, as it may obscure meaning conferred by the structure of the markup that is present in the *Accordion* pattern. Additionally, when not expanded, the content should not be available in any manner, but the content to be disclosed should be identified as a WAI-ARIA live region, ideally through the use of "`role="alert"`" so the content is announced when it is shown. Without the identification as a live region, there will be a potentially significant discoverability issue.

## Dropdown Listbox (Select) ✎

Many people find styling a native `select` difficult. As a result, they often turn to creating their own custom *Select* or *Dropdown Listbox* component. However, it is possible to create style rules for the HTML select element, even though you might need to add a vendor-specific property, such as `-webkit-appearance`, in order to get other CSS properties applied as easily as those properties can be applied to other input types. The difficulty associated with styling pales in comparison, however, to the difficulties associated with the creation of a custom *Select* interface.

☞ The form field styling available in *Best Practices* includes default styling for the `select` interface.

In order to create an custom select interface, you will need to use an WAI-ARIA widget role, specifically the *listbox* role. In addition, the use of that role will require the use of WAI-ARIA states and properties as well as the *option* child role.

After the markup is determined, a scripting layer must be added to control the interface and allow the selection of one, or more, of the options listed, and that scripting must not be device dependent.

🕸 Given the high probability of failure to create an accessible custom dropdown, it is strongly recommended that a native select interface be used whenever possible. This recommendation is so strong that no widget code will be provided in the *Code Examples*.

## Flyout ☐

A *Flyout* is related to the *Disclosure* and a *Tooltip* patterns. As such, the code necessary for the control as well as the section controlled need adequate markup. If the disclosed section has no other role, it should be given the role "region" as in the *Disclosure*.

In the *Flyout* pattern, more than text content is presented. In the example provided in the *Code Examples*, the content contains form elements in a checkbox group. Because the content of the flyout is closely associated with the control, it is important that it be sibling of the control and that the relationship be represented visually by a connecting arrow.

Because content is shown dynamically, content can either be clipped to hide it visually while it is still available to assistive technology, or it can be hidden both visually and from assistive technology. If the latter is the case, the disclosed section should be identified as a live region. This may be accomplished by altering the role of the disclosed section to "status" and setting the `aria-live` attribute to "polite".

# Link ⚓

A *Link* provides a way to navigate to a resource or a specific element within a resource that a human or a machine, such as a spider, crawler, or bot, can read and follow. Although it is a relatively common pattern, a *Link* should *not* be used to perform an action other than navigating to a resource; for example, a *Link* should not be used to open an *Accordion*, a *Button* should.

☞ A *Link* goes somewhere and a *Button* does something.

Because HTML has a native link that requires no further enhancement, there is no need for a widget or a widget role; however, the following must be followed or the accessibility of the link will be damaged or destroyed.

- Links *must* contain text and the text must be descriptive enough that it needs no additional context. For example, content such as "read more", "click here", or even "important information", is not sufficient. The content must *always* adequately identify the destination. Links must reference the same resources if they share the same link text.

  ☞ The text provided in the link may be in an `alt` attribute of an image or other form, but it must be present.

- Links *must* contain a valid URL in the `href` attribute, the attribute cannot reference the javascript protocol, e.g., "`href="javascript:helloWorld()"`" is not allowed.

- Links **must** activate with the *Enter* key and should not prevent the default behavior of the *Space* or arrow keys, *ArrowDown*, *ArrowLeft*, *ArrowRight*, or *ArrowUp*.

- Links should be easily identified by color and should be underlined.

☠ Some platforms do not announce text in the `aria-label` attribute in an anchor. If the link is to contain an icon without visible text, the text may be clipped; however, keep in mind that interactive items that are not clearly labeled with visible text may prove difficult to use for those using speech recognition assistance.

## Menu (Menubar) ☐

*Menus* and *Menubars*, a *Menu* displayed horizontally as a bar, follow the same pattern. There is no native HMTL implementation, so all implementations require HTML, CSS, and JavaScript to control the interactions and all use WAI-ARIA roles.

The *Menu* or *Menubar* use words for menu items rather than icons, and in the markup, the *Menu* and *Menubar* use the role "menu" and "menubar", respectively, while individual items are identified with the role "menuitem", "menuitemcheckbox", or

**Space Bears Menu**

Use full screen

▷ Space Bears

**Space Bears Menu**

Use full screen

▽ Space Bears

Not Space Bear 10
New Space Bear
Space Bear 2

"menuitemradio", depending on their interaction.

🕸 It is strongly recommended that a *Menu* not be used for navigation. There are significant differences between the interaction patterns, and most importantly, menus take an action on the page or one of its interface elements and navigation takes the user to a location. In short, a *Menu* should not contain a *Link*.

As mentioned previously, because WAI-ARIA roles are sometimes announced as such on many platforms, more knowledgeable users expect an interaction pattern that corresponds to the role announced, and those interactions are typically more complex than those given by native HTML. As always, those interactions must be coded using JavaScript. When coding a *Menu* or *Menubar*, the following interactions should be handled to maintain accessibility:

- The *Space* or *Enter* key should open the current item if it is a submenu, and move focus to the first item; otherwise, the key should activate the current menu item, causing action to be executed.

- The *Escape* key should close the current item and move focus to the parent menu item if it is an open submenu; otherwise, do nothing.

- The *Tab* or *ArrowRight* should close the current menu item if it is a submenu. If the current menu item is the last item, the focus should move to the first item in the current menu;

otherwise, focus should move to the next item in the menu. If the newly focused item is a submenu, it should be opened, but focus should be kept on the parent menu item.

- The *Shift + Tab* or *ArrowLeft* key should close the current menu item if it is a submenu. If the current menu item is the first item, focus should be moved to the last item; otherwise, focus should be moved to the previous item in the menu. If the newly focused item is a submenu, it should be opened, but focus should be kept on the parent menu item.

- The *ArrowDown* should open the submenu and move focus to the first item if the current menu item is a submenu; otherwise, focus should be moved to the next item. If the current item is the last item, focus should be moved to the first item.

- The *ArrowUp* should open the submenu and move focus to the last item if the current item is a submenu; otherwise, focus should be moved to the previous item. If the current item is the first item, focus should be moved to the last item.

- The *Home* key should move focus to first item in the current menu or submenu.

- The *End* key should move focus to last item in the current menu or submenu.

- Any character key should move focus to next item having a name that starts with the typed character.

- The *Shift + F10* key should open the menu.

☠ Although very common, it is strongly recommended that menus not be coded using WAI-ARIA but rather simply be native markup, CSS, and scripting to handle interactions. This approach will likely prevent issues that arise from unmet expectations and assistive technology that gets *stuck* when an interaction fails to signal that a menu or submenu is closed.

## Meter ☐

A *Meter* is a visualization of measurement data. As a visualization, it does not typically require scripting, but scripting may be used to automate transitions or some of the style rules applied to improve maintainability and scalability. *Meters* are typically separated into specific, identified segments with the current value identified both as a specific value and as existing within a range.

This pattern is especially common in financial services or other industries where payments or accounts are *aged*; 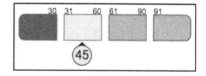 however, it is becoming increasingly common as a visualized measure of password strength where each segment represents a count of categories matched.

☞ Although a *Meter* has some similarity to *Progress Bar* items, not every *Meter* will have both maximum and minimum values as values can be in a *range* that is simply defined as greater-than or less-than. The potential lack of either a maximum or minimum makes this pattern a poor candidate for a *Progress Bar* as both maximum and minimum as well as a current value are required for a *Progress Bar*.

As this pattern is often a visual representation of information otherwise presented in the content, it does not necessarily pose accessibility issues, and in those cases where it is used as visual representation, it can be hidden from screen readers without impact. If, however, it is a stylized version of data not otherwise presented, it cannot be hidden. The example code provided in the *Code Examples* is an example of a financial services aged account where data is not otherwise presented in the content.

## Number ✎

Designing and constructing an input for numbers is one of the most challenging endeavors facing both designers and engineers. It seems simple at the outset, but given that number data is one of the three most likely types to cause errors, along with date and telephone, it should be easily deduced that creating an effective solution is likely difficult[34].

One of the reasons for this difficulty is that there are so many different number formats. Without the ability to convert the user's entry to a recognizable number, an interface is likely to mark an item as invalid even when it is not.

---

[34] There is a distinction between *numbers* and *numeric data*. Although numeric data, like account numbers or telephone numbers, is composed of digits, it is often not the same as a *number* which can be acted upon mathematically.

One alternative that is sometimes used is to the HTML number input; however, like other strongly typed inputs, it comes with its own accessibility problems and will impose a specific format and a less-than-ideal user experience. Further, unless the markup includes specific values, fractional units may be marked invalid.

☞ Although a "number" type input may be used in an international setting, it is strongly recommended that a "text" input be used instead and the value converted to a number. This will avoid many of the accessibility issues associated with the strongly-typed input and increase cognitive accessibility by allowing the user to enter numbers in a familiar format.

## Number Formats

A discussion of how best to construct a number input must start with a solid understanding of the different formats that might be used when entering numbers. The following table shows the features of the predominant number formats.

| Language or Region | Sample | Decimal | Thousands separator | Large Number Separator |
|---|---|---|---|---|
| Canada and Europe | 1 234 567 890,123 | , | space | space |
| Germany | 1 234 567.890,123 | , | . | space |
| Italy, Norway, and Spain | 1.234.567.890,123 | , | . | . |
| Unspecified | 1,234,567,890.123 | . | , | , |

## *Converting Numbers*

There are three primary features that have to be considered when converting between formats.

1. The decimal separator
2. The grouping character(s), both for thousands and for large numbers i.e., one million and more
3. The sign, for both positive and negative values

Once these three features are taken into account, converting a number becomes a matter of determining if grouping characters or a decimal character are present and separating the number into its integer and fractional portions and using the sign to convert the numeric portions into a floating-point number.

The JavaScript included in the *Code Examples* can be used with a text input to convert a user's entry to a number that can then be validated and manipulated. This JavaScript creates an additional property on the input object that is the JavaScript Number type and will be called "number", e.g., "`form.elements.amt.number`".

☞ It is important to remember that the class of the input must be number in order for this property to be assigned and that the property is not the same as the value, which will be submitted during a form submit. Additionally, the value entered by the user should not be modified as the value entered and accessed through the "`value`" property is the value accessed by assistive technology, and modification of the value will cause confusion.

## Pagination ⚓

There are two ways pagination can be addressed, and the interface built to handle it will depend on how the data is represented. The simplest determination is whether the items to be shown on a page are segregated at the resource level by page size. For example, if you can enter a page number or a starting and ending index in the address bar as part of the URL and the response contains only the items for that page, pagination is a navigational list that enables the user to navigate between pages. If the response contains more items than those for the specific page requested, the pagination is controlled by scripting through a button group. Building the interface is relatively straightforward once the model to use has been determined.

### *Navigational List*

In the navigational list model, the list of pages uses the "navigation" `role`. This will help assistive technology identify the list as possible destinations. In the example code in the *Code Examples*, the label of the anchors is overly simple when in reality, it would need additional content for non-visual users to provide context that is given through proximity or other cues available visually.

## *Button Group*

In the button group model, all buttons should be inside a container using the "group" role. Each button should be clearly labeled with the page number and the group should be described in such a manner that it is clear the buttons control the display of a specific page. As a page is selected in the page "group", the `aria-current` attribute on the button should be set to "page".

## Password ✎

*Passwords* are a special input case due to the often significant cognitive accessibility issues associated with them. These issues are often not included in the *Web Content Accessibility Guidelines*, and there are no test criteria associated with them that are not associated with other input types, so accessibility and usability in this form are often missed entirely.

While some input elements have a validation rule, or perhaps even a few validation rules, passwords generally have several validation rules, and often an entire list. The most common validation rules among these are:

- requiring a lowercase letter
- requiring an uppercase letter
- requiring a number
- requiring a minimum length

- requiring a maximum length
- restricting characters used to a specific set
- requiring a special character from a group of characters, e.g., a !, @, #, $, or *

As each password is likely to have a different list of validation rules that apply to a specific site, the number of possibilities becomes overwhelming. Adding the list of requirements as a description linked to your input will significantly improve the cognitive accessibility. As this recommended pattern uses native HTML, there is no need for a widget.

### *Enhancing accessibility*

To extend the accessibility, identify the list of requirements as a live region and update the list as requirements are met. Additionally, use a text input in place of the password type and give the user the ability to hide input by connecting a toggle button to the input that will toggle the type between text and password. By giving the user the ability to toggle between "text" and "password" types, the user is better able to manage cognitive accessibility while still being able to protect against a *Passerby Attack*.

### Progress Bar (Journey) ★

A *Progress Bar* is an interface that gives the user information about the current step in a process, and it may take one of several forms, depending on the type of process and how it may be navigated.

Processes can generally be placed in one of four different categories:

- *Linear Automatic Journey*: A Linear Automatic Journey is a process with one or more clearly defined, linear steps. Although each step or stage must be completed before the next, the process does not allow user input. A common example of this type of process is a file transfer.

  - ⚙ Although this pattern does not require the use of a WAI-ARIA role, *this is the only pattern that may use the WAI-ARIA role* **progressbar**, and the WAI-ARIA role should *only* be used if the action is a long-running task initiated by a user request, e.g., a file transfer.

- *Linear Manual Journey*: A Linear Manual Journey is a process with multiple, clearly defined, linear steps the user must complete. Some common examples of a Linear Manual Journey are road-trips and recipes, as well as highly regulated processes such as bank wire transfers.

- *Non-linear Manual Journey*: A Non-linear Manual Journey is a process with multiple, clearly defined steps, which the user may complete out of sequence. This process is often used for complex tasks, such as filing government forms or processes that require the option for review, such as forms that "cause legal commitments or financial transactions for the user to occur, that modify or delete user-controllable data in data storage systems, or that submit user test responses".

- *Non-linear Automatic Journey*: A Non-linear Automatic Journey is a process with multiple, clearly defined steps or stages which may be performed in parallel, or may be skipped, that are updated automatically, without user input. A common example of this type of process is synchronizing data across multiple platforms, such as when a status update is posted on multiple social media sites.

These four processes are typically shown using one of two interfaces: a *User Journey* or *Breadcrumbs*

### Linear Automatic Journey

This process is the simplest use-case, and there is an HTML5 native element that can be used for this purpose; however, the HTML native element, created using the `progress` element, may be animated on some platforms in a way that would violate the *Web Content Accessibility Guidelines*. For this reason, although examples of the native solution are available, it is recommended that a widget be used instead so updates to live regions and animation can be managed explicitly.

This pattern also allows the use of different visuals, such as an arc, as shown in the accompanying image where progress is approximately 50 percent.

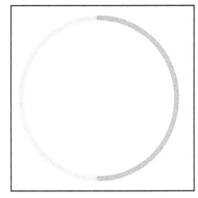

☞ Both the native element, and the widget provided in the *Code Examples*, can be updated by simply changing the value of the element directly, e.g., `"window.progress.value = 2;"`.

☠ If the value range of a progress element is not intended to represent a percentage, the value of the progress bar must be provided using the `aria-valuenow` attribute, otherwise the value of the progress bar will be treated as a percentage of the range.

### User Journeys

The remaining processes are significantly different than the pre-defined, automated process that is generally described by a progress element. The recommended design not only includes clear, concise text labels, but also includes a numeric indicator to improve cognitive accessibility, is shown below.

☞ The *Linear Manual Journey* and both *Non-linear* journey examples in the *Code Examples* use the same CSS and the same JavaScript;

however, the markup is different. The JavaScript provided will automatically update both the `aria-current` attribute and the associated container using the "alert" role and will also allow the specification of the default current item by either providing the `aria-current` attribute on the span or the `data-value` attribute containing either the text used as the `id` of the text element or the index of item. To provide compatibility with other progress bars, the current step can be updated by modifying the value of the widget using JavaScript, e.g., `"window.progress.value = 3;"`.

☠ The `aria-current` attribute must be included on the current step, and an accessible name should be provided for the list using either `aria-label` or `aria-labelledby`.

## Linear Manual Journey

Because a *Linear Manual Journey* does not contain a navigational component the way a *Non-linear Manual Journey* does, the HTML is a relatively simple description of the user's location in a process, a simple ordered list with a descriptive label, items containing descriptive text for the steps within a process, and a container using the "alert" role to identify when the value changes is sufficient. Additionally, the `aria-current` attribute should be used to identify the active step using the "step" value.

## Non-linear Manual Journey

Because a *Non-linear Manual Journey* contains a navigational component as the user can directly manipulate which step on the journey is active, the HTML is a little more complex than that of the *Linear Manual Journey*. Also note that because the steps are also navigational links, there is no need for an alert as the user will be directly involved in changing the value of the active step. In this case, the markup should contain the same ordered list with descriptive text and items containing text for the steps within a process; however, because the list is also navigational, it should be wrapped in the "`nav`" navigational element. Additionally, when the active step is changed, the `aria-current` attribute should be added to identify the current step.

## Non-linear Automatic Journey

Although the steps of a *Non-linear Automatic Journey* may be completed out of order, they are still ordered. As such, they should be identified using an ordered list with descriptive text that describes the list and items containing descriptive text for each step of the process. As in other user journey patterns, the currently active step should be identified using the `aria-current` attribute. Unlike other user journeys, the addition of the `aria-current` attribute, and especially the element using the "alert" `role` are critical as the current step may change in a non-linear manner.

☸ Although a *Non-linear Automatic Journey* lacks a navigation interface, the updates are automatic, so the use of JavaScript is required.

## Radio Button ✎

Like the *Checkbox*, a *Radio Button* is another native element that is difficult to style in the manner we want, and like the *Checkbox*, the solution to styling the element is relatively simple, using native HTML and CSS;

but, unlike the *Checkbox*, a *Radio Button* must always be in a group.

☞ See the *Checkbox* component for why the label in the HTML sample in the *Code Examples* is wrapped and what class is used to shift the visual portion to the right of the text label.

As with the *Checkbox*, the approach to developing an accessible, styled interface hides the native input using CSS with a `clip-path`, with `clip` as a fallback, visually hiding the element in place. This is important because moving an element outside the viewable area can cause a few focus issues in some instances.

Again, as with the Checkbox, a pseudo-element should be placed on a `span` wrapping the `label` for the `input`. This ensures that the accessible name of the input, generated by the label, is correct and does not include the pseudo-element content. Finally, setting the `height`, `line-height`, and `width` of the visual element to the standard line height will ensure the interface is as visible and accessible as the label and will align with the label appropriately.

## Search ✎

A *Search* input is an input that submits a query to a resource, or URL. The results of the query are then displayed to the user. Because the results of the query are dynamic, they must be provided to the users, to facilitate the

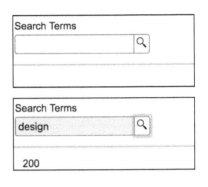

announcement of the results, the results section uses `aria-live` with an assertive setting so results are announced as soon as they are returned.

## Skip-To ⬍

A *Skip-To* is a navigational landmark that allows users to navigate from one part of the page to another. These commonly allow users to navigate directly to the main content of a page, skipping header information, or skip back to the top of a page from the bottom.

The pattern is relatively simple, but there are a few issues that can all be handled in three easy steps.

1.  Identify the section the link should point to and set the `id` attribute, e.g., "`id="main"`".

2. Create a link and set the `href` attribute to the identifier of the linked content, being sure to prefix the identifier with a hash (#), e.g., "`<a href="#main">Main content</a>`".

3. Add a style rule that hides the *Skip-to* until it receives focus so the link is hidden from users who are unlikely to need it, like those navigating with a pointing device such as a mouse.

Finally, there are a few quirky user-agents, some complain if a `tabindex` is hardcoded on an element and some leave focus on the anchor if there isn't a `tabindex` on the element that should be getting focus. The following JavaScript will address both of these quirks by dynamically setting and removing the `tabindex` when user events happen.

## Slider (Range) ✎

A *Slider* is an input where the user selects a value from within a given range. Sliders typically have a *thumb* that can be moved along a bar or track to change the value.

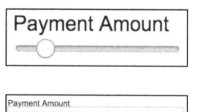

Although there are two available options, an HTML native option and a widget, as with most enhanced HTML input types, there are accessibility issues associated with the control that can be overcome through a carefully constructed widget. Unfortunately, not all accessibility issues associated with a component that is primarily designed to track a range of motion can be overcome even with careful construction.

☞ It is recommended that instead of a slider being used, a plain text input be used instead. Although every attempt has been made to ensure the *Slider* widget provided is accessible, there will likely be issues for those with motor or dexterity impairments.

When building a *Slider* widget, considering the following issues will help maintain accessibility.

- The touch target of the *Slider* must be at least 44 CSS pixels, or approximately 11 centimeters
- There must be adequate *negative* space around the slider
- Feedback must be given to the user indicating the value of the *Slider* as the "thumb" is moved along the bar.

In constructing a *Slider* widget, there are several components that will be necessary. First, and foremost, a *Slider* is an input, an input should be included in the markup and clipped using CSS. In addition to the input, a visual control should be constructed. The visual control should have a channel, a value indicator, and a "thumb", the sliding portion of the control.

In order to measure movement along the channel, the channel should listen for a click event, which is also triggered when a user touches a touch-sensitive device, and adjust the position of the "thumb" as the user moves the pointer. This approach will prevent difficulties by movement outside the range of the "thumb". As the "thumb" is moved, the value of the input should be adjusted, and the value should be announced to the user, both visually and verbally.

☞ As with other components, code that can be used to construct a *Slider* is available in the *Code Examples*.

## Stars ✎

A *Star* rating system is very common; however, creating an accessible interface that allows such a rating takes a little creativity.

☞ When creating a *Star* rating system, the first decision is if partial values, such as 3 and one-half stars, will be allowed. If fractional values are allowed, while the same general approach outlined below will work, the presentational portion will need to be modified to allow a partial fill pattern.

The *Stars* pattern is a group of radio buttons with a structure that is slightly different than the standard structure detailed in the *Radio Group*; however, the accessibility issues that need to be kept in mind are much the same.

For the *Stars* pattern, each radio button and its accompanying label are declared at the same level, as siblings. This approach allows the creation of CSS rules that select the label following the chosen value and apply properties to those label elements that identify them as "selected" or "unselected".

☞ There are two basic designs for a *Stars* input based on the lowest possible value. Additionally, the lowest possible value will determine whether or not it will be possible to set a "default" value for the input.

In the sample code, the CSS applied uses filled and unfilled stars as content in a pseudo-element to represent whole units. If fractional values are used, the presentation must represent fractional units; however, the same general approach can be used. If representing fractional values, it is recommended that the margins on fractional units be eliminated and margins be set on the boundaries between whole values.

☠ As a group of radio inputs, when the *Stars* pattern is used the entire group must be enclosed in a `fieldset` tag with an accompanying `legend` as shown in the group example. Additionally, if zero is the lowest possible value for stars, an input for zero must be provided, as once a radio button in a group has been selected, one of the options in that group must be selected, there is no way in which the user can reset the group after interacting with it.

## Stepper ✎

A *Stepper* is an input that increases or decreases a value *in discrete steps*. In

| Payment Amount | | |
|---|---|---|
| | - | + |

order for the input to be fully functional, JavaScript is required; however, by declaring the input as a text, the user is free to enter a value, not just click the increment or decrement buttons to adjust the value. This approach means the interface will degrade gracefully.

☞ A number input is often used when constructing a *Stepper*; however, a number input is designed for the input of *decimal* values and may not generate an integer. Additionally, a native number input carries with it a specific interface that is not necessarily accessible.

In this pattern, a simple text input is created, and two buttons are added, one to increase the value and one to decrease the value.

☠ Because focus is away from the input when the increase or decrease button is activated, it is important that the value is added to an alert that will announce the new value.

## Switch (Toggle) ✎

One rather common design is what we might call a *Toggle* or *Switch*. In reality, this is a stylized *Checkbox*, with "on" and "off" or "checked" and "unchecked" states, and as such, it can easily be done in native HTML with CSS without a need for JavaScript or an WAI-ARIA widget role that may introduce discoverability issues.

☞ Although the patterns *Toggle* and *Switch* are often used interchangeably, they have one major difference, a component using the "switch" role, regardless of its visual styling, will *affect the page it's on* **immediately**.

There are three basic types of *Toggles*, defined by whether or not the on and off states have labels and where those labels are placed. Because this pattern uses HTML and CSS with limited enhancement through JavaScript and WAI-ARIA, there are no additional accessibility issues to consider.

☞ Although it is possible to create a *Toggle* or a *Switch* using an HTML button, a checkbox is suggested because it sets and maintains its state, either "on" or "off", without the addition of either CSS or JavaScript, meaning it will gracefully degrade and will offer better performance overall.

### *Internal Labels*

In this implementation, there is not only a label for the input, but visual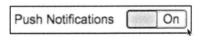

"state" labels for the "on" and "off" states as well. The visible state labels are on the inside of the channel in which the *Toggle* rests.

☠ This implementation is not recommended due to problems that will occur when the internal labels are longer.

## *Unlabeled*

In this implementation, there is only a label for the input, there are no visible state labels for the "on" and "off" states. This implementation is not recommended as it is less accessible than other options. If this is the desired design, it is recommended that the *External Labels* pattern below be used and the state labels be clipped and used for describing the value.

❧ Although this does not pose the internationalization challenges the *Internal Labels* model above does, this implementation is not recommended due to the potential for causing confusion because of the lack of visible state labels.

## *External Labels*

In this implementation, there is not only a label for the input, but visible state labels for the "on" and "off" states as well, just as with the *Internal Labels* model; however, unlike the *Internal Labels* model, the state labels are positioned *outside* the channel in which the *Toggle* is set.

Although in other components we have been clear that wrapping an input inside a label is an anti-pattern, it may be used in the *Toggle* to give the interface the expected interaction with less work in adding JavaScript with event handlers to manage the "click" turning the component "on" and "off". If the `label` element is used to maintain the interaction, the labeling content should be wrapped another element and bound to the input using an `id` and the `aria-labelledby` attribute of the input.

In the example code, all the *Toggle* types use the same CSS, with a "channel" that uses a background-color and a box-shadow to give the illusion of depth. The "button" inside the channel uses the opposite colors for background-color and box-shadow with a slight offset to give the illusion of height.

☞ Although JavaScript is not necessary for this design to work as expected, the example script will enhance the accessibility features for the *Toggle* by updating the described state using the existing position labels and switching the `aria-describedby` attribute to the base id plus the checked status of the input. This example script uses a naming convention that specifies the input identifier followed by "-label". The labeling element for the "off" or "false" position is identified by the input identifier followed by "-false" and the labeling element for the "on" or "true" position is identified by the input identifier followed by "-true". For example, the *Push Notifications* element uses "mytoggle" as the input identifier, as do the *Off* and *On* labels with "mytoggle-false" and "mytoggle-true", respectively.

## Tabs ☐

A *Tabs* component is used to show a series of content blocks with a skeuomorphic folder tab, typically at the top, that indicates which item is selected. It should be noted that although the image and the sample code use the common, top-aligned tab interface, the tabs need not be aligned horizontally at the top, they may be aligned vertically or positioned at the bottom.

The alignment and positioning of the tab list aside, there are a few requirements that must be address in order to maintain accessibility.

- The user must be able use the keyboard to activate each tab
- The control of the displayed panel is indicated both visually and programmatically.
- All controls have text labels, not just an icon that might be misunderstood.
- All controls have ample target area.

☞ There are two approaches identified here, a *plain HTML* approach and a *widget* approach. Programmatically, there is little difference between the two; however, use of the widget approach, which relies on WAI-ARIA roles to convey interaction details to the user, will move the *Tabs* into a different section of the assistive technology on some platforms, a section dedicated to WAI-ARIA widgets. Not all users will be aware of this practice, so use of the widget may leave some users confused. Because the widget approach raises discoverability issues, it is recommended that user monitoring include any section that uses a WAI-ARIA widget role.

## *Plain HTML*

The most important part
of the plain HTML
approach is that it uses

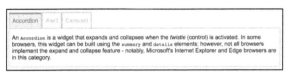

existing patterns without using WAI-ARIA roles. This practice
avoids the potential for assistive technology to segregate the *Tabs*,
and the potential issues that accompany such segregation, without
sacrificing usability.

The tab list contains anchors that use an `id` pattern to link to
markup in the page, in much the same way a *Skip-To* interface does.
The linked content is hidden, both visually and programmatically,
and the `aria-hidden` attribute is set to "true" until the content is
activated by the link being clicked. When the anchor is activated,
the `aria-selected` attribute is set to "true" and the `aria-`
`hidden` attribute on the paired content section is set to "false" or
removed, and the content is revealed. All sibling tab panels should
have the `aria-selected` attribute either set to "false" or removed
and the `aria-hidden` attribute set to "true".

🕸 Although much of the interaction can be controlled with HTML
and CSS, it is impossible to control the *entire* interaction using
only HTML and CSS, some scripting is required, as is
demonstrated in the sample code for the *Tabs* interface in the
*Code Examples*.

## *Widget*

☞ The *Tab* widget functions in much the same way a *Disclosure* interface does, with a few slight differences, in particular, the roles used by each. This widget follows the best current practice for development of a *Tab* control that uses the WAI-ARIA widget roles.

In the widget pattern, the *tablist* is a group of buttons that control which *tabpanel* is active at any time, and each *tabpanel* is labeled by its corresponding button in the *tablist* using `aria-labelledby`. Each button should also link to the associated *tabpanel* using the `aria-controls` attribute. This widget approach to constructing *Tabs* is another instance where the `aria-controls` attribute might be used to facilitate the show and hide functionality which must be implemented in JavaScript as well as providing an enhanced experience that allows users to jump to the *tabpanel* on some platforms.

Accessibility issues such as enabling keyboard navigation and hiding or revealing content both visually and to assistive technology have been addressed in the sample code provided for the *Tabs* in the *Code Examples*.

☞ Constructing the tablist with buttons in the widget pattern and anchors in the plain HTML pattern makes the tablist completely accessible by keyboard.

# Table ☐

One of the most basic components of a web page is a *Table*.
Although they are sometimes erroneously used for layout, their
true purpose is to provide a structure to data, and use of a *Table* for
layout is considered an accessibility error. Because of the
complexity inherent in constructing a *Table*, examples of several
types of layout are available in the *Code Examples*, as are some
interfaces identified below.

## *Types of Layout*

There are several
different layouts a table
may have. The most
common layout is a
*Simple* layout, which has

| 10 Busiest Airports | | | |
|---|---|---|---|
| **Airport Name** | **Airport Code** | **Country** | **Passengers** |
| Hartsfield-Jackson Atlanta International Airport | ATL | US | 104,000,000 |
| Beijing Capital International Airport | PEK | CN | 96,000,000 |
| Dubai International Airport | DXB | AE | 88,000,000 |
| Los Angeles International Airport | LAX | US | 84,600,000 |
| Tokyo Haneda International Airport | HND | JP | 85,000,000 |
| Chicago O'Hare International Airport | ORD | US | 80,000,000 |
| London Heathrow Airport | LHR | GB | 78,000,000 |
| Hong Kong International Airport | HKG | CN | 73,000,000 |
| Shanghai Pudong International Airport | PVG | CN | 70,000,000 |
| Aéroport de Paris-Charles de Gaulle | CDG | FR | 69,000,000 |

one row of headings at the top of the table and rows of data in the
body of the table. If this layout is used, the *Sortable* interface can be
used, allowing the data in the body of the table to be sorted. The
*Sortable* interface can also be used with the next-most-common
layout, *Simple Multi-level Header*. In the *Simple Multi-level Header*
layout, not only do the column headings act as headers, each row
also has a heading in the first column.

## Complex Multi-level Header

The next-most-common layout for tables is a *Complex Multi-level Header* layout. In this layout, the data in the body of the table is not

| 10 Busiest Airports | | | |
|---|---|---|---|
| Airport Name | Airport Code | Country | Passengers |
| Domestic | | | |
| Hartsfield-Jackson Atlanta International Airport | ATL | US | 104,000,000 |
| Los Angeles International Airport | LAX | US | 84,600,000 |
| Chicago O'Hare International Airport | ORD | US | 80,000,000 |
| International | | | |
| Beijing Capital International Airport | PEK | CN | 96,000,000 |
| Dubai International Airport | DXB | AE | 88,000,000 |
| Tokyo Haneda International Airport | HND | JP | 85,000,000 |
| London Heathrow Airport | LHR | GB | 78,000,000 |
| Hong Kong International Airport | HKG | CN | 73,000,000 |
| Shanghai Pudong International Airport | PVG | CN | 70,000,000 |
| Aéroport de Paris-Charles de Gaulle | CDG | FR | 69,000,000 |

only labeled by column headings, but also by a heading applied to a group of rows. For example, data about the number of passengers traveling through airports might be grouped according to the country the airport is in or whether the travelers are traveling to a domestic or international location.

⚙ Because of the complexity inherent in the layout, use of the *Sortable* interface is not recommended for the *Complex Multi-level Header* layout.

## Complex Group

The next-most-common layout for tables is a *Complex Group* layout. In this layout, the data in the body of the table is described not only by

| | | Sales | | | | | |
|---|---|---|---|---|---|---|---|
| | | Q1 | | | Q2 | | |
| | Region | January | February | March | April | May | June |
| Product A | | | | | | | |
| North | | 345 | 370 | 370 | 345 | 370 | 354 |
| East | | 245 | 320 | 270 | 288 | 325 | 204 |
| South | | 222 | 297 | 255 | 325 | 226 | 250 |
| West | | 145 | 220 | 170 | 188 | 225 | 114 |
| Product B | | | | | | | |
| North | | 145 | 170 | 170 | 145 | 170 | 154 |
| East | | 145 | 120 | 170 | 188 | 125 | 104 |
| South | | 122 | 197 | 155 | 125 | 126 | 150 |
| West | | 145 | 120 | 170 | 188 | 125 | 114 |

grouping rows but also by grouping columns. This layout, although offering the highest granularity available, is also very complex, not only from a construction standpoint but also from a comprehension standpoint. Users are typically better served by a greater degree of aggregation of the data with the ability to explore a specific group through another interface.

☠ Because of the complexity inherent in the layout, use of the *Sortable* interface is not recommended for the *Complex Group* layout. If the *Sortable* interface is necessary, the row groups must be identified by the value in the first column, with the table cell spanning all relevant rows.

| | | | Sales | | |
|---|---|---|---|---|---|
| | | | Q1 | | |
| Product | Region | January | February | March | |
| Product A | North | 345 | 370 | 370 | |
| | East | 245 | 320 | 270 | |
| | South | 222 | 297 | 255 | |
| | West | 145 | 220 | 170 | |
| Product B | North | 145 | 170 | 170 | |
| | East | 145 | 120 | 170 | |
| | South | 122 | 197 | 155 | |
| | West | 145 | 120 | 170 | |

### Types of Interfaces

In addition to layout, there are other features, or *interfaces*, that can be added to a *Table*, many of which can affect its accessibility. One of the simplest interfaces that can be added to a *Table* using *any* of the mentioned layouts is a *Caption*.

☠ Be cautious when adding interfaces to a *Table*, as interfaces can be added in a way that damages accessibility or violates accessibility guidelines. *All* accessibility guidelines, including guidelines for line, or row, height and device independence.

## Banding

Banded rows, also commonly called *zebra striping*, can help users scan data while also reducing the risk of confusing data in different rows. The risks to accessibility are low with the addition of banding, being primarily limited to *Luminance Contrast Ratio* issues. The advantages so outweigh the risks that it is generally recommended that either *Banding* or row borders be used.

## Caption

A caption can significantly enhance the accessibility of a *Table* by providing additional context or information; however, not all platforms treat captions created with the `caption` tag equally, and because of this inconsistency, it is recommended that the caption be linked to the table itself through the use of the `aria-labelledby` attribute and not just the `caption` tag. Additionally, each column header should use the `scope` attribute with the value "col" to bind the content as a column heading.

## Dive Down

There are several design approaches that have been used to dive deeper into a specific row of data. All the *Dive Down* approaches fall into one of two categories: an expandable row or a *Dialog*. Of the two, the *Dialog*, or modal approach, whether it is placed alongside the *Table* in a preview pane or above the *Table* as a traditional modal, is most common. It must be noted that the *Dialog* has its own interface requirements that must be followed if that approach is used, and if the *Dialog* is used detail for only one row can be shown at a time. Because of the risks associated with use of a Dialog, along with the opportunity to have multiple expanded rows, the expanded row approach is the recommended approach for a *Dive Down* interface.

## Editing

No discussion of a Table would be complete without consideration of the ability to allow inline editing. Although it might be done in a manner that makes the input interfaces inaccessible, Editing itself is not a challenge to accessibility.

| Region | Sales | | | | | |
| | Q1 | | | Q2 | | |
| | January | February | March | April | May | June |
| Product A | | | | | | |
| North | 345 | 370 | 370 | 345 | 370 | |
| East | 245 | 320 | 270 | 288 | 325 | |
| South | 222 | 297 | 265 | 325 | 228 | |
| West | 145 | 220 | 170 | 188 | 225 | |
| Product B | | | | | | |
| North | 145 | 170 | 170 | 145 | 170 | |
| East | 145 | 120 | 170 | 188 | 125 | |
| South | 122 | 197 | 155 | 125 | 126 | |
| West | 145 | 120 | 170 | 188 | 125 | |

☞ When adding the ability to edit data in a table, use the `aria-labelledby` attribute to identify all the labels that apply to the data element.

## Filter

On particularly large sets of data, many would implement a method to *Filter* or hide data that either matches the filter or does not match the filter. Although a *Filter* does not pose any more accessibility concerns than other methods of hiding information, nor would the interface used to implement it, it does change the data available in the *Table*. Because a *Filter* changes the content of the *Table*, a *Table* with a *Filter* is a live region and requires a mechanism to report changes, such as a status message, created by giving a container the role "status".

☠ Dynamically hiding data in a *Table* might pose accessibility issues as the updates are unlikely to be announced to visually impaired users without the addition of such a status message or identifying the *Table* as a live region.

### Pagination

Although *Pagination* is often included in discussions about a Table component, its complexities render it a topic unto itself. *Pagination* is covered as a topic below.

### Popover

Increasing the z-index of a row or column to make it appear closer, also known as a *Popover*, is a common technique used to draw focus to a specific row or column in the data of a *Table*. Often a *Popover* interface is triggered by hovering over a row or column; however, binding an interface to a specific device or device type, like a mouse or pointing device, violates one of the key principles of accessibility.

### Scrollable

Another common pattern in use with *Tables*

is making a table scrollable with a sticky header row or column, keeping the heading, or headings, in place while the body of the *Table* scrolls along the vertical or horizontal axis.

Unfortunately, the *Scrollable* pattern poses significant accessibility issues, first among them is the issue that user-agents do not allow a set height on a *Table* body which would allow a single element with proper markup that also scrolls. Because it is impossible to set a height on a the body, the appropriate method for constructing a *Scrollable* interface requires two pieces, a container with the headings that act as a *visual presentation* followed by a size-constrained container, that allows scrolling, with a properly constructed *Table*, complete with headings that are visually clipped.

☠ Although the approach for a *Scrollable* interface is fairly straightforward, the visual heading must be identified as presentational only and hidden from assistive technology and the visually hidden heading must be properly constructed so it is available to assistive technology

## Sortable

In addition to identifying the scope of the headings, if the table is sorted, it is recommended that a

| 10 Busiest Airports | | | |
|---|---|---|---|
| Airport Name ↕ | Airport Code ↕ | Country ↕ | Passengers ↕ |
| Hartsfield-Jackson Atlanta International Airport | ATL | US | 104,000,000 |
| Beijing Capital International Airport | PEK | CN | 96,000,000 |
| Dubai International Airport | DXB | AE | 88,000,000 |
| Los Angeles International Airport | LAX | US | 84,600,000 |
| Tokyo Haneda International Airport | HND | JP | 85,000,000 |
| Chicago O'Hare International Airport | ORD | US | 80,000,000 |
| London Heathrow Airport | LHR | GB | 78,000,000 |
| Hong Kong International Airport | HKG | CN | 73,000,000 |
| Shanghai Pudong International Airport | PVG | CN | 70,000,000 |
| Aéroport de Paris-Charles de Gaulle | CDG | FR | 69,000,000 |

description of the sort pattern be linked to the table through the use of the `aria-describedby` attribute, providing further insight into what can be complex data.

At the time of this writing, the HTML table does not have a native mechanism that allows the sorting of the data contained in it; however, that does not preclude the creation of a sorting mechanism. Because a *Sort* interface results in changes to a *Table*, the *Table* is a live region and requires a mechanism to report changes, such as a status message, created by giving a container the role "status".

※ Dynamically sorting data in a table might pose accessibility issues as the updates are unlikely to be announced to visually impaired users without the addition of such a status message or identifying the table as a live region. An example of this approach is included in the *Code Examples*, along with code that makes columns *sortable*.

## Trimmed Text

Because data tables can be a challenge to horizontal scrolling, a *Trimmed Text* interface, in which text is truncated and an ellipsis is shown indicating text is hidden, is a frequent theme. As with all hidden content, the *Trimmed Text* interface will pose cognitive accessibility issues, and may affect overall accessibility if the method of revealing the hidden text is not built in an accessible manner.

☠ Because of the accessibility issues inherent in the *Trimmed Text* interface, it is not recommended.

## Timer (Stopwatch) ★

*Timers* typically fall into one of two categories: *Elapsed Time*, sometimes called a *Stopwatch*, and *Countdown Clock*, sometimes called a *Timer*; however, there is a third category that combines these two functions, a dual-purpose timer. These dual-purpose timers might be used in situations where customers are waiting and should be notified when a certain period has passed...like when the "on hold" message repeats while customers are on hold.

☞ The primary concern with a *Timer* is the general lack of user interaction. There are elements within the *Web Content Accessibility Guidelines* that deal specifically with timed events, so those overall guidelines must be taken into account before any of the patterns described here are implemented.

In addition to accessibility concerns that might be raised when timed events are included in a web page or process, in order for a *Timer* to be accessible, there are a few additional requirements we must keep in mind.

- Information conveyed by visual cues of the timer, e.g., color changes to indicate state, must be conveyed in another way.
- Updates must not be announced more frequently than every fifteen seconds, to allow adequate time for the device to

announce the new value and also take into account the speech rate and language. This holds true even if the visual interface is updated more frequently.

- Animation that runs continuously must have a mechanism that allows the user to pause or stop the animation.

The timer pattern is relatively straightforward, there are two content areas, one for visual updates and a second used for updating assistive technology. All other components, such as a mechanism for controlling the animation, are not part of the timer and are outside the scope of this topic.

In addition to the accessibility concerns identified above, care should be exercised in determining which format will be used and how the information is announced as not all platforms announce numbers as numbers, but rather as digits. For example, while humans might read 12 as "twelve", some platforms might announce it as "one two", leaving it to the user to determine what the number is. Additionally, the time period separator, which is often a colon in western cultures, might not be appropriately announced if announced at all.

Once the various issues have been resolved, constructing an all-purpose timer is relatively easy, using two separate elements that have no other semantic meaning, typically a `div` or `span`, to contain the two time values: the visual element and the assistive element and identifying the visual element as hidden from assistive technology using `aria-hidden` and labeling the assistive element.

### A Dual-Purpose Timer

When creating a *Dual-purpose Timer*, two timers must be created, a *Stopwatch* and a *Countdown Clock*, and there must be a scripting mechanism that listens for the Countdown Clock to expire, which will trigger the event that made a *Dual-purpose Timer* necessary.

Code that demonstrates this approach, as well as code for the *Stopwatch* and *Countdown Clock*, is provided in the *Code Examples*. The widgets in the example in the *Code Examples* expose two properties: "elapsed" and "remaining", two methods, "start" and "stop", and two events: "expired" and "tick", to scripting and enables three attributes: `data-expired`, a message to be used in an "alert" when time is expired; `data-remaining`, the amount of time to use in the countdown clock, specified either as a number of seconds or as a time duration in the format hh:mm:ss; and `data-use`, the time value to be used for the display, either "elapsed" or "remaining".

### Toolbar ▢

A *Toolbar* follows much of the same pattern as a *Menu* or *Menubar*. For the *Toolbar*, as with the *Menubar*, there is no native HMTL implementation, so all implementations require HTML, CSS, and JavaScript to control the interactions. The difference between a *Toolbar* and a *Menubar* is that a *Toolbar* uses images as the visual label for the buttons and other controls that act as menu items rather than words. In the markup, a *Toolbar* uses the WAI-ARIA role "toolbar" rather than the "menu" or "menubar" role, and items in a toolbar are not identified using a "menuitem", "menuitemcheckbox", or "menuitemradio" role as they would be in a *Menu* or *Menubar*.

The interactions that go along with the WAI-ARIA "toolbar" role are almost identical to those of the *Menubar*, with the exception of the interaction for *Shift + F10*, and those interactions must be coded using JavaScript. As a reminder, the following keys should be handled: *Space* and *Enter*, *Escape*, *Tab* and *ArrowRight*, *Shift + Tab* and *ArrowLeft*, *ArrowDown*, *ArrowUp*, *Home*, *End*, and character keys; and all icons must be labeled.

☠ Although very common, it is strongly recommended that toolbars not be coded using WAI-ARIA but rather simply be native markup, CSS, and scripting to handle interactions. This will likely prevent issues that arise from unmet expectations and assistive technology that gets "stuck" when an interaction fails to signal that a *Menu* contained in a *Toolbar* is closed.

## Tooltip ☐

The *Tooltip* pattern, content that appears dynamically, showing additional information intended to

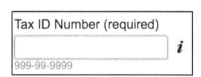

explain or describe something that may cause confusion, such as "why is this needed" content, is not recommended because of the potential for accessibility issues it generates.

As with any content that appears dynamically, such as the *Dialog*, there must be a mechanism available to dismiss the content without changing which element has focus. For the *Tooltip* pattern, changing focus is the common interface, which makes navigating this particular accessibility requirement particularly tricky. For example, many tooltips are shown when a specific item gets focus and hidden when the item loses focus; however, once the tooltip is shown, there must be a secondary method, other than the item losing focus, that will hide the tooltip.

Additionally, in the *Tooltip* pattern, content intended to reduce cognitive load is hidden until a user interaction determined by the designer/developer rather than when the user might find it helpful. In nearly all cases it would improve cognitive accessibility if the content were not hidden.

☠ Dynamically showing or hiding content is not only likely to cause confusion, especially to those users who are visually impaired and be faced without shifting focus and interrupted vocalization, it may be a form of the *Usurping the User* anti-pattern.

If the *Tooltip* pattern is used, it is recommended that the construction be in native HTML and CSS, and use the following patterns to maintain proper structure and organization. More information about the input pattern can be found in Best Practices.

☞ By adding the role of "alert" to the content container inside the Tooltip, assistive technology that may be in use will announce the tooltip content when the tooltip is displayed, without the need to manage focus. This approach is the easiest manner in which to make the dynamic display of a tooltip accessible; however, it does not address the ability to dismiss the tooltip without changing focus, a requirement if the tooltip hides or replaces other content.

## Placement

In common practice, the tooltip is placed next to the element it describes. Keeping a tooltip next to the element it describes maintains a logical structure, which is important for accessibility; however, it is possible to place the Tooltip next to the label without introducing a significant impact to the accessibility of the interface, and in some instances, placement of a tooltip before the input it describes is preferable.

| Tax ID Number (required) *i* |
| --- |
| &#124; |
| 999-99-9999 |

## Showing tooltips when a user hovers

Showing a tooltip, or any content, when a user hovers over a specific element is especially dangerous. Not only is the display of content restricted to those users who are using a pointing device, a subset of non-mobile users, but it also poses a significant risk of creating an experience that includes rapidly flashing, or strobing, content as the hover state switches in and out and content is dynamically displayed. Flashing content is not only distracting but also has the potential to cause seizures.

☠ Because the risk of accidentally creating a flashing element is very high and the potential effects severe, tooltips should never be displayed using the "hover" method.

### Showing tooltips when an input has focus

Your interaction design might call for tooltips to show up when a field has focus. This pattern is only available without additional JavaScript when the *Tooltip* is after the input in the markup, and it is important that if the content is displayed dynamically, especially when an item has "focus", the user must be able to dismiss it without moving focus.

### Showing tooltips by adding a class

In order to show a *Tooltip* regardless of its placement and what other element has focus, you will need to add a style rule for an "open" class and a mechanism, typically a scripted mechanism to add the "open" class to the *Tooltip* when it should be open and remove it when it should be closed.

# Tree ⚓

A *Tree* is a list of items, each item optionally containing a further list, that can be collapsed, expanded, or navigated using the arrow keys or the *Tab* and *Shift + Tab*, as well as the *Enter* key to select. Because there is no native HTML implementation of the tree role, when creating a *Tree* there are accessibility issues that must be kept in mind.

```
[-] Account Profile
   [-] Contact Information
      [+] Addresses
      [-] Email
         Work noname-work@mailinator.com
         Personal noname-personal@mailinator.com
      [+] Telphone
   Balances
      USD: $0.00
   Funding Instruments
      Card 9999
```

```
[-] Account Profile
   [-] Contact Information
      [-] Addresses
         My Company
         123 Any St
         Anytown AZ 85999
         999 E Notalane Rd
         Anytown AZ 85999
      [-] Email
         Work noname-work@mailinator.com
         Personal noname-personal@mailinator.com
      [-] Telphone
         Work (999) 555-1212
         Personal (602) 555-1212
   Balances
      USD: $0.00
   Funding Instruments
      Card 9999
```

- *Space* or *Enter*: activates the current node on the tree, activating the link or expanding its content.
- *ArrowDown*: moves focus to the next item that is focusable without expanding or collapsing the current item.
- *ArrowUp*: moves focus to the previous item that is focusable without expanding or collapsing the current item.
- *ArrowRight*: opens the current item if it is closed, or moves focus to the first item.
- *ArrowLeft*: closes the current item if it is opened, or moves focus to its parent.
- *Home*: moves focus to first item without opening or closing the item.

- *End*: moves focus to the last item that can be focused without expanding any items that are closed.

- *Character*: moves focus to the next item with a name that starts with the typed character, looping back to the beginning of the tree if no match is found. Closed items are ignored.

- *: expands all closed items that are at the same level as the current item.

- All expanded items are identified using `aria-expanded`

- Each item has the WAI-ARIA "treeitem" role

Care should be taken to ensure that the *Tree* is expanded by default, without CSS or JavaScript, otherwise content may be hidden by accident.

## Video ▢

There are a number of accessibility issues that must be addressed when providing video. While there is a native video element, as with many of the HTML5 elements, accessibility has gotten a bit lost in the development. In the case of the native HTML5 video element, a little extra work building a widget gets it back on the correct path. While it is possible to build a *Video* element, it will be much more efficient to use a video platform, such as YouTube, for delivery. This will reduce the possibility of inadvertently introducing technical issues and allow focus to be shifted to authoring issues such as providing adequate captioning and other media alternatives such as transcripts or a synopsis.

☞ It is strongly recommended that a text alternative, such as a transcript or synopsis, be provided and linked to the video using the `aria-describedby`.

If a video platform is not being used, one of the most significant issues is the use of the native controls for the player. The native controls, those provided by the HTML5 element, are not accessible, which means a widget  approach that uses JavaScript to handle the playback interface is the best alternative. For the best possible interface for visually impaired users, the following pattern has drawn on guidance from a number of sources, most notably, the American Foundation for the Blind.

❀ If the widget provided in the *Code Examples* is used, any shortcut keys identified with the `accessKey` attribute should be announced and described. If the `accessKey` attribute is not included, no such announcement is necessary.

☞ As with other widgets provided in this resource, the HTML and class attributes are tied directly to the CSS and JavaScript provided. Other images may be provided for the control buttons; however, the CSS and the JavaScript might need to be altered to accommodate those changes.

🔉 Although the example video does not have a track, videos provided in the wild must have captioning available. Captioning can be provided for multiple languages and must be labeled accordingly. For example, the track in English might look like "`<track kind="captions" label="English" src="https://mytracks.com/bigbuckbunny.vtt" srclang="en-US">`".

# Testing and Evaluating Accessibility

Accessibility testing has a bit of a troubled past and as a result, the first questions brought to the fore any time accessibility testing is mentioned are "when", "how", and "what". To get an idea of when, an understanding of the five typical phases of development is needed. Not all projects or organizations will have all five phases, but these are the most common.

1. *Ideation*: Ideation is the initial phase of product development, it's the development of the *idea* of the product or feature.

2. *Design and Content*: In the design and content phases, which likely happen in parallel, the overall design is created and content is developed[35].

3. *Development*: In the development phase, engineers take the design specification and the content that has been written and combine them into a unified interface.

4. *Quality Assurance*: In the quality assurance phase, the output of the development phase is tested to ensure it matches the design and content and is without any observable flaws.

5. *Release*: In the release phase, users are able to use the product.

---

[35] Approximately sixty percent of accessibility issues are injected into a product at this phase, making it the single largest contributor to issues.

# When Testing is Done

Accessibility testing has typically been performed after a page, site, or app has been released and has been reactive rather than proactive. There are two good reasons for this: (a) accessibility is affected, not only by the design and content, but the code used to mark up, style, and script the interface, so all development must be complete in order for accurate testing to occur; and (b) testing has typically been intended to offer proof of compliance as a legal protection or as a reaction to a complaint.

Because testing is often used to offer proof of compliance, it has primarily been focused on meeting or exceeding the A and AA level *Success Criteria* of the *Web Content Accessibility Guidelines*. Establishing the *Web Content Accessibility Guidelines* Success Criteria as *the measure* also allows organizations to rely on automated testing rather than the more costly manual testing.

☞ It should be noted that while passing tests identified by the *Web Content Accessibility Guidelines* Success Criteria *might* offer legal protection, it does not ensure your page, site, or app is accessible and legal protection is not *guaranteed*.

The important practice to follow is to *shift it left*, move testing and evaluation earlier in the process[36] whenever possible. If testing and evaluation is typically done after *release*, shift it to the *quality assurance* phase; if testing is currently done during the *quality assurance* phase, shift it to the *development* phase.

## How Testing is Done

Accessibility testing for web pages, sites, and apps is typically separated between *automated* and *manual* testing, and there is a strong industry trend to move all testing to automated methods. Most organizations believe automated testing is more reliable, but that bias is clouded by the significantly lower cost associated with automated testing.

Automated testing is like autocorrect. Automated testing can check the validity of the code to ensure syntax is followed, and it can check for known bad patterns, like transforming text to all uppercase. However, it cannot always perform more complex tasks, like ensuring the correct code has been used or completing more complex tasks, like calculating a *Luminance Contrast Ratio* with a mixed background.

---

[36] The development process is typically a five-phase cycle: ideation, the development of the idea of the product or feature; design and content creation; development, which is when engineers take the design specification and the content that has been written and combine them into a unified interface; quality assurance, when the output of the development phase is tested by someone other than those involved in build the interface to ensure it is without any observable flaws; and release, when users are able to use the product.

Manual testing is like proofreading. Unlike automated testing, manual testing and evaluation can ensure the correct code has been used rather than the correct syntax. For example, it can ensure that a heading is identified as a heading rather than as another element type. Manual testing also identifies less common bad patterns, like an incorrect structure or tab order, and validates more complex cases, like calculating a *Luminance Contrast Ratio* with a mixed background.

## Automated Testing

Automated testing has become increasingly uncomplicated, and there are a variety of tools available that can be easily integrated at various points in the product development process. An approach to *shift it left* is especially important where automation, and the resulting lower testing costs, is involved because the cost-to-benefit ratio is so heavily skewed. Many of the easily solved problems can be highlighted by automated testing and resolved before they work their way into phases where correction becomes costly.

☞ The addition of automated testing *does not* mean manual testing is not needed. Both types of testing are important in ensuring the accessibility of a product.

## Manual Testing

When testing for accessibility manually, there are several tests that should be performed. Each of the tests listed below will test for major or common accessibility issues. Because manual testing is typically time-consuming and costly, it is recommended that this be performed after all other testing has been performed and the identified issues resolved.

- Test without a pointing device, e.g., unplug your mouse or turn off your trackpad
- Test with High Contrast mode on
- Test with images turned off
- Test with CSS turned off
- Test with speakers turned off
- Test with a larger and smaller default font size
- Test the ability to change the font size
- Test the form field labels by clicking or tapping on them
- Test the tab order through the entire document

## What Testing is Done

Having generally identified how testing should be performed, it becomes a question of what should be tested and evaluated. In general, the elements that should be tested are:

- Content: Is the content legible and readable?
- Links: Are they clearly identifiable through color and decoration and do they notify users when opening in a new window?
- Media: Are there alternatives for audio, images, and video?

- Navigation: Does the tab order match the visual and logical structure of the document? Are landmarks clearly identified?

- Structure: Are the page title, headings, and lists correct, or are these elements incorrectly identified?

- Text: Can the text be resized? Is there sufficient contrast for all text, including links?

The final area that should be tested are forms. Forms, by their nature, are the most complex of testing situations because of the various layers of accessibility. Labeling, descriptions, help text, and feedback should all be evaluated; however, there are few hard and fast rules related to exactly how each of the elements should function. It is recommended that the guidance provided in this resource under both *Best Practices* and *Design Patterns* be reviewed before evaluation.

## Frequent Errors

When a number of websites are reviewed, we begin to see emerging patterns, patterns that help identify which mistakes are most frequently made. The good news is that many of the flaws that fall into the "most frequent" category can be caught with proper code evaluation, via linting, and automated testing, and can also frequently be prevented by adhering to the recommendations in *Best Practices* and avoiding all practices listed as *Anti-Patterns*.

## Color Alone

Most interfaces have a strong visual component, leading to the desire to minimize or eliminate labels. When diagrams, images, and data visualizations are in full color, the temptation to separate the colors from their labels is often strong; however, color alone cannot be used to convey meaning.

## Device Dependence

All interfaces must be usable regardless of the device being used. Although the *Web Content Accessibility Guidelines* note keyboard accessibility specifically, it is worth noting that the use of pointer devices, such as a mouse, or touch devices, such as a touch screen on a smartphone or tablet, must be supported as well.

## Insufficient Contrast

Insufficient contrast, or a low *Luminance Contrast Ratio*, occurs when the difference in lightness or brightness between adjacent foreground and background pixels does not meet a specific threshold, and is important regardless of whether the adjacent pixels are part of text or not. Although the computation of the difference ratio is somewhat complex, this value can, in most cases, be easily checked through the use of a variety of tools.

## Missing Alternative Text

Alternative text, whether that text is captioning in a video, audio descriptions of media, or written transcripts, must be provided for all media. While there are some automated tests available to ensure alternative text is provided in some cases, there are not automated tests for all cases. It is worthy of note that data visualizations, such as graphs and charts, also require alternative text.

## Missing Focus Indicators

Removing focus indicators, whether for all devices or a subset of devices, causes cognitive accessibility issues. Many designers will remove the default focus outline, and some accessibility researchers recommend this; however, if the outline is removed, a supplementary focus indicator *must* be provided, and that focus indicator must meet accessibility guidelines such as the guidelines for *Luminance Contrast Ratio*.

## Non-semantic Markup

Non-semantic markup is one of the most significant barriers to accessibility. Although the validation of HTML can be done with automated tools, there are very few automated tests that can identify the lack of *semantic* markup, with the exception of specific accessibility landmarks. One issue of note related to non-semantic markup, the attempt to provide semantic meaning to non-semantic markup through the use of WAI-ARIA roles is misguided as there are multiple issues associated with that practice.

## Placeholders without Labels

The use of placeholder or ghost text is an anti-pattern; however, using a placeholder without an associated label is also a common error in *Web Content Accessibility Guidelines* automated tests. All interfaces must have an accessible name, and the accessible name is rarely provided by the content in the placeholder attribute.

## Accessibility Audits

There is a special category of testing, an Accessibility Audit. When testing as part of an Accessibility Audit, it is critical issues are correctly identified. The primary focus during the audit will be manual testing that focuses on identifying issues that cannot be identified through automated testing.

The following issues are common issues identified during an audit:

- Alternative text in images may be missing or incorrect. This is especially the case for those images inside a link. Verify that the alternative text is present and describing the correct resource.

- Descriptive text for audio is often missing from caption tracks. While it is possible to partially automate caption tracks using speech recognition technology, this will not include descriptive text like "[ominous music]" or "[birds chirping]" that must be present in order to meet AA level *Success Criteria* in the *Web Content Accessibility Guidelines*.

- Headings may be missing, not convey the structure of a document, or contain irrelevant content. This issue can be especially frequent when pages are constructed without an understanding of the hierarchy, as they typically are when a JavaScript framework is used. Headings must be (a) present,

(b) convey the structure of the page, and (c) contain relevant content. All headings must be clear, descriptive, and unique.

- Color cannot be the only element used to convey meaning. The Success Criteria relating to color will be critical if the page tested has a data visualization, such as a chart or graph, included. It is important to note that automated tools can be confused and offer false positives or false negatives if the background color cannot be determined. This commonly happens when a background image is provided for a text block.

- Keyboard accessibility is critical; however, it is not limited to whether or not all interactive elements, links, form elements, and widget controls, can be accessed and activated using the keyboard, they must perform the expected action when activated. For example, skip links must actually skip to the correct content.

- Focus is another area where errors are common, having three distinct areas that must be tested: (a) a visible indicator showing focus is present and has a sufficient *Luminance Contrast Ratio* of at least 3:1; (b) the tab order corresponds to the document structure; and (c) the focus is not shifted unexpectedly either when focus is moved by the user or when the user interacts with a control.

☞ Carrying out an Accessibility Audit presents a good opportunity to increase capacity and technical skills within an organization around accessibility, regardless of whether it is led by an in-house expert or an external consultant.

An Accessibility Audit uses a number of tests to establish what elements of the website fulfill the testing requirements and which elements do not, and therefore need to be modified and improved. Some audits are more in-depth than others; however, all audits should include the test criteria from the latest *Web Content Accessibility Guidelines Recommendation*. Because of the inadequacy of automated testing, it is imperative that an audit include manual testing.

The final output of an audit will likely be a report, though in-house audits may have different requirements. The audit should: (a) show where the evaluated item or items, whether it be a sample or an entire site, stands in conforming with the *Web Content Accessibility Guidelines*, (b) indicate how accessibility can be improved, (c) give an implementation plan, and (d) give a basis for deciding whether to fix the identified issues or recreate the items through redesign or development. Although the decision to either fix or rebuild will depend on the resources available, the audit should provide valuable insight into the amount of effort necessary for each option.

A full Accessibility Audit report will typically have the following sections:

- *Summary*: The summary should contain the overall conformance rating of the website with the *Web Content Accessibility Guidelines* and a high-level, prioritized summary of issues that need to be addressed. Keep in mind that accessibility follows the adage "as strong as its weakest link", it is not an average or scored item; the lowest conforming member establishes the conformance level for the whole.

- *Background and Methodology*: The background and methodology section is the who, what, when, where, why, and how of the audit and will answer such questions as: who carried out the audit, what methodology was used, when the audit was carried out, where the audit was performed, i.e., what the sample was, why the audit was performed, and how testing and evaluation was performed.

- *Findings*: The findings section is a snapshot or summary of test results that gives not only the overall result, such as the *Web Content Accessibility Guidelines* conformance level met, but also a summary of the greatest issues

- *Prioritized Action List*: the prioritized action list contains the resolution to issues and will typically be either specific directed action, such as "change the font-size to relative values", or generic actions such as "ensure content providers understand the need for media alternatives"

- *Appendix*: the appendix contains the detailed list of issues, identifying both the issue, such as an insufficient *Luminance Contrast Ratio*, and the location

## Organizing an Audit

When organizing an audit, whether it will be done in-house or by an external party, consider the following:

- what conformance standards must be met, typically this will be a *Web Content Accessibility Guidelines* level but it may include other criteria such as specific government standards
- whether to audit the entire site or a sample of pages, keep in mind that because not all testing can be automated, the greater the scope the greater the cost
- if a sample is being used, what sampling approach should be used, samples should include pages most frequently accessed by site users, any pages with forms or tables, pages that are static and pages that are generated, pages that include graphics and data visualizations such as charts or diagrams, and interactive pages that use scripting or process user input
- what the final output should be, not every organization needs a detailed report as described above
- who will perform the audit, address what level of experience with accessibility, examples of work in the area, references,

professional qualifications, and what specific expertise might be required

☞ Some organizations will opt for an external resource because of the sensitivity around critical evaluation of work product. It is important that regardless of the source of the audit report, staff are briefed about the importance of accessibility to the organization *and* that all findings are presented in a manner that identifies the exercise as an opportunity for improvement rather than blame-attribution.

## Performing an Audit Yourself

☞ If an audit is to be performed by in-house staff, it is still important that all the requirements identified above are evaluated, as the degree of experience with accessibility and testing is critical to the success of the audit.

The necessary resources for performing an audit internally, both the relevant automation software and manual testing directions, including a checklist, are provided below.

# Testing and Evaluation Tools

There are several different tools available in the testing and evaluation toolbox, and different organizations use some, all, or even none of these tools. The tools listed provide a means of testing and/or evaluating different parts, or steps, of the design and construction process. The tools listed here are listed in the general order in which they would be used, beginning with the evaluation of content, through the development and creation of code, to evaluation of the final product.

## Roking-A11y Color Tuner and Roking-A11y Color Matrix

Numerous resources exist to analyze the *Luminance Contrast Ratio*; however, these two tools, which can easily be used during the design phase, perform specific functions not typically found in other resources. The *Roking-A11y Color Tuner*[37] not only analyzes a foreground and background color to determine if the *Luminance Contrast Ratio* passes the tests for normal and large text or adjacent non-text colors, but also manipulates the foreground and background colors to provide the nearest passing possibility. The *Roking-A11y Color Matrix*[38], on the other hand, analyzes a color palette and creates a readable table with color values and their *Luminance Contrast Ratio*, giving a designer the ability to see at a glance which colors can be used alongside or on top of other colors.

## Roking-A11y Readability Tool

Content is often difficult to test or evaluate to ensure it is clear and concise and sound from a cognitive accessibility perspective. One of the few tools available, other than direct user testing, is the

---

[37] The Roking-A11y Color Tuner is available at
https://hrobertking.github.io/roking-a11y/color-tuner.htm
[38] The Roking-A11y Color Matrix is available at
https://hrobertking.github.io/roking-a11y/color-matrix.htm

Läsbarhetsindex. As mentioned in the *Best Practices*, the Läsbarhetsindex is preferred over other algorithms, like the *Flesch Reading Ease Score*, because scores vary little across languages, making boundaries easier to determine. The *Roking-A11y Readability Tool*[39] analyzes text you provide according to the language you specify.

## Markup Validation

The HTML specification was developed by the W3C, so there is no better tool to use for validation of your markup than the W3C HTML validation service[40].

There are command-line interfaces for several validators, including the W3C's Nu project; however, care should be taken when validating via command-line because the entire document must be validated. With the use of JavaScript frameworks, like AngularJs or ReactJs, it is tempting to validate portions of code. While validating portions of code has its use, portions may be correct while the whole is invalid.

## CSS Linting

There are two tools of note that can be used to evaluate CSS as a standalone: *stylelint-a11y* and *roking-csslint*. These tools are command-line, automated services only. While *stylelint-a11y* will evaluate preprocessor files, it uses a different internal toolset to

---

[39] The Roking-A11y Readability Tool is available at
https://hrobertking.github.io/roking-a11y/readability.htm
[40] The W3C HTML validation service is available at https://validator.w3.org/

perform evaluations and has a more limited rule set than *roking-csslint*. The *roking-csslint* package is a variant of *CSSLint*, written by Nicole Sullivan and Nick Zakas, and therefore only evaluates pure CSS, but has a much more comprehensive rule set.

## Automation Tools

There are a number of full automation tools available to perform automation testing, however, three are worthy of note: *aXe*, by Deque Systems; the *Automated Accessibility Testing Tool* by PayPal; and the *Accessibility Viewer* by the Paciello Group. These tools vary in the manner in which they can be used and the how comprehensive they are. It should also be noted that they might or might not have updated rule sets matching the latest *Web Content Accessibility Guidelines* Recommendation.

## Screen Readers

There are several screen readers, software that converts the text in a web page or application to voice, however, the most prominent is *JAWS* (pronounced jaws). Nearly all screen readers have navigational shortcuts such as allowing the user to navigate by links, *navigation shortcuts should be tested alongside the announcement of content*. Although it is likely impossible to test all screen readers, *VoiceOver*, which is available on Apple devices, *TalkBack*, which is available on Android devices, *JAWS*, which is available for Windows devices, and *NVDA*, which is available for Windows devices, should all be tested. At the time of this writing, of these packages, *JAWS* is the only package with a fee-based license.

## Speech Recognition Software

Speech recognition software, sometimes called voice-to-text, is software that converts speech into an input method, enabling users to use voice commands to control their device. Speech recognition software aids individuals with a number of different impairments, including motor or dexterity impairments such as carpal tunnel syndrome and cognitive or neurological impairments such as dyslexia.

Of the options available in the market, the *Dragon NaturallySpeaking* line of products from Nuance are the most prominent, with offerings for both Windows and Mac, and even a smartphone dictation app, called *Dragon Anywhere*. One important feature of speech recognition software that may not be available in more limited voice-to-text is the ability of the software to interact with programs and devices.

The difficulties inherent in the development of speech recognition software means it is currently trailing other assistive technology such as screen readers. This important interaction assistant often has less support for features such as WAI-ARIA, and may even fail when some common practices, such as using an `aria-label` instead of a `label`.

# Checklist

The final tool in the toolbox, the checklist, is perhaps the most significant, because it can only be used with manual testing. Undoubtedly, there are potential problems with using a checklist, most stemming from two irrefutable facts: checklists are written by people and checklists are read by people. Both steps, writing and reading, involve people and therefore bias. The checklist provided as part of this resource is intended to be comprehensive and clear; however, as the possibility for bias exists, it should be used only in conjunction with other methods.

☠ This checklist should not be used as a substitute for the *Web Content Accessibility Guidelines*, as that particular specification carries a legal weight not covered here. However, there are issues identified in this checklist that are not present in the *Web Content Accessibility Guidelines* that are also important for accessibility, even though they may not be covered by statute.

## *Animation*
- o  All animations are clear and meaningful
- o  All animations can be removed, prevented, or stopped at the user's request
- o  All animations have a duration of at least one second

## *ARIA Roles, States, and Properties*
- o  WAI-ARIA roles are only used when there is no HTML alternative

- WAI-ARIA states and properties are used with the appropriate role
- WAI-ARIA states and properties have valid values

## *Color*

- Text has a sufficient *Luminance Contrast Ratio* for its relative size
- Non-text adjacent colors have a sufficient *Luminance Contrast Ratio*
- Color is not used as the lone differentiation between similar elements
- Pure white and pure black are not used

## *Content*

- All content belongs to a landmark
- All statuses, including error messages, have been identified as a live region using either a status or alert role
- All exclusive or inflammatory language, such as he, she, or master, has been removed
- Captions and transcripts have been provided for all video content
- Clear error messages have been provided for all invalid input
- Content is readable, with a *Läsbarhetsindex* lower than 70
- Content is not placed inside images
- Hidden content is hidden for all users

- Interfaces use with the same terminology for the same functionality
- Only abbreviations and acronyms are entirely in uppercase
- Text alternatives have been provided for all visualizations, such as graphs and pie charts
- Text alternatives have been provided for all images that do not a presentation role
- Text alternatives have been provided for all abbreviations and acronyms the first time they are used
- The same content is available across different devices and platforms
- Transcripts have been provided for all audio content

## Controls

- All controls look like controls, with strong perceived affordance
- All controls that can receive focus have a focus style
- Editable inputs are shown on a non-white, or non-empty background
- Editable inputs have a white, or empty background
- Input is validated when possible
- Links are underlined
- Validity of user-provided information is clearly provided
- Visible and announceable labels are provided for all controls

## CSS

- o A link tag is used in place of @import

- o A print stylesheet has been provided

- o All redundant and unused styles have been removed

- o All sizes, including borders, margin and padding, are provided in relative units

- o All stylesheets have been minified and compressed

- o Use of absolute position is limited or non-existent

- o Use of display, font-variant, and text-transform is limited or non-existent

## HTML

- o A language code is provided for all languages used

- o All HTML is accessible to both screen reader and keyboard

- o All redundant and unused HTML has been removed

- o Div-itis has been removed

- o HTML semantics are matched to behavior

- o HTML has been minified and compressed

- o Tables are used for data only, not layout

## Icons

- o All icons are labeled

- o Commonly used and understood icons are used

## Images

- o All raster images have been compressed

o   Inline images, rather than background images, have been used

o   SVG path data has been optimized

o   Well-established icons and symbols have been used

## *Interaction*

o   All states, e.g., current, expanded, invalid, or selected, are communicated to all users

o   CAPTCHA is not used

o   Complexity is reduced by shortcuts like autocompleting addresses using a quick address search

o   Device dependence in interactions has been eliminated

o   Empty space between touch targets is sufficiently large (at least forty-four pixels)

o   Focus can be moved to scrollable elements using the keyboard

o   Focus is not set on page load

o   Focus styles are clear and unambiguous

o   Hidden elements do not receive focus

o   Infinite scroll is not used

o   Links with unusual behavior, such as opening in a new window, are identified to users

o   Standard scrolling behavior is not hijacked

o   Supported and expected user-agent behaviors have not be recreated with scripting

- o Touch targets are sufficiently large (at least .46 inches or 11.6 millimeters)
- o User action reveals content only by exception

### *JavaScript*

- o All redundant and unused JavaScript has been removed
- o JavaScript is not required for interaction
- o JavaScript is not used to recreate supported and expected user-agent behaviors
- o JavaScript has been minified and compressed

### *Media*

- o All content provided in media is present in markup
- o Alternative and descriptive text is provided for media

### *Performance*

- o All applicable assets are cached
- o Devices are provided images using srcset
- o Large images use lazy loading
- o Styles and scripts do not render blocking

### *Privacy*

- o The use of accessibility features or software is not tracked
- o The Do Not Track header (DNT header) is honored
- o Third-party resources that compromise user privacy are not included

### *Structure*

- o All grouped elements have a group label

- All headings describe a logical section or subsection
- All logical sections and subsections are described by a heading
- Focus order follows the displayed and written structure
- Forms are as short as possible
- Labels are place above their input elements
- Long documents have a table of contents
- Long documents and complex forms are broken up into discrete sections

## Typography

- All fonts have sufficient stroke width, a minimum of approximately one-eighth the height
- Language-specific paragraph justification, left or right, is used
- Line height is at least 150 percent of font height
- No absolute units are used for font size
- Serif fonts are limited in use
- Special fonts use a subset of just the characters needed
- The font size used for primary content is no smaller than the default user-agent size
- Uppercase and smallcaps are used only for abbreviations and acronyms

# Accessibility Statements

As a part of your testing and evaluation, your organization should develop and publish an *Accessibility Statement*.

An *Accessibility Statement* is a web page that describes the policy, goals, and accomplishments related to an organization's web accessibility efforts. Although in the US it is often a part of a legal action that is an alternative to filing a lawsuit, called *Structured Negotiations*, it need not be, and an organization need not be facing legal action to develop an *Accessibility Statement*. In fact, developing and publishing an *Accessibility Statement* might result in some of the same benefits seen in the *Business Case for Accessibility* by demonstrating a commitment to accessibility and inclusion.

## Sections to Include

For some organizations, such as public sector bodies in the EU, not only is an *Accessibility Statement* required, it must meet certain guidelines. This section is not intended to function as a replacement for requirements within a specific jurisdiction but to function as general guidance in the formation of an *Accessibility Statement*.

### A Commitment

The *Commitment* section is often the introductory statement and identifies an organization as committed to digital accessibility. The section should include acknowledgement that accessibility is not a one-time fix but is an on-going improvement and maintenance process.

## The Standard Applied

In the *Standard Applied* section, not only should the standard which was used in testing, such as the *Web Content Accessibility Guidelines 2.1*, *Section 504*, or *Section 508*, be cited, but the section should also include the environments in which the content was tested and any technical prerequisites, such as supported user-agents.

## Contact Information

The *Contact Information* section should offer clear instructions regarding how a user can provide feedback about content that does not meet accessibility requirements or is difficult to use due to an impairment.

## Goals

The *Goals* section should include any known points of failure, a list of any parts of the web page or website that have been identified as not being accessible. This section should also include an explanation of why these portions are not accessible, and if possible, a link to accessible alternatives[41].

---

[41] It is important to note that the presence of accessible alternative may not be sufficient. In 2018, the US Department of Transportation fined Scandinavian Airline System for violating the Department's web accessibility requirements by creating a separate website for "individuals with disabilities" rather than ensuring the primary website met the *Web Content Accessibility Guidelines*.

☞ It is important that this section use clear, concise language. For example, rather than referring to "Success Criterion 1.2.4", refer to "captions for live audio content".

## Accomplishments

The *Accomplishments* section should list those measures an organization has taken to ensure accessibility, such as including accessibility in the organizational mission statement or internal policies, establishing accessibility-focused roles or providing training, or quality assurance methods.

## Recourse and References

The *Recourse and References* section should identify any applicable national or local laws and policies as well as any enforcement procedure, or procedures, which might offer recourse.

☠ This section is often *required* for public sector bodies, be sure to review the relevant statues in your jurisdiction.

## Where to put the Accessibility Statement

The final step in creating an *Accessibility Statement* is determining how it fits best in your site navigation. Common wisdom might suggest a single link in the footer is sufficient; however, the *Accessibility Statement* will work best when users can find it easily. The *Accessibility Statement* should be linked in all navigation where it unlikely to cause confusion such as help menus, site maps, and the *about* section.

# Hiring and Utilizing Accessibility Resources

One of the first actions most organizations undertake when actively pursuing accessible solutions is hiring accessibility resources. The reason most choose to hire rather than promote from within is the amount of knowledge required to be effective takes a significant amount of time to acquire. The difference between platforms and the sometimes competing needs for the variety of impairments addressed implies a significant breadth of knowledge is often required. A successful plan will almost always require hiring resources while also developing skills among existing resources.

## Certifications

There are few formal programs for accessibility education or certification; however they do exist. The International Association of Accessibility Professionals has two primary certifications, the *Certified Professional in Accessibility Core Competencies* and the *Web Accessibility Specialist*, and a special certification, the *Certified Professional in Web Accessibility*, for those individuals who have completed both certifications. Additionally, the US government will certify an individual as a tester for *Section 508* compliance with a *508 Trusted Tester Certification*[42]. Finally, the University of

---

[42] It should be noted that prior to June 2018 *Section 508* and the *Web Content Accessibility Guidelines* were separate entities with *Section 508* applying

Missouri Columbia has a *ADA Coordinator Training Certification Program*; however, much of the training is focused on the Americans with Disabilities Act (ADA) and may or may not include digital accessibility and may or may not be applicable to a specific role.

In addition to the general certifications, individuals may have certification with a specific assistive technology. For example, an individuals might have received certification from Vispero, for JAWS, or NV Access, for NVDA; however, those certifications are not accessibility certifications per se, but specific to their respective software.

## Interview Questions

One of the most difficult tasks in evaluating an individual for an accessibility role or outlook is interviewing. For many questions asked to assess outlook there seldom is a right or wrong answer in the way there are with many technical questions, leaving interpretation to the individual performing the interview. For this reason, many of the questions listed here do not offer guidance about what the answer should be.

☞ It is important to note that although the questions here need not be asked by an expert, it will be extremely helpful to include

---

specifically to US government providers, so a 508 Trusted Tester Certification may or may not be applicable to a specific role.

one if at all possible. If including them in the interview is not possible, record the answers so they can be evaluated at a later point. Do not assume everyone performing an interview has the same level of knowledge about accessibility.

## Questions for all roles

No one is born knowing about accessibility, not even something as simple as why a screen reader might needed. The most basic of questions should evaluate how a person learned or is learning about accessibility. Questions like who benefits from accessibility and are you familiar with assistive technology are good starting points, as is a question about the motivation for any previous emphasis on accessibility, but **do not ask about medical conditions**. As you dive deeper into accessibility, you might wish to ask general opinion-type questions to ensure a candidate's opinions match your own, questions like what would you add or take out of the *Web Content Accessibility Guidelines* or is WAI-ARIA helpful or harmful will often provide insight into a candidate's thought process and experience.

More specific questions, like what are some of the tools available for testing, are important; however, keep in mind that not all organizations will have given the same level of access to tools to all employees and not all organizations treat accessibility or testing in the same way. For example, it is unwise to assume that everyone will know about the majority of the resources described in the

*Testing Toolbox* section, let alone what each does or how best to use it.

## Questions for Specific Roles

In addition to general questions, if you are evaluating someone for a specific role and wish to assess their knowledge about accessibility relative to their role, there are several questions that might be asked. You may wish to delve deeper into a specific thread as needed. These questions also are divided into opinion-based questions and fact-based questions. For fact-based questions, quick answers that can be used for comparison have been provided.

### *Questions for Designers and Content Writers*

To get a general feel for the accessibility opinions of a designer, you might ask how they define inclusiveness in design, how responsive design can affect accessibility, or what concerns might arise from the use of iconography in a user interface. For a content writer, you might ask what makes a heading a heading, why headings are useful, or how language can affect accessibility. In the responses, the more shallow or surface answers will reveal the lack of deeper thought about accessibility.

Familiarity with skip links, why `rem` and `em` are preferable to `px` or `pt`, the importance of the *Luminance Contrast Ratio*, and why color alone is insufficient to convey meaning will generally indicate some exposure to accessibility, but are not likely to indicate deeper thought about accessibility

## *Questions for Technical Resources*

For technical resources, otherwise known as web developers or UI engineers, the questions are a little easier because they are more likely to have right and wrong answers. For example, if the question asked was what is the difference between a link and a button the correct answer is that a link *goes somewhere* or points to a resource but a button *does something*. Likewise, questions about what every input or image needs have specific answers, i.e., a label or alternative text, respectively.

More specific questions, such as what is the *Accessibility Tree*, what would you use to indicate an element's or component's state, and what is the difference between "`hidden`", "`aria-hidden`", and "`role="presentation"`" will give an indication to whether or not an individual has more experience with accessibility; however, it should be noted that more experience and better experience are two different things. Someone can be more experienced with poor habits.

Finally, just as there are for designers and content writers, there are opinion-based questions that reveal deeper thought patterns about accessibility for UI engineers. Questions such as what issues should be addressed when content is hidden from sighted users but not screen readers and vice versa, and if a website has successfully passed all *Web Content Accessibility Guidelines* tests is the interface accessible, can give insight to how deeply a candidate has thought about accessibility and possibly the extent to which they are familiar with testing.

## Questions for Leaders

If the candidate is being considered for a leadership position, it is important to ask several *what if* questions and that you get an answer that fits the organization. You should ask questions such as what would you do if there are accessibility issues open when a release is scheduled, because that is more likely to be a *when* than *if*, and what would you do if the designer, content writer, or manager refused to fix a *Level A* defect, again a situation that is more likely a when than an if. Thoughtful answers here should demonstrate an understanding of priority, complexity, and possible work-arounds rather than be superficial.

# Utilizing Accessibility Resources

Often, organizations are tempted to decree accessibility to be a global responsibility. While such decrees are well-intentioned, they are unrealistic. Designers, content writers, and UI engineers have not been taught and are not being taught about accessibility, and no decree will alter that fact. Even if an organization makes such a decree, they will still face challenges in maintaining skills and education, similar to other annual skills training such as the annual business ethics and compliance training common in the financial industry. The alternative is to leverage the passion that exists, fan the spark into a flame, and to build processes to integrate that knowledge and passion into the greater whole.

## Identifying Resources

There are a number of ways in which an organization can utilize accessibility resources, but all of the ways begin by identifying the accessibility resources that already exist in an organization. If there are no resources that exist in an organization, there are outside resources available, organizations that can provide accessibility consultation and training to develop internal resources, and organizations can add individuals with skills in accessibility skills by adding screening questions to interviews. Once resources have been identified, an organization can determine how best to integrate those resources, often using one of the following models for accessibility roles[43].

## The Accessibility Champion Model

Perhaps the most common way accessibility is integrated into an organization is when an *individual* expresses an interest in accessibility and is then identified, or perhaps self-identifies, as a resource, an *Accessibility Champion*. The *Accessibility Champion* builds and maintains skills outside of their normal workload and

---

[43] Regardless which model is chosen, there will be instances when there are irreconcilable differences between design, development, or product teams and the accessibility resource. For this reason, the organization should provide guidance regarding how to reconcile those differences *before they arise*.

fields questions in addition to their normal workload. As a reactive model, this often leads to frustration because the questions typically arise after planning has already occurred, the *Accessibility Champion* has little time to maintain their skills, and the *Accessibility Champion* feels an even greater responsibility, often without the corresponding authority or compensation. In order for this model to function properly, an organization must recognize the amount of effort involved in the *Accessibility Champion*'s work and make corresponding changes in the recognition they receive.

## The Accessibility Lab Model

A second way in which organizations can utilize accessibility resources is through an *Accessibility Lab*. This approach identifies a *group* of individuals who perform research and training for the enterprise as well as act as general consultants. This approach offers several advantages, including (a) providing better, more complete answers to queries that are valid enterprise-wide and (b) addressing some of the issues an *Accessibility Champion* faces in skill maintenance, authority, and compensation by spreading the cost and demand over multiple individuals. This approach takes a significant commitment from the organization to both grow internal resources and dedicate resources to research and training as well as running the risk of not providing highly technical consultation because of their focus on user experience. In order for this model to function properly, all aspects of product development, from ideation through development must be covered.

## The Accessibility Architect Model

Yet a third way in which organizations can utilize accessibility resources is through an *Accessibility Architect*. This *individual* is responsible for ensuring a product, or products if the area of responsibility is enterprise-wide, are designed and built to be as accessible as possible. Although the *Accessibility Architect* is likely to have strengths in either design, content writing, or development, they are familiar with all three areas and accessibility issues that may arise in any of them as well as how to address those issues. To be most successful, the *Accessibility Architect* should not directly be a part of a single product team but part of a larger accessibility collective that is embedded in product teams in much the same way journalists are embedded with operational military units. This will minimize the risk of excessively constraining the *Accessibility Architect*'s authority and creating an authority-to-responsibility imbalance.

If an organization has design, content, or UI engineering teams embedded in product teams already, this can be a natural fit; however, to be successful, it requires the development of an enterprise-wide accessibility collective and has the potential for greater overhead if not managed well, just as embedded design, content, or UI engineering teams do.

The embedded *Accessibility Architect* approach has the advantage of offering consistency across an organization for issues that are open to interpretation, such as what counts as incidental text, in much the same way an *Accessibility Lab* does, as well as decreasing the amount of time required to get answers and guidance. As an added bonus, the task of team education can easily be shifted to the *Accessibility Architect*, improving the education as it will have greater focus and relevance compared to an enterprise-wide solution such as an *Accessibility Lab*.

To be successful, the *Accessibility Architect* will need to be a full member of the local team, getting on the email distribution lists and being identified as someone who is not only available, but someone team members should consult.

## Beyond Utilization

Too often, those with a passion for accessibility and inclusion face organizations that encourage them to shift their focus or lower their standards, and even in those cases where organizations encourage the utilization of accessibility resources, whether they be an *Accessibility Champion*, members of an *Accessibility Lab*, or an *Accessibility Architect*, the task can seem a Sisyphean one. It is important for the success of the resource(s) that they be included at every possible step to make the task easier and that the inclusion be more than just a tick mark on a to-do list and that the organization mature in its treatment of accessibility along the way.

Organizationally, accessibility might be treated in much the same way the SEI Capability Maturity Model treats software development. This approach, like the Digital Accessibility Maturity Model[44], sees approaches to accessibility within an organization along a continuum, where efforts at the initial stage are undocumented or varying across the enterprise, often with uncontrolled processes that are reactive and event driven and at the highest level of maturity is a state where everyone in the organization understands accessibility, and is continually improving performance through incremental change.

In real-world scenarios; however, this highest level is not maintainable at the present. The lack of education and real-world emphasis along with the demand of continuing education to address constantly-changing basic skills create a situation in which individuals often do not have the time to understand accessibility to any greater degree than absolutely necessary. The highest level an organization is likely to attain is one in which accessibility is adjusted and adapted for particular projects without significant, measurable losses of quality or deviations from specifications.

That organizations cannot achieve the impossible does not mean they should abandon all efforts to improve. On the contrary, the existence of the wide gap between the initial stages of poorly-

---

[44] More information about the Digital Accessibility Maturity Model can be found at https://www.levelaccess.com/the-digital-accessibility-maturity-model-maturity-levels/

defined chaos and consistent evaluation indicates just how much room there is to improve, and every improvement to accessibility will improve the bottom line.

# Appendix: Code Examples

The CSS provided for inputs assumes the use of the generalized *field* CSS provided above.

# Accordion 🔨

## HTML

```
<section class="accordion">
  <header id="accordion-label">© Copyright 2018</header>
  <p aria-labelledby="accordion-label">
    All content on this site is controlled and licensed by its author
    under the Artistic-2.0 license.
  </p>
</section>
```

## CSS

```
/*
the line-height of the header is set to zero because the UTF-8 triangle,
which is visually the same as the twistie used by the HTML5 summary tag,
is not the same height as the text in the header. Additionally, the
twistie symbol does not have the same width as height, so the width is set
to prevent the text from jumping up and down or left and right when the
section is expanded or collapsed and the twistie twists
*/
.accordion > header {
  cursor: pointer;
}
.accordion > header button {
  border: none;
  margin-right: 0.5em;
}
.accordion > header button[aria-expanded="false"]::before {
  content: '▶';
}
.accordion > header button[aria-expanded="true"]::before {
  content: '▼';
}
.accordion > header + [aria-expanded="false"] {
  border: 0 !important;
  clip: rect(0, 0, 0, 0);
  clip-path: polygon(0 0, 0 0, 0 0, 0 0);
  left: -200% !important;
  overflow: hidden;
  position: absolute !important;
}
```

## JavaScript

```
/*
By adding the aria-expanded attribute using JavaScript, there is no risk
the component will be stuck in the collapsed state
*/
[].slice.call(document.getElementsByClassName('accordion'))
.forEach(function init(el) {
```

```
  var attr = 'aria-expanded',
    btn = document.createElement('button'),
    header = el.getElementsByTagName('header').item(0),
    labels = {
      'false': 'expand',
      'true': 'collapse'
    },
    sibling = header.nextElementSibling,
    onActivate = function activate(e) {
      var activate = !e.key || (e.key && /enter|space| /i.test(e.key)),
        expanded = btn.expanded === 'true';

      if (activate) {
        btn.expanded = String(!expanded);
      }
    };

  Object.defineProperty(btn, 'expanded', {
    enumerable: true,
    get: function () {
      return this.getAttribute(attr);
    },
    set: function (value) {
      this.setAttribute(attr, value);
      this.setAttribute('aria-label', labels[value]);
      sibling && sibling.setAttribute(attr, value);
    }
  });

  header.insertBefore(btn, header.firstChild);
  btn.addEventListener('click', onActivate);
  btn.expanded = 'false';
});
```

# Alert

## HTML

```
<section aria-live="assertive" role="alert">
  <header id="alert-header">System notice</header>
  <p id="alert-content">
    System shutdown will begin in 20 minutes.
  </p>
</section>
```

# AlertDialog ⚠

## *HTML*

```
<div class="overlay" id="alertdialog">
  <section
    aria-describedby="alertdialog-content"
```

```
      aria-labelledby="alertdialog-header"
      role="alertdialog"
      tabindex="-1"
  >
    <header>
      <h2 id="alertdialog-header">System notice</h2>
      <button class="close" aria-label="Close" type="button">X</button>
    </header>
    <section id="alertdialog-content">
      <p>
        System shutdown will begin in 20 minutes
      </p>
    </section>
  </section>
</div>
```

# CSS

```
.overlay {
  align-items: center;
  background: hsla(204, 0%, 80%, 0.7);
  bottom: 0;
  display: flex;
  left: 0;
  position: fixed;
  right: 0;
  top: 0;
  /* the z-index must be set to the highest z-index + 1 */
  z-index: 999;
}
.overlay > [role="alertdialog"] {
  background-color: hsl(204, 0%, 100%);
  margin-left: auto;
  margin-right: auto;
  padding: 1rem;
}
.overlay > [role="alertdialog"] > header {
  align-items: center;
  display: flex;
}
.overlay > [role="alertdialog"] > header > h2 {
  flex: 1;
}
```

```css
.overlay > [role="alertdialog"] > header > button {
  align-self: flex-start;
  background-color: transparent;
  border: 0;
  color: hsl(204, 0%, 0%);
  font-size: 1.5rem;
  margin: 0;
  padding: 0;
  width: 2rem;
}
```

# JavaScript

```javascript
[].slice.call(document.getElementsByClassName('overlay'))
.forEach(function init(modal) {
  var body = modal.getElementsByTagName('section').item(0),
    id = modal.id,
    position,
    close = function close() {
      document.body.style.position = position;
      modal.style.display = 'none';
    },
    open = function open() {
      position = document.body.style.position;
      document.body.style.position = 'fixed';
      modal.style.display = 'flex';
      body.focus();
    },
    trap = function trap(e) {
      var dest = e.relatedTarget;

      if (!modal.contains(dest)) {
        body.focus();
      }
    };

  if (!id) {
    id = 'dialog-' + (new Date()).getTime();
    modal.setAttribute('id', id);
  }
  modal.open = open;

  modal.addEventListener('keydown', function (e) {
    if (e.key === 'Escape' || e.keyCode === 27) {
      close();
    }
  });

  [].slice.call(modal.getElementsByClassName('close'))
  .forEach(el => {
    el.addEventListener('click', close);
  });

  [].slice.call(modal.getElementsByTagName('*'))
  .forEach( el => {
    el.addEventListener('blur', trap);
  });
```

```
  body.addEventListener('click', function (e) {
    e.stopPropagation();
  });

  window[id] = modal;
  if (window[id] === modal) {
    close();
  }
});
```

# Autocomplete ⚠

## HTML

```
<span class="field">
  <label for="myautocomplete" id="myautocomplete-label">
    Favorite Fruit
  </label>
  <span class="autocomplete">
    <span
      aria-expanded="false"
      aria-haspopup="true"
      aria-owns="myautocomplete-list"
      id="myautocomplete-combo"
      role="combobox"
    >
      <input
        aria-autocomplete="list"
        aria-controls="myautocomplete-list"
        autocomplete="off"
        id="myautocomplete"
        type="text"
      >
    </span>
    <ol
      aria-labelledby="myautocomplete-label"
      id="myautocomplete-list"
      role="listbox"
      tabindex="-1"
    >
      <li role="option" id="apple">Apple</li>
      <li role="option" id="apricot">Apricot</li>
      <li role="option" id="banana">Banana</li>
      <li role="option" id="cherry">Cherry</li>
      <li role="option" id="date">Date</li>
    </ol>
    <span class="listlength" role="status"></span>
  </span>
</span>
```

# CSS

```css
.autocomplete {
  display: inline-flex;
  flex-direction: column;
  /* this width should be the same as the .field width */
  width: 168.2px;
}
.autocomplete [role="combobox"],
.autocomplete [role="listbox"] {
  flex-basis: 100%;
}
.autocomplete [role="combobox"] input {
  /*
   * this style rule will make the input the same width as the list
   * by subtracting the left and right margin and the left and right
   * padding as defined on the .field input from 100%
   */
  width: calc(100%  1.5125em);
}
.autocomplete [role="listbox"] {
  border-color: hsl(0, 0%, 75%);
  border-radius: 0;
  cursor: pointer;
  list-style-type: none;
  margin: 0;
  max-height: 3.5rem;
  overflow-y: scroll;
  padding: 0 0.125rem;
}
.autocomplete [aria-expanded="false"] + [role="listbox"] {
  display: none;
}
.autocomplete [aria-expanded="true"] + [role="listbox"] {
  display: initial;
}
.autocomplete [role="listbox"] [aria-hidden="true"] {
  height: 0;
  overflow: hidden;
}
.autocomplete [role="listbox"] [aria-selected="true"] {
  background-color: hsl(204, 100%, 90%);
}
.autocomplete [role="listbox"] > li:hover {
  background-color: hsl(204, 100%, 30%);
  color: hsl(0, 0%, 100%);
}
.autocomplete [role="status"] {
  clip: rect(0, 0, 0, 0);
  clip-path: polygon(0 0, 0 0, 0 0, 0 0);
  position: absolute;
  left: -200%;
}
```

# JavaScript

```
[].slice.call(document.getElementsByClassName('autocomplete'))
.forEach(function init(autocomplete) {
  var activeIndex = 0,
    status = autocomplete.getElementsByClassName('listlength').item(0),
    match = function match(el, value) {
      var text = el.innerText.toLowerCase();
      return el.innerText
        .toLowerCase()
        .indexOf(value.toLowerCase()) === 0;
    },
    onInput = function onInput() {
      if (!autocomplete.isOpen()) {
        autocomplete.open();
      }
      autocomplete.filter();
    },
    onKeyDown = function onKeyDown(e) {
      switch (e.key) {
        case 'ArrowDown':
          e.preventDefault();
          if (autocomplete.isOpen()) {
            autocomplete.items().next();
          }
          break;
        case 'ArrowUp':
          e.preventDefault();
          if (autocomplete.isOpen()) {
            autocomplete.items().previous();
          }
          break;
        case 'Backspace':
        case 'Delete':
          onInput();
          break;
        case 'Enter':
          autocomplete.input.setValue();
          break;
        case 'Escape':
          e.preventDefault();
          autocomplete.close();
          autocomplete.input.value = '';
        default:
      }
    },
    select = function select(e) {
      var target = e.target;
      if (target) {
        autocomplete.items().reset();
        target.setAttribute('aria-selected', 'true');
        autocomplete.input.setValue();
      }
    };

  autocomplete.close = function open(e) {
    autocomplete.combobox.setAttribute('aria-expanded', 'false');
    autocomplete.listbox.setAttribute('tabindex', -1);
  };
```

```javascript
autocomplete.filter = function filter() {
  var value = autocomplete.input.value,
    items = [].slice.call(autocomplete.listbox.data),
    active;

  autocomplete.items().reset();
  items.forEach(function filterList(item) {
    if (item.innerText) {
      item.setAttribute('aria-hidden', !match(item, value));
    }
  });

  active = items.filter(function active(el) {
    return el.getAttribute('aria-hidden') !== 'true';
  });

  if (active.length === 1) {
    autocomplete.items().select(active[0], true);
  }

  autocomplete.setAttribute('data-count', active.length);
  status.innerHTML = active.length;
};
autocomplete.isOpen = function isOpen() {
  return autocomplete.combobox.getAttribute('aria-expanded') === 'true';
};
autocomplete.items = function items() {
  var value = autocomplete.input.value,
    lis = [].slice.call(autocomplete.listbox.data),
    listItems = lis.map(function unselect(li) {
        if (li) {
          li.setAttribute('aria-hidden', !match(li, value));
        }
        return li;
      }).filter(function filteredItems(li) {
        return li && li.getAttribute('aria-hidden') !== 'true';
      });

  listItems.first = function first() {
    var list = autocomplete.listbox.data,
      count = list.length - 1,
      target = 0;

    while (count > -1) {
      if (list.item(count).getAttribute('aria-hidden') !== 'true') {
        target = count;
      }
      count -= 1;
    }
    count = list.length - 1;
    while (count > -1) {
      listItems.select(count, count === target);
      count -= 1;
    }

    return list.item(target);
  };
```

```
listItems.last = function last() {
  var list = autocomplete.listbox.data,
    count = list.length - 1,
    target = 0;

  while (count > -1) {
    if (list.item(count).getAttribute('aria-hidden') !== 'true') {
      target = count;
      break;
    }
    count -= 1;
  }
  count = list.length - 1;
  while (count > -1) {
    listItems.select(count, count === target);
    count -= 1;
  }

  return list.item(target);
};
listItems.next = function next() {
  var list = autocomplete.listbox.data,
    i = list.length - 1,
    selected,
    target;

  while (i > -1 && !selected) {
    if (list.item(i).getAttribute('aria-selected') === 'true') {
      selected = listItems.select(i, false);
    }
    i -= 1;
  }

  if (selected) {
    selected = selected.nextElementSibling;
    while (selected) {
      if (selected.getAttribute('aria-hidden') !== 'true') {
        selected = listItems.select(selected, true);
        break;
      }
      selected = selected.nextElementSibling;
    }
  }

  if (!selected) {
    selected = listItems.first();
  }
  return selected;
};
```

```javascript
listItems.previous = function prev() {
  var list = autocomplete.listbox.data,
    i = list.length - 1,
    selected,
    target;

  while (i > -1 && !selected) {
    if (list.item(i).getAttribute('aria-selected') === 'true') {
      selected = listItems.select(i, false);
    }
    i -= 1;
  }

  if (selected) {
    selected = selected.previousElementSibling;
    while (selected) {
      if (selected.getAttribute('aria-hidden') !== 'true') {
        selected = listItems.select(selected, true);
        break;
      }
      selected = selected.previousElementSibling;
    }
  }

  if (!selected) {
    selected = listItems.last();
  }

  return selected;
};
listItems.reset = function reset() {
  var i = autocomplete.listbox.data.length - 1;
  while (i > -1) {
    autocomplete.listbox.data.item(i).setAttribute(
      'aria-hidden',
      false
    );
    autocomplete.listbox.data.item(i).removeAttribute(
      'aria-selected'
    );
    i -= 1;
  }
};
listItems.select = function select(n, value) {
  var list = autocomplete.listbox.data
    node = n && n.nodeName ? n : list.item(n);

  if (node) {
    if (value) {
      node.setAttribute('aria-selected', 'true');
      node.scrollIntoView();
    } else {
      node.removeAttribute('aria-selected');
    }

    return node;
  }
};
return listItems;
};
```

```
autocomplete.open = function open(e) {
  autocomplete.combobox.setAttribute('aria-expanded', 'true');
  autocomplete.listbox.setAttribute('tabindex', 0);
  autocomplete.filter();
};
autocomplete.selected = function selected() {
  var i = autocomplete.listbox.data.length - 1,
    item;

  while (i > -1) {
    item = autocomplete.listbox.data.item(i);
    if (item.getAttribute('aria-selected') === 'true') {
      return { id: item.id, text: item.innerText };
    }
    i -= 1;
  }
};

autocomplete.input = autocomplete.getElementsByTagName('input').item(0);
if (autocomplete.input) {
  autocomplete.input.setValue = function setValue() {
    var item = autocomplete.selected(),
      input = autocomplete.input,
      value = input.value;
    if (item.text.toLowerCase().indexOf(value.toLowerCase()) > -1) {
      input.setAttribute('aria-activedescendant', item.id);
      input.value = item.text;
    }
    autocomplete.close();
  };
  autocomplete.input.addEventListener('keydown', onKeyDown);
  autocomplete.input.addEventListener('input', onInput);
}

autocomplete.combobox = autocomplete.input.parentNode;

autocomplete.listbox = autocomplete.getElementsByTagName('ol').item(0);
if (autocomplete.listbox) {
  autocomplete.listbox.data =
    autocomplete.listbox.getElementsByTagName('li');
  autocomplete.listbox.addEventListener('blur', autocomplete.close);
  autocomplete.listbox.addEventListener('keydown', onKeyDown);

  [].slice.call(autocomplete.listbox.data).forEach(function f(i) {
    i.addEventListener('click', select);
  });
}
});
```

# Breadcrumbs

## HTML

```html
<nav aria-labelledby="banner">
    <ol class="breadcrumb">
      <li>
        <a href="/components">Components</a>
      </li>
      <li>
        <a href="/components/input">Input</a>
      </li>
      <li>
        <span>Breadcrumb</span>
      </li>
    </ol>
</nav>
```

## CSS

```css
.breadcrumb {
  display: inline-flex;
  list-style-type: none;
  margin: 0;
  padding: 0;
}
.breadcrumb > li {
  align-items: center;
  cursor: default;
  display: inline-flex;
  line-height: 1.2em;
}

.breadcrumb > li:not(:first-of-type)::before {
  border-bottom: 0.3em solid transparent;
  border-left: 0.5em solid hsl(204, 100%, 60%);
  border-top: 0.3em solid transparent;
  content: "\202f";
  display: inline-block;
  flex-shrink: 0;
  font-size: inherit;
  height: 0;
  margin: 0 0.25em;
  width: 0;
}
.breadcrumb > li:last-of-type {
  margin-right: 0;
}
```

# Button 📻

## HTML for a Request Button

```html
<button
  aria-busy=""
  aria-labelledby="button-label"
  class="request"
  data-oncomplete="Data received"
  data-onfail="Request failed"
  data-url="http://example.com/movies.json"
  type="button"
>
  <span id="button-label">Request Data</span>
  <span role="presentation"></span>
</button>
<span role="status"></span>
```

## CSS for a Request Button

```css
/*
 * the color of the 'spinner' is light,
 * so the button background has to be
 * dark
 */
button {
  background-color: hsl(204, 100%, 30%);
  border-radius: 0.25rem;
  color: hsl(0, 0%, 90%);
  font-size: 1rem;
  line-height: 1.5rem;
  min-height: 44px;
  min-width: 44px;
}
button:disabled {
  background-color: hsl(0, 0%, 60%);
}

button[aria-busy] {
  display: inline-block;
}
button[aria-busy] > [role="presentation"] {
  border-radius: 50%;
  font-size: 1.5em;
  height: 0.1em;
  margin: -0.5em 0;
  position: absolute;
  text-indent: -9999em;
  width: 0.1em;
}
button[aria-busy="true"] > :not([role="presentation"]) {
  visibility: hidden;
}
button[aria-busy="true"] > [role="presentation"] {
  animation: spin 1.1s infinite ease;
  transform: translateZ(0);
}
```

```css
button[aria-busy=""] + [role="status"],
button[aria-busy="true"] + [role="status"] {
  display: none;
}

/*
 * the color of the 'spinner' is light,
 * so the button background has to be dark
 */
@keyframes spin {
  0%,
  100% {
    box-shadow: 0 -0.26em 0 0 hsla(204, 0%, 100%, 1),
      0.18em -0.18em 0 0 hsla(204, 0%, 100%, 0.2),
      0.25em 0 0 0 hsla(204, 0%, 100%, 0.2),
      0.175em 0.175em 0 0 hsla(204, 0%, 100%, 0.2),
      0 0.25em 0 0 hsla(204, 0%, 100%, 0.2),
      -0.18em 0.18em 0 0 hsla(204, 0%, 100%, 0.2),
      -0.26em 0 0 0 hsla(204, 0%, 100%, 0.5),
      -0.18em -0.18em 0 0 hsla(204, 0%, 100%, 0.7);
  }
  12.5% {
    box-shadow: 0 -0.26em 0 0 hsla(204, 0%, 100%, 0.7),
      0.18em -0.18em 0 0 hsla(204, 0%, 100%, 1),
      0.25em 0 0 0 hsla(204, 0%, 100%, 0.2),
      0.175em 0.175em 0 0 hsla(204, 0%, 100%, 0.2),
      0 0.25em 0 0 hsla(204, 0%, 100%, 0.2),
      -0.18em 0.18em 0 0 hsla(204, 0%, 100%, 0.2),
      -0.26em 0 0 0 hsla(204, 0%, 100%, 0.2),
      -0.18em -0.18em 0 0 hsla(204, 0%, 100%, 0.5);
  }
  25% {
    box-shadow: 0 -0.26em 0 0 hsla(204, 0%, 100%, 0.5),
      0.18em -0.18em 0 0 hsla(204, 0%, 100%, 0.7),
      0.25em 0 0 0 hsla(204, 0%, 100%, 1),
      0.175em 0.175em 0 0 hsla(204, 0%, 100%, 0.2),
      0 0.25em 0 0 hsla(204, 0%, 100%, 0.2),
      -0.18em 0.18em 0 0 hsla(204, 0%, 100%, 0.2),
      -0.26em 0 0 0 hsla(204, 0%, 100%, 0.2),
      -0.18em -0.18em 0 0 hsla(204, 0%, 100%, 0.2);
  }
  37.5% {
    box-shadow: 0 -0.26em 0 0 hsla(204, 0%, 100%, 0.2),
      0.18em -0.18em 0 0 hsla(204, 0%, 100%, 0.5),
      0.25em 0 0 0 hsla(204, 0%, 100%, 0.7),
      0.175em 0.175em 0 0 hsla(204, 0%, 100%, 1),
      0 0.25em 0 0 hsla(204, 0%, 100%, 0.2),
      -0.18em 0.18em 0 0 hsla(204, 0%, 100%, 0.2),
      -0.26em 0 0 0 hsla(204, 0%, 100%, 0.2),
      -0.18em -0.18em 0 0 hsla(204, 0%, 100%, 0.2);
  }
  50% {
    box-shadow: 0 -0.26em 0 0 hsla(204, 0%, 100%, 0.2),
      0.18em -0.18em 0 0 hsla(204, 0%, 100%, 0.2),
      0.25em 0 0 0 hsla(204, 0%, 100%, 0.5),
      0.175em 0.175em 0 0 hsla(204, 0%, 100%, 0.7),
      0 0.25em 0 0 hsla(204, 0%, 100%, 1),
      -0.18em 0.18em 0 0 hsla(204, 0%, 100%, 0.2),
      -0.26em 0 0 0 hsla(204, 0%, 100%, 0.2),
      -0.18em -0.18em 0 0 hsla(204, 0%, 100%, 0.2);
  }
```

```
  }
  62.5% {
    box-shadow: 0 -0.26em 0 0 hsla(204, 0%, 100%, 0.2),
      0.18em -0.18em 0 0 hsla(204, 0%, 100%, 0.2),
      0.25em 0 0 0 hsla(204, 0%, 100%, 0.2),
      0.175em 0.175em 0 0 hsla(204, 0%, 100%, 0.5),
      0 0.25em 0 0 hsla(204, 0%, 100%, 0.7),
      -0.18em 0.18em 0 0 hsla(204, 0%, 100%, 1),
      -0.26em 0 0 0 hsla(204, 0%, 100%, 0.2),
      -0.18em -0.18em 0 0 hsla(204, 0%, 100%, 0.2);
  }
  75% {
    box-shadow: 0 -0.26em 0 0 hsla(204, 0%, 100%, 0.2),
      0.18em -0.18em 0 0 hsla(204, 0%, 100%, 0.2),
      0.25em 0 0 0 hsla(204, 0%, 100%, 0.2),
      0.175em 0.175em 0 0 hsla(204, 0%, 100%, 0.2),
      0 0.25em 0 0 hsla(204, 0%, 100%, 0.5),
      -0.18em 0.18em 0 0 hsla(204, 0%, 100%, 0.7),
      -0.26em 0 0 0 hsla(204, 0%, 100%, 1),
      -0.18em -0.18em 0 0 hsla(204, 0%, 100%, 0.2);
  }
  87.5% {
    box-shadow: 0 -0.26em 0 0 hsla(204, 0%, 100%, 0.2),
      0.18em -0.18em 0 0 hsla(204, 0%, 100%, 0.2),
      0.25em 0 0 0 hsla(204, 0%, 100%, 0.2),
      0.175em 0.175em 0 0 hsla(204, 0%, 100%, 0.2),
      0 0.25em 0 0 hsla(204, 0%, 100%, 0.2),
      -0.18em 0.18em 0 0 hsla(204, 0%, 100%, 0.5),
      -0.26em 0 0 0 hsla(204, 0%, 100%, 0.7),
      -0.18em -0.18em 0 0 hsla(204, 0%, 100%, 1);
  }
}
```

# JavaScipt for a Request Button

```javascript
[].slice.call(document.getElementsByClassName('request'))
.forEach(function initRequestor(el) {
  var isButton = el.nodeName.toLowerCase() === 'button' ||
      el.type.toLowerCase() === 'button' ||
      el.type.toLowerCase() === 'submit';

  if (isButton) {
    var btnStatus = el.nextElementSibling,
      url = el.getAttribute('data-url');

    while (
      btnStatus &&
      !/^(status|alert)$/i.test(btnStatus.getAttribute('role'))
    ) {
      btnStatus = btnStatus.nextElementSibling;
    }

    el.send = function onRequest() {
      if (el.getAttribute('aria-busy') !== 'true') {
        /* you may optionally disable the button here,
           but it's not necessary */
        el.setAttribute('aria-busy', true);
        el.disabled = true;

        /* this is the function to execute when the request is issued */
        fetch(url).then(function onSuccess(response) {
          /* process the response */
          if (btnStatus) {
            btnStatus.innerHTML = el.getAttribute('data-oncomplete');
          }
        }).catch(function onFailure(error) {
          /* process the error */
          if (btnStatus) {
            btnStatus.innerHTML = el.getAttribute('data-onfail');
          }
        }).finally(function done(status) {
          /* twenty seconds should be sufficient for people
             to read the status */
          var seconds = 20;

          /* turn the 'busy' indicator off */
          el.setAttribute('aria-busy', false);

          /* set a timeout so the status message displays for a set
             period of time before disappearing */
          setTimeout(function () {
            el.setAttribute('aria-busy', '');
            el.disabled = false;
          }, seconds * 1000);
        });
      }
    };

    el.addEventListener('click', el.send);
  }
});
```

# Carousel ⚠

## HTML

```html
<section class="carousel" data-delay="3" id="mycarousel">
  <div class="gallery">
    <button aria-label="Previous" name="previous" type="button">❮</button>
    <ul class="viewer">
      <li aria-labelledby="mc-tab1" id="mc-panel1" role="tabpanel">
        <figure>
          <img alt="Widgets R Us, product one"
            src="_resources/product-one.png"/>
          <figcaption>
            Product One is our most basic version.
          </figcaption>
        </figure>
      </li>
      <li aria-labelledby="mc-tab2" id="mc-panel2" role="tabpanel">
        <figure>
          <img alt="Widgets R Us, product two"
            src="_resources/product-two.png"/>
          <figcaption>
            Product Two has all the features of Product One
            <em>plus</em> a large grin.
          </figcaption>
        </figure>
      </li>
      <li aria-labelledby="mc-tab3" id="mc-panel3" role="tabpanel">
        <figure>
          <img alt="Widgets R Us, product three"
            src="_resources/product-three.png"/>
          <figcaption>
            Product Three has all the features of Product Two
            <em>plus</em> sunglasses, a Hawaiian shirt, and a
            drink in a coconut.
          </figcaption>
        </figure>
      </li>
    </ul>
    <button aria-label="Next" name="next" type="button">❯</button>
  </div>
  <div class="indicator">
    <ul role="presentation">
      <li role="presentation">
        <button aria-label="play" name="play" type="button"></button>
      </li>
    </ul>
    <ul aria-label="Product Gallery" role="tablist">
      <li role="presentation">
        <button
          aria-controls="mc-panel1"
          aria-selected="true"
          id="mc-tab1"
          role="tab"
          type="button"
        >1</button>
      </li>
```

```
        <li role="presentation">
          <button
            aria-controls="mc-panel2"
            aria-selected="false"
            id="mc-tab2"
            role="tab"
            type="button"
          >2</button>
        </li>
        <li role="presentation">
          <button
            aria-controls="mc-panel3"
            aria-selected="false"
            id="mc-tab3"
            role="tab"
            type="button"
          >3</button>
        </li>
      </ul>
    </div>
</section>
```

# CSS

```css
.carousel {
  align-items: center;
  display: flex;
  flex-direction: column;
}
.carousel .gallery {
  align-items: center;
  display: flex;
}
.carousel .viewer {
  display: flex;
  list-style-type: none;
  margin: 0;
  padding: 0;
}
.carousel figure {
  align-items: center;
  display: inline-flex;
  flex-direction: column;
  height: 500px;
  width: 500px;
}
.carousel img {
  display: inline-block;
  max-height: 500px;
  max-width: 500px;
}
.carousel li[aria-hidden="true"] {
  display: none;
}
```

```css
button[name="play"]::before {
  content: '▶';
  display: inline;
}
button[name="pause"]::before {
  content: '▐▐';
  display: inline;
}

.carousel .indicator,
.carousel .indicator ul {
  display: flex;
  justify-content: center;
  list-style-type: none;
  margin: 0;
  padding: 0;
}
.carousel .indicator ul:not(:last-of-type) {
  margin-right: 1rem;
}
.carousel .indicator li button {
  border-radius: 100%;
  display: inline-block;
  height: 1.2rem;
  line-height: 0;
  margin: 0 0.25rem;
  padding: 0;
  text-align: center;
  width: 1.2rem;
}
.carousel .indicator li [aria-selected="true"] {
  box-shadow: 0 0 0.25rem currentColor;
  font-weight: bold;
}
```

## JavaScript

```javascript
[].slice.call(document.getElementsByClassName('carousel'))
.forEach(function CarouselInterface(el) {
  var ANIMATION_DELAY = Number(el.getAttribute('data-delay')) * 1000,
    btnNext = [].slice.call(el.getElementsByTagName('button'))
      .filter(function isNext(btn) {
        return btn.name === 'next';
      }).pop(),
    btnPrev = [].slice.call(el.getElementsByTagName('button'))
      .filter(function isNext(btn) {
        return btn.name === 'previous';
      }).pop(),
    index = 0,
    panels = [].slice.call(
      el.getElementsByClassName('viewer').item(0)
        .getElementsByTagName('li')
    ),
    tablist = [].slice.call(
      el.getElementsByTagName('ul')
    ).filter(list => list.getAttribute('role') === 'tablist')[0],
```

```javascript
    tabs = [].slice.call(
      tablist.getElementsByTagName('li')
    ).map(li => li.getElementsByTagName('button').item(0)),
    next = function next() {
      index += 1;
      index %= tabs.length;
      tabs[index].click();
    },
    previous = function previous() {
      index -= 1;
      index = index < 0 ? index + tabs.length : index;
      tabs[index].click();
    },
    timer;

function play() {
  timer = setInterval(next, ANIMATION_DELAY);
}
function stop() {
  clearInterval(timer);
}

if (btnNext) {
  btnNext.addEventListener('click', next);
}
if (btnPrev) {
  btnPrev.addEventListener('click', previous);
}

[].slice.call(
  el.getElementsByTagName('button')
).filter(btn => btn.name === 'play')
.pop()
.addEventListener('click', (e) => {
  if (timer) {
    e.target.name = 'play';
    stop();
  } else {
    e.target.name = 'pause';
    play();
  }
});
tabs.forEach(function initTab(btn, i) {
  btn.addEventListener('click', (e) => {
    var target = e.target,
      activePanel = document.getElementById(
        target.getAttribute('aria-controls')
      );

    tabs.filter(tab => tab !== target)
    .forEach(tab => {
      var panel = document.getElementById(
        tab.getAttribute('aria-controls')
      );

      panel && panel.setAttribute('aria-hidden', true);
      tab.setAttribute('aria-selected', false);
    });
```

```
      activePanel && activePanel.setAttribute('aria-hidden', false);
      target.setAttribute('aria-selected', true);
    });

    if (btn.getAttribute('aria-selected') === 'true') {
      btn.click();
    }
  });
});
```

# Checkbox ⚓

## HTML

```html
<span class="field">
  <input id="single" type="checkbox" />
  <span>
    <label for="single">Checkbox Foo</label>
  </span>
</span>
```

## HTML for a Checkbox Group

```html
<fieldset class="checkbox">
  <legend id="grp-label">Fruits I like to eat</legend>
  <p>
    Please select all the fruits you like to eat.
  </p>
  <span class="field">
    <input aria-describedby="grp-label" id="grp-apple" type="checkbox" />
    <span>
      <label for="grp-apple">Apple</label>
    </span>
  </span>
  <span class="field">
    <input aria-describedby="grp-label" id="grp-banana" type="checkbox" />
    <span>
      <label for="grp-banana">Banana</label>
    </span>
  </span>
 <span class="field">
    <input aria-describedby="grp-label" id="grp-cherry" type="checkbox" />
    <span>
      <label for="grp-cherry">Cherry</label>
    </span>
  </span>
  <span class="field">
    <input aria-describedby="grp-label" id="grp-date" type="checkbox" />
    <span>
      <label for="grp-date">Date</label>
    </span>
  </span>
</fieldset>
```

# HTML for a Checkbox Group with a Tristate

## Descriptor

```html
<fieldset class="checkbox tristate">
  <legend id="tri-label">
    <span class="field">
      <input id="tri-grp" type="checkbox" />
      <span>
        <label for="tri-grp">Fruits I like to eat</label>
      </span>
    </span>
  </legend>
  <p>
    Please select all the fruits you like to eat.
  </p>
  <span class="field">
    <input aria-describedby="tri-label" id="tri-apple" type="checkbox" />
    <span>
      <label for="tri-apple">Apple</label>
    </span>
  </span>
  <span class="field">
    <input aria-describedby="tri-label" id="tri-banana" type="checkbox" />
    <span>
      <label for="tri-banana">Banana</label>
    </span>
  </span>
  <span class="field">
    <input aria-describedby="tri-label" id="tri-cherry" type="checkbox" />
    <span>
      <label for="tri-cherry">Cherry</label>
    </span>
  </span>
  <span class="field">
    <input aria-describedby="tri-label" id="tri-date" type="checkbox" />
    <span>
      <label for="tri-date">Date</label>
    </span>
  </span>
</fieldset>
```

## CSS

```css
/*
Although the following CSS uses aria-checked, it is highly recommended
that the aria-checked attribute not be used on a native checkbox unless a
tristate checkbox is being used and the aria-checked attribute is set via
scripting.
*/
fieldset.checkbox {
  align-items: baseline;
  display: flex;
  flex-direction: column;
}
```

```css
fieldset.checkbox > .field {
  margin-left: 0;
}

:not(.toggle) [type="checkbox"] {
  border: 0;
  clip: rect(0, 0, 0, 0);
  clip-path: polygon(0 0, 0 0, 0 0, 0 0);
  left: -200%;
  overflow: hidden;
  outline: none;
  position: absolute;
}
:not(.toggle) [type="checkbox"] + span {
  align-items: center;
  display: inline-flex;
}
:not(.toggle) [type="checkbox"] + span.trailing::after,
:not(.toggle) [type="checkbox"] + span:not(.switch):not(.trailing)::before
{
  background-color: hsl(0, 0%, 99%);
  border: 0.0625rem solid hsl(0, 0%, 60%);
  border-radius: 0.25rem;
  color: hsl(0, 0%, 1%);
  content: '\202F';
  display: inline-block;
  height: 1.2rem;
  line-height: 1.2rem;
  margin: 0 0.5rem;
  text-align: center;
  width: 1.2rem;
}
:not(.toggle) [type="checkbox"][aria-checked="mixed"] +
span.trailing::after,
:not(.toggle) [type="checkbox"][aria-checked="mixed"] +
span:not(.switch):not(.trailing)::before,
:not(.toggle) [type="checkbox"][aria-checked="true"] +
span.trailing::after,
:not(.toggle) [type="checkbox"][aria-checked="true"] +
span:not(.switch):not(.trailing)::before,
:not(.toggle) [type="checkbox"]:checked + span.trailing::after,
:not(.toggle) [type="checkbox"]:checked +
span:not(.switch):not(.trailing)::before {
  background-color: hsl(204, 100%, 40%);
  border-color: transparent;
  color: hsl(204, 100%, 99%);
}
:not(.toggle) [type="checkbox"][aria-checked="true"] +
span.trailing::after,
:not(.toggle) [type="checkbox"][aria-checked="true"] +
span:not(.switch):not(.trailing)::before,
:not(.toggle) [type="checkbox"]:checked + span.trailing::after,
:not(.toggle) [type="checkbox"]:checked +
span:not(.switch):not(.trailing)::before {
  content: '√';
}
```

```css
:not(.toggle) [type="checkbox"][aria-checked="mixed"] +
span.trailing::after,
:not(.toggle) [type="checkbox"][aria-checked="mixed"] +
span:not(.trailing)::before {
  content: '-';
}
:not(.toggle) [type="checkbox"]:focus + span:before {
  border-color: hsl(204, 100%, 40%);
}
:not(.toggle) [type="checkbox"]:focus + span > label {
  text-shadow: 0 0 0.5em hsl(204, 100%, 75%);
}
```

# JavaScript

```javascript
[].slice.call(document.getElementsByClassName('tristate'))
.forEach(function TristateCheckboxInterface(group) {
  var legend = group.getElementsByTagName('legend').item(0),
    indicator = [].slice.call(legend.getElementsByTagName('input'))
      .filter(function (el) { return el.type === 'checkbox'; }).pop(),
    inputs = [].slice.call(group.getElementsByTagName('input'))
      .filter(function (el) { return el !== indicator }),
    update = function update() {
      var checked = inputs.checked;

      indicator.checked = checked;
      if (checked === true || checked === false) {
        indicator.indeterminate = false;
        indicator.removeAttribute('aria-checked');
      } else {
        indicator.indeterminate = true;
        indicator.setAttribute('aria-checked', 'mixed');
      }
    };

  Object.defineProperty(inputs, 'checked', {
    enumerable: true,
    get: function () {
      var count = this.filter(function (el) {
          return el.checked;
        }).length;

      if (count === 0) {
        return false;
      } else if (count === this.length) {
        return true;
      }
      return null;
    },
    set: function (value) {
      this.forEach(function (input) {
        input.checked = value;
      });
      update();
    }
  });
```

```
  indicator.addEventListener('change', function (e) {
    inputs.checked = e.target.checked;
  });
  inputs.forEach(function (input) {
    input.addEventListener('change', update);
  });
});
```

# ComboBox ⚠

## HTML

```
<span class="field">
  <label for="mycombobox" id="mycombobox-label">
    Side item
  </label>
  <span class="combobox">
    <span role="group">
      <input
        aria-autocomplete="list"
        aria-expanded="false"
        aria-haspopup="true"
        aria-owns="mycombobox-list"
        autocomplete="off"
        id="mycombobox"
        role="combobox"
        type="text"
      >
      <span class="listlength" role="status"></span>
      <button
        aria-label="show fruit options"
        tabindex="-1"
        type="button"
      >
        ▼
      </button>
    </span>
    <ol
      aria-labelledby="mycombobox-label"
      id="mycombobox-list"
      role="listbox"
      tabindex="-1"
    >
      <li role="option" id="apple">Apple</li>
      <li role="option" id="apricot">Apricot</li>
      <li role="option" id="banana">Banana</li>
      <li aria-selected="true" role="option" id="cherry">Cherry</li>
      <li role="option" id="date">Date</li>
      <li role="option" id="nonsense">
        Supercalifragilisticexpialodocius
      </li>
    </ol>
  </span>
</span>
```

# CSS

```css
.combobox {
  display: inline-flex;
  flex-direction: column;
}
.combobox [role="group"] {
  display: flex;
}
.combobox [role="group"] input {
  flex-grow: 1;
}
.combobox [role="group"] input {
  border-top-right-radius: 0;
  border-bottom-right-radius: 0;
}
.combobox [role="group"] input[aria-expanded="true"] {
  border-bottom-left-radius: 0;
}
.combobox [role="group"] input[aria-expanded="true"] + button {
  border-bottom-right-radius: 0;
}
.combobox [role="group"] button {
  border-bottom-left-radius: 0;
  border-left: 0;
  border-top-left-radius: 0;
  flex-grow: 0;
  font-size: 1.02em;
}
.combobox [role="listbox"] {
  border-top-left-radius: 0;
  border-top-right-radius: 0;
  border-top: 0;
  cursor: pointer;
  left: -200%;
  list-style-type: none;
  margin: 0;
  max-height: 3.5rem;
  overflow-y: scroll;
  padding: 0 0.125rem;
  position: relative;
}
.combobox [role="listbox"].open {
  border: 0.0625em solid hsl(204, 100%, 90%);
  border-top: 0;
  left: 0;
}
.combobox [role="listbox"] [aria-hidden="true"] {
  height: 0;
  overflow: hidden;
}
.combobox [role="listbox"] [aria-selected="true"] {
  background-color: hsl(204, 100%, 90%);
}
.combobox [role="listbox"] > li:focus,
.combobox [role="listbox"] > li:hover {
  background-color: hsl(204, 100%, 30%);
  color: hsl(0, 0%, 100%);
}
```

```css
.combobox input:not([aria-invalid]) + [role="status"] {
  border: 0;
  clip: rect(0, 0, 0, 0);
  clip-path: polygon(0 0, 0 0, 0 0, 0 0);
  left: -200%;
  outline: none;
  overflow: hidden;
  position: absolute;
}
```

## JavaScript

```javascript
[].slice.call(document.getElementsByClassName('combobox'))
.forEach(function ComboboxInterface(combobox) {
  var activeIndex = 0,
    listlength = combobox.getElementsByClassName('listlength').item(0),
    match = function match(el, value) {
      return el.innerText
        .toLowerCase()
        .indexOf(value.toLowerCase()) === 0;
    },
    onInput = function onInput() {
      if (!combobox.isOpen) {
        combobox.open();
      }
      combobox.filter();
    },
    onKeyDown = function onKeyDown(e) {
      switch (e.key) {
        case 'ArrowDown':
          e.preventDefault();
          if (!combobox.isOpen) {
            combobox.open();
            combobox.items().first();
          } else {
            combobox.items().next();
          }
          break;
        case 'ArrowUp':
          e.preventDefault();
          if (!combobox.isOpen) {
            combobox.open();
            combobox.items().last();
          } else {
            combobox.items().previous();
          }
          break;
        case 'Enter':
          e.preventDefault();
          combobox.input.setValue();
          break;
        case 'Escape':
          e.preventDefault();
          combobox.close();
          combobox.input.value = '';
      }
    },
```

```javascript
  select = function select(e) {
    var target = e.target;
    if (target) {
      combobox.items().reset();
      target.setAttribute('aria-selected', 'true');
      combobox.input.setValue();
    }
  };
Object.defineProperty(combobox, 'isInvalid', {
  enumerable: true,
  get: function() {
    return combobox.input.getAttribute('aria-invalid') === 'true';
  },
  set: function(value) {
    combobox.input.setAttribute('aria-invalid', !!value);
  }
});
Object.defineProperty(combobox, 'isOpen', {
  enumerable: true,
  get: function () {
    return combobox.input.getAttribute('aria-expanded') === 'true';
  }
});

combobox.close = function (e) {
  combobox.input.setAttribute('aria-expanded', 'false');
  combobox.listbox.setAttribute('tabindex', -1)
  combobox.listbox.className = combobox.listbox.className
    .replace(/\s*open\s*/, ' ').trim();
};
combobox.filter = function () {
  var value = combobox.input.value,
    items = [].slice.call(combobox.listbox.data),
    active;

  combobox.items().reset();
  items.forEach(function filterList(item) {
    item.setAttribute('aria-hidden', !match(item, value));
  });

  active = items.filter(function active(el) {
    return el.getAttribute('aria-hidden') !== 'true';
  });

  if (active.length === 1) {
    combobox.items().select(active[0], true);
  }

  combobox.listbox.setAttribute('data-count', active.length);
  listlength.innerHTML = active.length;
};
```

```
combobox.items = function () {
  var value = combobox.input.value,
    lis = [].slice.call(combobox.listbox.data),
    listItems = lis.map(function (li) {
        if (li) {
            li.setAttribute('aria-hidden', !match(li, value));
        }
        return li;
    }).filter(function (li) {
        return li && li.getAttribute('aria-hidden') !== 'true';
    });

  listItems.first = function () {
    var list = combobox.listbox.data,
      count = list.length - 1,
      target = 0;
    while (count > -1) {
      if (list.item(count).getAttribute('aria-hidden') !== 'true') {
        target = count;
      }
      count -= 1;
    }
    count = list.length - 1;
    while (count > -1) {
      listItems.select(count, count === target);
      count -= 1;
    }

    return list.item(target);
  };
  listItems.last = function () {
    var list = combobox.listbox.data,
      count = list.length - 1,
      target = 0;

    while (count > -1) {
      if (list.item(count).getAttribute('aria-hidden') !== 'true') {
        target = count;
        break;
      }
      count -= 1;
    }
    count = list.length - 1;
    while (count > -1) {
      listItems.select(count, count === target);
      count -= 1;
    }

    return list.item(target);
  };
  listItems.next = function () {
    var list = combobox.listbox.data,
      i = list.length - 1,
      selected,
      target;
```

```javascript
    while (i > -1 && !selected) {
      if (list.item(i).getAttribute('aria-selected') === 'true') {
        selected = listItems.select(i, false);
      }
      i -= 1;
    }

    if (selected) {
      selected = selected.nextElementSibling;
      while (selected) {
        if (selected.getAttribute('aria-hidden') !== 'true') {
          selected = listItems.select(selected, true);
          break;
        }
        selected = selected.nextElementSibling;
      }
    }

    if (!selected) {
      selected = listItems.first();
    }
    return selected;
};
listItems.previous = function () {
  var list = combobox.listbox.data,
    i = list.length - 1,
    selected,
    target;

    while (i > -1 && !selected) {
      if (list.item(i).getAttribute('aria-selected') === 'true') {
        selected = listItems.select(i, false);
      }
      i -= 1;
    }

    if (selected) {
      selected = selected.previousElementSibling;
      while (selected) {
        if (selected.getAttribute('aria-hidden') !== 'true') {
          selected = listItems.select(selected, true);
          break;
        }
        selected = selected.previousElementSibling;
      }
    }

    if (!selected) {
      selected = listItems.last();
    }

    return selected;
};
```

```
listItems.reset = function () {
  var i = combobox.listbox.data.length - 1;
  while (i > -1) {
    combobox.listbox.data.item(i).setAttribute('aria-hidden', false);
    combobox.listbox.data.item(i).removeAttribute('aria-selected');
    i -= 1;
  }
};
listItems.select = function (n, value) {
  var list = combobox.listbox.data
    node = n && n.nodeName ? n : list.item(n);

  if (node) {
    if (value) {
      node.setAttribute('aria-selected', 'true');
      node.scrollIntoView();
    } else {
      node.removeAttribute('aria-selected');
    }

    return node;
  }
};

return listItems;
};
combobox.open = function (e) {
  combobox.input.setAttribute('aria-expanded', 'true');
  combobox.listbox.setAttribute('tabindex', 0);
  combobox.listbox.className = [
    combobox.listbox.className,
    'open',
  ].join(' ').trim();
  combobox.filter();
};
combobox.selected = function () {
  var i = combobox.listbox.data.length - 1,
    item;

  while (i > -1) {
    item = combobox.listbox.data.item(i);
    if (item.getAttribute('aria-selected') === 'true') {
      return { id: item.id, text: item.innerText };
    }
    i -= 1;
  }
};
```

```
combobox.input = combobox.getElementsByTagName('input').item(0);
if (combobox.input) {
  combobox.input.setValue = function () {
    var item = combobox.selected(),
      input = combobox.input,
      value = input.value;
    if (item.text.toLowerCase().indexOf(value.toLowerCase()) > -1) {
      input.setAttribute('aria-activedescendant', item.id);
      input.value = item.text;
    }
    combobox.close();
  };
  combobox.input.addEventListener('keydown', onKeyDown);
  combobox.input.addEventListener('input', onInput);
}
combobox.controller = combobox.getElementsByTagName('button').item(0);
if (combobox.controller) {
  combobox.controller.addEventListener('click', combobox.open);
  combobox.controller.addEventListener('keydown', onKeyDown);
}
combobox.listbox = combobox.getElementsByTagName('ol').item(0);
if (combobox.listbox) {
  combobox.listbox.data = combobox.listbox.getElementsByTagName('li');
  combobox.listbox.addEventListener('blur', combobox.close);
  combobox.listbox.addEventListener('keydown', onKeyDown);

  [].slice.call(combobox.listbox.data).forEach(function (i) {
    i.addEventListener('click', select);
  });
}
});
```

# Date 📵⚠

## HTML for Multiple Inputs

```
<fieldset>
  <legend id="dob-label">Date of birth</legend>
  <section role="group">
    <span class="field">
      <select aria-describedby="dob-label" id="dobDay">
        <option>January</option>
        <option>February</option>
        <option>March</option>
        <option>April</option>
        <option>May</option>
        <option>June</option>
        <option>July</option>
        <option>August</option>
        <option>September</option>
        <option>October</option>
        <option>November</option>
        <option>December</option>
      </select>
```

```html
        <span class="status"></span>
        <label for="dobDay">Day</label>
      </span>
      <span class="field">
        <select aria-describedby="dob-label" id="dobMonth">
          <option>01</option>
          <option>02</option>
          <option>03</option>
          <option>04</option>
          <option>05</option>
          <option>06</option>
          <option>07</option>
          <option>08</option>
          <option>09</option>
          <option>10</option>
          <option>11</option>
          <option>12</option>
          <option>13</option>
          <option>14</option>
          <option>15</option>
          <option>16</option>
          <option>17</option>
          <option>18</option>
          <option>19</option>
          <option>20</option>
          <option>21</option>
          <option>22</option>
          <option>23</option>
          <option>24</option>
          <option>25</option>
          <option>26</option>
          <option>27</option>
          <option>28</option>
          <option>29</option>
          <option>30</option>
          <option>31</option>
        </select>
        <span class="status"></span>
        <label for="dobMonth">Month</label>
      </span>
      <span class="field">
        <input aria-describedby="dob-label" class="year" id="dobYear"
          maxlength="4" type="text"
        />
        <span class="status"></span>
        <label for="dobYear">Year</label>
      </span>
    </section>
</fieldset>
```

## HTML for a Single Input

```html
<span class="field date">
  <label for="dob-single">
    Date of birth
    <span class="data-format">dd/mm/yyyy</span>
  </label>
```

```html
<input aria-describedby="dob-label" class="year"
  data-lang="de-DE" id="dob-single" type="text"
/>
<span role="status"></span>
<span class="hint"></span>
</span>
```

## JavaScript for a Single Input

```javascript
[].slice.call(document.getElementsByClassName('date'))
.forEach(function DateInterface(el) {
  var convert = function convert(dt) {
      if (typeof dt !== 'undefined' &&
        typeof dt.year !== 'undefined' &&
        typeof dt.month !== 'undefined' &&
        typeof dt.day !== 'undefined') {
        var d = new Date(dt.year, dt.month - 1, dt.day),
          dtz = d.toISOString().substr(11).split(':')
            .reduce(function (t, v, i) {
              var mods = [60, 1, 1],
                mod = mods.slice(i).reduce(function (min, seg) {
                  return min *= seg;
                }, 1),
                n = Number(v.replace(/[a-z]/ig, ''));

              return t += n * mod;
            }, 0),
          tzo = d.getTimezoneOffset();
        return new Date(d.getTime() + (dtz !== tzo ? tzo * 60000 : 0));
      }
    },
    dfe = el.getElementsByClassName('data-format').item(0),
    hint = el.getElementsByClassName('hint').item(0),
    input = el.getElementsByTagName('input').item(0),
    isLeap = function (yy) {
      return (yy % 400 === 0) || (yy % 100 !== 0 && yy % 4 === 0);
    },
    dfa = input.getAttribute('data-format') || 'dd/mm/yyyy',
    lang = input.getAttribute('data-lang') || 'en-US',
    options = {
      weekday: 'long',
      year: 'numeric',
      month: 'long',
      day: 'numeric'
    };

  if (input) {
    input.format = dfe ? dfe.innerHTML : dfa;
    input.parse = function (value) {
      var name = {
        d: 'day',
        dd: 'day',
        m: 'month',
        mm: 'month',
        yy: 'year',
        yyyy: 'year'
      };
```

```javascript
  var keys = input.format.split(/[^ymd]/i),
    parts = {};

  keys.map(function (v, i) {
    parts[name[v]] = (value || '').split(/\D/)[i];
  });

  return parts;
};
input.toString = function (dt, fmt) {
  var formatter = fmt || input.format,
    iso = typeof dt === 'string' &&
      /(\d{4})\D(\d{2})\D(\d{2})/.test(dt) ?
      dt.split(/\D/g).map(function (n) { return Number(n); }) :
      null,
    keys = formatter.split(/[^ymd]/i),
    trFromDate = {
      d: function () {
        return dt.getDate();
      },
      dd: function () {
        return ('0' + dt.getDate()).substr(-2);
      },
      m: function () {
        return dt.getMonth() + 1;
      },
      mm: function () {
        return ('0' + (dt.getMonth() + 1)).substr(-2);
      },
      yy: function () {
        return dt.getFullYear().substr(-2);
      },
      yyyy: function () {
        return dt.getFullYear() + '';
      }
    },
    trFromIso = {
      d: function () {
        return iso[2];
      },
      dd: function () {
        return ('0' + iso[2]).substr(-2);
      },
      m: function () {
        return iso[1];
      },
      mm: function () {
        return ('0' + iso[1]).substr(-2);
      },
      yy: function () {
        return iso[0] % 100;
      },
      yyyy: function () {
        return iso[0];
      }
    },
    str = dt instanceof Date || iso.length ? formatter : '';
```

```javascript
        if (dt instanceof Date) {
          keys.forEach(function (key) {
            str = str.replace(key, trFromDate[key]());
          });
        } else if (iso.length) {
          keys.forEach(function (key) {
            str = str.replace(key, trFromIso[key]());
          });
        }

        return str;
      };
      input.validate = function (dt) {
        var dim,
          msPerDay = 1000 * 60 * 60 * 24,
          parts = Object.keys(dt),
          required = ['year', 'month', 'day'],
          valid = required.reduce(function (ttl, part) {
            var value = dt[part];

            if (Number.isNaN(value) || typeof value === 'undefined') {
              ttl = false;
            }
            return ttl;
          }, true);

        if (!valid) {
          return;
        }

        if (dt.month < 1 || dt.month > 12) {
          return false;
        }

        dim = (new Date(dt.year, dt.month, 1).getTime() -
          new Date(dt.year, dt.month - 1, 1).getTime()) / msPerDay;
        if (dt.day < 1 || dt.day > dim) {
          return false;
        }
        return true;
      };

      input.addEventListener('input', (e) => {
        var val = input.parse(e.target.value),
          converted = convert(val),
          iso = [val.year, val.month, val.day].join('-'),
          valid = input.validate(val);

        input.setAttribute('aria-invalid', typeof valid === 'undefined' ?
          '' : !valid);
        if (valid) {
          input.setAttribute('data-value', iso);

          if (hint) {
            hint.innerHTML = converted.toLocaleDateString(lang, options);
          }
        }
      });
    }
  });
```

# DatePicker ⚠

## HTML

```
<span class="field datepicker date">
  <label for="dob">
    Date of birth
    <span class="data-format">dd/mm/yyyy</span>
  </label>
  <span class="input">
    <input aria-describedby="dob-hint" data-lang="de-DE"
      id="dob" type="text"
    />
    <span role="status"></span>
  </span>
</span>
<span class="hint" id="dob-hint">
  Please enter month, day, and year, separated by a stroke,
  e.g., December 31 as 12/31/2018.
</span>
```

## CSS

```
.datepicker.field {
  margin-bottom: 0;
}
.datepicker .input input {
  border-right: 0;
  border-radius: 0.25em 0 0 0.25em;
}
.datepicker .input button {
  border-radius: 0 0.25em 0.25em 0;
  margin-left: -0.6em;
  position: relative;
  width: 2em;
}
.datepicker + [role="region"][aria-hidden="true"] {
  display: none;
}
.datepicker + [role="region"]::before {
  border-bottom: 0.5em solid hsl(204, 100%, 30%);
  border-left: 0.5em solid transparent;
  border-right: 0.5em solid transparent;
  content: '';
  display: block;
  margin-left: 2em;
  width: 0;
}

.calendar {
  border: 0.0625em solid hsl(204, 100%, 30%);
}
.calendar tbody td {
  border: 0.0625em solid hsl(204, 100%, 60%);
  width: 14%;
}
```

```css
.calendar tbody td > button {
  border: 0;
  text-align: right;
  width: 100%;
}
.calendar tbody td > button::after {
  content: '';
  display: block;
  padding-bottom: 50%;
}
.calendar thead td,
.calendar thead th {
  text-align: center;
}
```

# JavaScript

```javascript
[].slice.call(document.getElementsByClassName('datepicker'))
.forEach(function DatePickerInterface(field) {
  var input = [].slice.call(field.getElementsByTagName('input'))
        .filter(function (el) { return el.type === 'text' }).pop(),
    bcp47 = input.getAttribute('data-lang') || 'en-US',
    calendar = document.createElement('table'),
    calendarId = input.id + '-calendar',
    controller = document.createElement('button'),
    disclosure = document.createElement('div'),
    focusFrom,
    months = document.createElement('select'),
    next = document.createElement('button'),
    prev = document.createElement('button'),
    sibling = input.nextElementSibling,
    tbody = document.createElement('tbody'),
    thead = document.createElement('thead'),
    weekdays = document.createElement('tr'),
    weeks = tbody.getElementsByTagName('tr'),
    year = document.createElement('input');

  sibling = sibling.getAttribute('role') === 'status' ? sibling : input;

  calendar.className = 'calendar';
  calendar.appendChild(thead);
  calendar.appendChild(tbody);
  Object.defineProperty(calendar, 'draw', {
    enumerable: true,
    value: function () {
      var DAY = 1000 * 60 * 60 * 24,
        PERIOD = new Date(calendar.year, calendar.month, 1),
        START = new Date(calendar.year, calendar.month, 1),
        WEEK = DAY * 7;

      months.selectedIndex = calendar.month;
      year.value = calendar.year;

      while (START.getDay() > 0) {
        START = new Date(START.getTime() - DAY);
      }
```

```javascript
[].slice.call(weeks).forEach(function (row, week) {
  [].slice.call(row.getElementsByTagName('td'))
    .forEach(function (col, day) {
      var button = col.getElementsByTagName('button').item(0),
        d = new Date(START.getTime() + (week * WEEK) + (day * DAY)),
        iso = [
          d.getFullYear(),
          ('0' + (d.getMonth() + 1)).substr(-2),
          ('0' + d.getDate()).substr(-2)
        ].join('-'),
        isAfter = d.getFullYear() > PERIOD.getFullYear() ||
          d.getMonth() > PERIOD.getMonth(),
        isBefore = d.getFullYear() < PERIOD.getFullYear() ||
          d.getMonth() < PERIOD.getMonth();

      col.className = [
        col.className.replace(/\b(before|after)\b/, ''),
        isAfter ? 'after' : '',
        isBefore ? 'before' : ''
      ].join(' ').trim();
      button.setAttribute('aria-label', iso);
      button.innerHTML = ('0' + d.getDate()).substr(-2);
    });
  });
}
});
Object.defineProperty(calendar, 'lang', {
  enumerable: true,
  get: function () {
    return bcp47;
  },
  set: function (value) {
    var analyze = /^([a-z]{2})(-[A-Z]{2})?$/i,
      code = function () {
        return analyze.test(value) &&
          value.replace(analyze, function (m, lang, country) {
            var l = (lang||'').toLowerCase(),
              c = (country||'').toUpperCase();

            return l + c;
          });
      };

    if (code) {
      bcp47 = code;
      setDaysAndMonths();
      input.setAttribute('data-lang', bcp47);
      calendar.setAttribute('lang', bcp47);
    }
  }
});
Object.defineProperty(calendar, 'month', {
  enumerable: true,
  get: function () {
    var mo = calendar.getAttribute('data-month'),
      num = mo ? Number(mo) : Number('-');

    return Number.isNaN(num) || num < 0 ? new Date().getMonth() : num;
  },
```

```
  set: function (value) {
    var n = Number(value);

    if (!Number.isNaN(n)) {
      months.selectedIndex = n;
      calendar.setAttribute('data-month', n);
      calendar.draw();
    }
  }
});
Object.defineProperty(calendar, 'year', {
  enumerable: true,
  get: function () {
    var yr = calendar.getAttribute('data-year'),
      num = yr ? Number(yr) : Number('-');

    return Number.isNaN(num) || num < 0 ?
      new Date().getFullYear() :
      num;
  },
  set: function (value) {
    var n = Number(value);

    if (!Number.isNaN(n)) {
      year.value = n;
      calendar.setAttribute('data-year', n);
      calendar.draw();
    }
  }
});

controller.setAttribute('aria-controls', calendarId);
controller.setAttribute('aria-expanded', false);
controller.type = 'button';
controller.innerHTML = '🕒';
input.parentNode.insertBefore(controller, sibling.nextElementSibling);

disclosure.close = function () {
  controller.setAttribute('aria-expanded', false);
  disclosure.setAttribute('aria-hidden', true);
  document.removeEventListener('keydown', function  (e) {
    if (e.key === 'Escape') {
      disclosure.close();
    }
  });
  controller.focus();
};
disclosure.open = function () {
  var parsed = input.parse(input.value);

  if (parsed && parsed.month && parsed.year) {
    calendar.month = Number(parsed.month) - 1;
    calendar.year = Number(parsed.year);
  }
```

```javascript
        calendar.draw();
        disclosure.setAttribute('aria-hidden', 'false');
        document.addEventListener('keydown', function (e) {
          if (e.key === 'Escape') {
            disclosure.close();
          }
        });
      };
      disclosure.setAttribute('id', calendarId);
      disclosure.setAttribute('aria-hidden', true);
      disclosure.setAttribute('role', 'region');
      disclosure.appendChild(calendar);
      field.parentNode.insertBefore(disclosure, field.nextElementSibling);

      next.innerHTML = '▶';
      prev.innerHTML = '◀';
      year.setAttribute('maxlength', 4);

      function DatePickerCalendar() {
        var clicked = function (e) {
            var target = e.target,
              label = target ? target.getAttribute('aria-label') : '';

            if (label) {
              input.setAttribute('value', input.toString(label));
              disclosure.close();
            }
          },
          idx = 0,
          row = thead.insertRow(-1),
          col = row.insertCell(-1),
          btn;

        col.appendChild(prev);

        col = row.insertCell(-1);
        col.setAttribute('class', 'period');
        col.setAttribute('colspan', 5);
        col.appendChild(months);
        col.appendChild(year);

        col = row.insertCell(-1);
        col.appendChild(next);

        weekdays.setAttribute('role', 'row');
        thead.appendChild(weekdays);

        for (var c = 0; c < 7; c += 1) {
          row = document.createElement('tr');
          row.setAttribute('role', 'row');
```

```
    for (var i = 0; i < 7; i += 1) {
      btn = document.createElement('button');
      btn.setAttribute('type', 'button');
      btn.setAttribute('aria-describedby', 'day-' + i);
      btn.addEventListener('click', clicked);

      col = document.createElement('td');
      col.appendChild(btn);
      row.appendChild(col);
    }
    tbody.appendChild(row);
  }
  setDaysAndMonths();
  calendar.draw();
}

function setDaysAndMonths() {
  var dayCols = Array.apply(null, new Array(7))
    .map(function (val, i) {
      var d = new Date(1970, 0, 4 + i),
        lng = d.toLocaleString(bcp47, { weekday: 'long' }),
        sht = d.toLocaleString(bcp47, { weekday: 'short' });

      return '<th scope="col" role="columnheader">' +
        '<span aria-label="' + lng + '" id="day-' + i + '">' +
        sht +
        '</span>' +
        '</th>';
    }),
    monthNames = Array.apply(null, new Array(12))
      .map(function (val, i) {
        var d = new Date();
        d.setMonth(i);
        return d.toLocaleString(bcp47, { month: 'long' });
      }),
    monthOpts = monthNames.map(function (val, i) {
        return '<option value="' + i + '">' +
          val +
          '</option>';
      });

  months.innerHTML = monthOpts.join('');
  next.setAttribute('aria-label', monthNames[calendar.month + 1]);
  prev.setAttribute('aria-label', monthNames[calendar.month - 1]);
  weekdays.innerHTML = dayCols.join('');
}

DatePickerCalendar();

controller.addEventListener('click', function () {
  var isOpen = controller.getAttribute('aria-expanded') === 'true';

  controller.setAttribute('aria-expanded', !isOpen);
  isOpen && disclosure.close();
  !isOpen && disclosure.open();
});
months.addEventListener('change', function (e) {
  calendar.month = months.selectedIndex;
});
```

```javascript
  next.addEventListener('click', function () {
    if (calendar.month === 11) {
      calendar.year += 1;
      calendar.month = 0;
      return;
    }
    calendar.month += 1;
  });
  prev.addEventListener('click', function () {
    if (calendar.month === 0) {
      calendar.year -= 1;
      calendar.month = 11;
      return;
    }
    calendar.month -= 1;
  });
  year.addEventListener('change', function (e) {
    var target = e.target,
      value = target ? target.value : null,
      num = value ? Number(value) : Number('-');

    if (Number.isNaN(num)) {
      year.value = calendar.year;
    } else {
      calendar.year = num;
    }
  });
});
```

# Dialog ⚠

## HTML

```html
<div class="dialog" id="mydialog">
  <section
    aria-describedby="dialog-content"
    aria-labelledby="dialog-label"
    role="dialog"
    tabindex="0"
  >
    <header>
      <h2 id="dialog-label">System Notification</h2>
      <button aria-label="close" class="close" type="button">
        x
      </button>
    </header>
    <section id="dialog-content">
      <p>
        System shutdown in 3 minutes. Please save your data and exit.
      </p>
      <button class="close" type="button">
        Cancel
      </button>
    </section>
  </section>
</div>
```

## CSS

```css
.dialog {
  align-items: center;
  background: hsla(204, 0%, 80%, 0.7);
  bottom: 0;
  display: flex;
  left: 0;
  position: fixed;
  right: 0;
  top: 0;
  z-index: 9999; /* this _must_ be the highest z-index used */
}
.dialog > section {
  background-color: hsl(204, 0%, 100%);
  margin-left: auto;
  margin-right: auto;
  padding: 1rem;
  width: 50%;
}
.dialog > section > header {
  align-items: center;
  display: flex;
}
.dialog > section > header > h2 {
  flex: 1;
}
.dialog > section > header > button {
  background-color: transparent;
  border-radius: 50%;
  color: hsl(204, 0%, 0%);
  font-size: 1.5rem;
  height: 2rem;
  line-height: 0;
  text-align: center;
  width: 2rem;
}
```

## JavaScript

```javascript
[].slice.call(document.getElementsByClassName('dialog'))
.forEach(function DialogInterface(overlay) {
  var position;

  overlay.cancel = function cancel() {
    if (overlay.opener && overlay.opener.focus) {
      overlay.opener.focus();
    }

    document.body.style.position = position;
    overlay.style.display = 'none';
```

```javascript
    if (typeof overlay.onCancel === 'function') {
      overlay.onCancel();
    }
  };
  overlay.confirm = function confirm() {
    if (overlay.opener && overlay.opener.focus) {
      overlay.opener.focus();
    }

    document.body.style.position = position;
    overlay.style.display = 'none';

    if (typeof overlay.onConfirm === 'function') {
      overlay.onConfirm();
    }
  };
  overlay.open = function open() {
    position = document.body.style.position;
    document.body.style = 'fixed';

    overlay.opener = document.activeElement;
    overlay.style.display = 'flex';
    overlay.dialog.focus();
  };
  overlay.trap = function trap(blurred) {
    var focused = blurred.relatedTarget;
    if (!overlay.contains(focused)) {
      overlay.dialog.focus();
    }
  };

  if (!overlay.id) {
    overlay.setAttribute('id', 'dialog-' + (new Date()).getTime());
  }

  overlay.dialog = overlay.getElementsByTagName('section').item(0);

  overlay.dialog.addEventListener('click', function stopClick(e) {
    e.stopPropagation();
  });

  [].slice.call(overlay.dialog.getElementsByTagName('*'))
    .forEach(function assignTrap(el) {
      el.addEventListener('focusout', overlay.trap);
    });

  [].slice.call(overlay.dialog.getElementsByClassName('close'))
    .forEach(function assignClose(el) {
      el.addEventListener('click', overlay.cancel);
    });
  [].slice.call(overlay.dialog.getElementsByClassName('confirm'))
    .forEach(function assignConfirm(el) {
      el.addEventListener('click', overlay.confirm);
    });

  overlay.addEventListener('click', overlay.cancel);
  overlay.addEventListener('keydown', function keydown(e) {
    if (e.key === 'Escape' || e.keyCode === 27) {
      overlay.cancel();
    }
```

```
  });

  overlay.style.display = 'none';
  /* allows you to call window[overlay.id].open(); */
  window[overlay.id] = overlay;
});
```

# Disclosure ⚠

## HTML

```
<button
  aria-controls="show-hide"
  aria-expanded="false"
  class="disclosure"
  type="button"
>
  Open Disclosure
</button>

<p>
  This content is not part of the disclosure, but represents content that
  is displayed by default.
</p>
<!--
  other content goes here
-->

<div aria-hidden="true" aria-live="assertive" class="disclosed"
  id="show-hide" role="alert"
>
  Lorem ipsum dolor sit amet, consectetur adipiscing elit, sed do eiusmod
  tempor incididunt ut labore et dolore magna aliqua. Ut enim ad minim
  veniam, quis nostrud exercitation ullamco laboris nisi ut aliquip ex ea
  commodo consequat. Duis aute irure dolor in reprehenderit in voluptate
  velit esse cillum dolore eu fugiat nulla pariatur. Excepteur sint
  occaecat cupidatat non proident, sunt in culpa qui officia deserunt
  mollit anim id est laborum.
</div>
```

## CSS

```
.disclosed[aria-hidden="true"] {
  display: none !important;
}
```

## JavaScript

```javascript
[].slice.call(document.getElementsByClassName('disclosure'))
.forEach(function DisclosureInterface(ctrl) {
  var region = document.getElementById(
      ctrl.getAttribute('aria-controls')),
    initialState = region ?
      region.getAttribute('aria-hidden') === 'true' :
      false;

  if (ctrl && region) {
    region.className = [region.className.replace(/\bdisclosed\b/, ''),
      'disclosed'].join(' ');
    ctrl.setAttribute('aria-expanded', !initialState);

    ctrl.addEventListener('click', function () {
      var hidden = region.getAttribute('aria-hidden') === 'true';

      region.setAttribute('aria-hidden', !hidden);
      ctrl.setAttribute('aria-expanded', hidden);
    });
  }
});
```

# Dropdown Listbox ⚠

## HTML

```html
<ul
  aria-expanded="false"
  aria-label="Font Family"
  id="font-list"
  role="listbox"
  tabindex="0"
>
  <li role="option">
    <span style="font-family: sans-serif">
      Sans-serif
    </span>
  </li>
  <li role="option">
    <span style="font-family: serif">
      Serif
    </span>
  </li>
  <li role="option">
    <span style="font-family: monspace">
      Monospace
    </span>
  </li>
  <li role="option">
    <span style="font-family: fantasy">
      Fantasy
    </span>
  </li>
```

```html
  <li role="option">
    <span style="font-family: cursive">
      Cursive
    </span>
  </li>
</ul>
```

# CSS

```css
[role="listbox"] {
  display: inline-flex;
  flex-direction: column;
  list-style-type: none;
  padding: 0;
  position: relative;
}
[role="listbox"] [role="option"] {
  padding-right: 2em;
}
[role="listbox"][aria-expanded="true"] [aria-current="true"] {
  background-color: hsl(204, 100%, 95%);
}
[role="listbox"][aria-expanded="false"]:not([aria-multiselectable]) {
  height: 1.5em;
  overflow: hidden;
}
[role="listbox"][aria-expanded]:not([aria-multiselectable])::after {
  content: '▼';
  margin: 0.25em;
  position: absolute;
  right: 0;
}
[role="listbox"][aria-expanded="true"]:not([aria-multiselectable])::after
{
  color: transparent;
}
[role="listbox"][aria-expanded="false"][data-selectedIndex]:not([aria-
multiselectable])
[role="option"]:not([aria-selected]) {
  height: 0;
}
[role="listbox"][aria-expanded="false"] [role="option"] {
  white-space: nowrap;
}
[role="listbox"] [role="option"] {
  line-height: 1.5em;
}
[role="listbox"] [aria-selected="true"] {
  background-color: hsl(204, 100%, 90%);
}
```

## JavaScript

```javascript
function ListboxInterface(ddlb) {
  var activeIndex = 0,
    evtChange = new CustomEvent('change', { detail: ddlb }),
    defaultSelected =
[].slice.call(ddlb.querySelectorAll('[role="option"]'))
      .find(function (opt) {
        return opt.getAttribute('aria-selected') === 'true';
      }),
    isDisabled = false;

  function activate(index) {
    var c = ddlb.options.length - 1,
      node = ddlb.options.item(index);

    activeIndex = index;
    while (c > -1) {
      ddlb.options.item(c).setAttribute('aria-current', false);
      c -= 1;
    }

    if (node) {
      node.setAttribute('aria-current', true);
      ddlb.active = node.id;
    }
    return node;
  }
  function bool(value) {
    switch (typeof value) {
      case 'boolean':
        return value;
      case 'bigint':
      case 'number':
        return !!value;
      case 'function':
      case 'symbol':
        return true;
      case 'object':
        return !!Object.keys(value || {}).length;
      case 'string':
        return Boolean(
          JSON.parse(
            value.split(/\W/).reduce(function (t, v) {
              if (/^(false|no|n|off)$/i.test(v)) {
                t = 'false';
              }
              return t;
            }, 'true')
          )
        );
      case 'undefined':
        return false;
    }
    return false;
  }
  function close() {
    ddlb.expanded = false;
  }
```

```javascript
function first() {
  return activate(0);
}
function last() {
  return activate(ddlb.options.length - 1);
}
function next() {
  return activate(activeIndex + 1);
}
function open() {
  ddlb.expanded = true;
}
function previous() {
  return activate(activeIndex - 1);
}
function select(node) {
  var c = ddlb.options.length - 1
    el = node || ddlb.options.item(activeIndex),
    selected = bool(el.getAttribute('aria-selected'));

  if (!ddlb.multiple) {
    while (c > -1) {
      ddlb.options.item(c).removeAttribute('aria-selected');
      c -= 1;
    }
  }
  el.setAttribute('aria-selected', !selected);
  if (ddlb.selectedIndex > -1) {
    ddlb.setAttribute('data-selectedIndex', ddlb.selectedIndex);
  } else {
    ddlb.removeAttribute('data-selectedIndex');
  }
  !ddlb.multiple && close();
  ddlb.dispatchEvent(evtChange);
}

Object.defineProperty(ddlb, 'active', {
  enumerable: true,
  get: function () {
    return this.getAttribute('aria-activedescendant');
  },
  set: function (value) {
    if (document.getElementById(value)) {
      this.setAttribute('aria-activedescendant', value);
    }
  }
});
Object.defineProperty(ddlb, 'add', {
  enumerable: true,
  value: function (option, index) {
    this.options.add(option, index);
  }
});
Object.defineProperty(ddlb, 'autofocus', {
  enumerable: true,
  get: function () {
    return;
  },
```

```
      set: function () {
        return;
      }
    });
    Object.defineProperty(ddlb, 'disabled', {
      enumerable: true,
      get: function () {
        return;
      },
      set: function () {
        return;
      }
    });
    Object.defineProperty(ddlb, 'expanded', {
      enumerable: true,
      get: function () {
        return bool(this.getAttribute('aria-expanded'));
      },
      set: function (value) {
        this.setAttribute('aria-expanded', bool(value));
      }
    });
    Object.defineProperty(ddlb, 'form', {
      enumerable: true,
      get: function () {
        return;
      }
    });
    Object.defineProperty(ddlb, 'length', {
      enumerable: true,
      get: function () {
        return this.options.length;
      }
    });
    Object.defineProperty(ddlb, 'multiple', {
      enumerable: true,
      get: function () {
        return bool(this.getAttribute('aria-multiselectable'));
      },
      set: function (value) {
        var b = bool(value);

        if (b) {
          this.setAttribute('aria-multiselectable', true);
        } else {
          this.removeAttribute('aria-multiselectable');
        }
      }
    });
    Object.defineProperty(ddlb, 'name', {
      enumerable: true,
      get: function () {
        return this.getAttribute('name');
      },
      set: function (value) {
        if (typeof value === 'string') {
          this.setAttribute('name', value);
        }
      }
    });
```

```
Object.defineProperty(ddlb, 'options', {
  enumerable: true,
  get: function () {
    var opts = this.querySelectorAll('[role="option"]'),
      items = [].slice.call(opts);

    items.forEach(function (opt, idx) {
      if (!opt.hasOwnProperty('defaultSelected')) {
        Object.defineProperty(opt, 'defaultSelected', {
          enumerable: true,
          value: defaultSelected ?
            opt.id === defaultSelected.id :
            undefined
        });
      }
      if (!opt.hasOwnProperty('disabled')) {
        Object.defineProperty(opt, 'disabled', {
          enumerable: true,
          get: function () {
            return bool(this.getAttribute('aria-disabled'));
          },
          set: function (value) {
            this.setAttribute('aria-disabled', !!value);
          }
        });
      }
      if (!opt.hasOwnProperty('form')) {
        Object.defineProperty(opt, 'form', {
          enumerable: true,
          get: function () {
            return;
          }
        });
      }
      if (!opt.hasOwnProperty('html')) {
        Object.defineProperty(opt, 'html', {
          enumerable: true,
          get: function () {
            return this.innerHTML;
          },
          set: function (value) {
            this.innerHTML = value;
          }
        });
      }
      if (!opt.hasOwnProperty('index')) {
        Object.defineProperty(opt, 'index', {
          enumerable: true,
          value: idx
        });
      }
      if (!opt.hasOwnProperty('label')) {
        Object.defineProperty(opt, 'label', {
          enumerable: true,
          get: function () {
            return this.text;
          },
```

```
        set: function (value) {
          this.text = value;
        }
      });
    }
    if (!opt.hasOwnProperty('selected')) {
      Object.defineProperty(opt, 'selected', {
        enumerable: true,
        get: function () {
          return bool(this.getAttribute('aria-selected'));
        },
        set: function (value) {
          this.setAttribute('aria-selected', !!value);
        }
      });
    }
    if (!opt.hasOwnProperty('text')) {
      Object.defineProperty(opt, 'text', {
        enumerable: true,
        get: function () {
          return this.innerText;
        },
        set: function (value) {
          this.innerHTML = value;
        }
      });
    }
    if (!opt.hasOwnProperty('value')) {
      Object.defineProperty(opt, 'value', {
        enumerable: true,
        get: function () {
          return this.getAttribute('value');
        },
        set: function (arg) {
          this.setAttribute('value', arg);
        }
      });
    }
  });
  if (!opts.hasOwnProperty('add')) {
    Object.defineProperty(opts, 'add', {
      enumerable: true,
      value: function (option, index) {
        var reference = this.item(index);

        if (/^li$/i.test(option.nodeName)) {
          option.setAttribute('role', 'option');
          this.insertBefore(option, reference);
        }
      }
    });
  }
  if (!opts.hasOwnProperty('namedItem')) {
    Object.defineProperty(opts, 'namedItem', {
      enumerable: true,
      value: function (id) {
        return this.querySelector('[id="' + id + '"]');
      }
    });
  }
```

```javascript
      if (!opts.hasOwnProperty('selectedIndex')) {
        Object.defineProperty(opts, 'selectedIndex', {
          enumerable: true,
          get: function () {
            var b = false,
              n = this.length - 1;

            while (!b && n > -1) {
              b = this.item(n).getAttribute('aria-selected') === 'true';
              n -= b ? 0 : 1;
            }
            return n;
          },
          set: function (value) {
            select(this.item(Number(value)));
          }
        });
      }
      if (!opts.hasOwnProperty('remove')) {
        Object.defineProperty(opts, 'remove', {
          enumerable: true,
          value: function (index) {
            var reference = /^(number|string)$/.test(typeof index) ?
              this.item(Number(index)) :
              index;

            if (reference) {
              this.removeChild(reference);
            }
          }
        });
      }
      return opts;
    }
  });
  Object.defineProperty(ddlb, 'remove', {
    enumerable: true,
    value: function (index) {
      this.options.remove(index);
    }
  });
  Object.defineProperty(ddlb, 'selectedIndex', {
    enumerable: true,
    get: function () {
      return this.options.selectedIndex;
    },
    set: function (value) {
      this.options.selectedIndex = Number(value);
    }
  });
  Object.defineProperty(ddlb, 'selectedOptions', {
    enumerable: true,
    get: function () {
      var qs = '[role="option"][aria-selected="true"]';
      return this.querySelectorAll(qs);
    }
  });
```

```javascript
Object.defineProperty(ddlb, 'size', {
  enumerable: true,
  get: function () {
    return;
  },
  set: function () {
    return;
  }
});
Object.defineProperty(ddlb, 'type', {
  enumerable: true,
  get: function () {
    return 'listbox-' + (this.multiple ? 'multiple' : 'one');
  }
});
Object.defineProperty(ddlb, 'value', {
  enumerable: true,
  get: function () {
    var selected = [].slice.call(this.selectedOptions);

    if (selected) {
      return selected[0].value;
    }
  },
  set: function (arg) {
    var c = 0,
      opts = [].slice.call(this.options),
      reference = opts.find(function (opt) {
        opt.value === arg;
      });

    if (reference) {
      select(reference);
    }
  }
});

ddlb.addEventListener('blur', function (e) {
  e.target.expanded = false;
});
ddlb.addEventListener('click', function (e) {
  var opt = e.target,
    role = /^option$/i;

  if (ddlb.expanded) {
    while (opt && !role.test(opt.getAttribute('role'))) {
      opt = opt.parentNode;
    }

    if (role.test(opt.getAttribute('role'))) {
      select(opt);
    }
  } else {
    open();
  }
});
ddlb.addEventListener('focus', function (e) {
  e.target.expanded = true;
});
```

```
ddlb.addEventListener('keydown', function (e) {
  if (ddlb.expanded) {
    switch (e.key) {
      case 'ArrowDown':
        return next() || first();
      case 'ArrowLeft':
        return previous() || last();
      case 'ArrowRight':
        return next() || first();
      case 'ArrowUp':
        return previous() || last();
      case 'End':
        return last();
      case 'Enter':
      case ' ':
        return select();
      case 'Escape':
        return close();
      case 'Home':
        return first();
    }
  } else {
    switch (e.key) {
      case 'ArrowDown':
      case 'ArrowRight':
      case 'End':
      case 'Enter':
        return open();
    }
  }
});
ddlb.setAttribute('tabindex', 0);

  first();
}

[].slice.call(document.getElementsByTagName('*'))
.filter(function (el) {
  return /^listbox$/i.test(el.getAttribute('role'));
})
.forEach(function (listbox) {
  return ListboxInterface(listbox);
});
```

# Flyout ⚠

## HTML

```html
<button
  aria-controls="fruit-group"
  aria-describedby="group-label"
  aria-expanded="false"
  class="flyout"
  type="button"
>
  Fruits
</button>
<section
  aria-hidden="true"
  aria-labelledby="group-label"
  aria-live="polite"
  class="flyout-content checkbox"
  id="fruit-group"
  role="status"
>
  <fieldset class="checkbox">
    <legend id="group-label">Fruits I like to eat</legend>
    <p>
      Please select all the fruits you like to eat.
    </p>

    <span class="field">
      <input aria-describedby="group-label" id="group-apple"
        type="checkbox" />
      <span>
        <label for="group-apple">Apple</label>
      </span>
    </span>
    <span class="field">
      <input aria-describedby="group-label" id="group-banana"
        type="checkbox" />
      <span>
        <label for="group-banana">Banana</label>
      </span>
    </span>
    <span class="field">
      <input aria-describedby="group-label" id="group-cherry"
        type="checkbox" />
      <span>
        <label for="group-cherry">Cherry</label>
      </span>
    </span>
    <span class="field">
      <input aria-describedby="group-label" id="group-date"
        type="checkbox" />
      <span>
        <label for="group-date">Date</label>
      </span>
    </span>
  </fieldset>
</section>
```

## CSS

```css
.flyout {
  display: inline-block;
  flex-grow: 0;
  flex-shrink: 0;
}
.flyout-content {
  background: hsl(204, 0%, 99%);
  border: 0.0625em solid hsl(204, 100%, 30%);
  border-radius: 0.25em;
  box-shadow: 0.2em 0.2em 1em hsl(204, 100%, 30%);
  flex: 0;
  margin-top: 0.75em;
  padding: 0.25em;
}
.flyout-content::before {
  border-bottom: 0.7em solid hsl(204, 100%, 30%);
  border-left: 0.3em solid transparent;
  border-right: 0.3em solid transparent;
  content: '';
  display: block;
  height: 0;
  margin: -1em 0.5em 0;
  width: 0;
}
.flyout-content[aria-hidden="true"] {
  display: none;
}
.flyout-content fieldset {
  border: 0;
  margin: 1em;
  padding: 0;
}
```

## JavaScript

```javascript
[].slice.call(document.getElementsByClassName('flyout'))
.forEach(function FlyoutInterface(ctrl) {
  var region = document.getElementById(
      ctrl.getAttribute('aria-controls')),
    initialState = region ?
      region.getAttribute('aria-hidden') === 'true' :
      false,
    list = region.querySelectorAll(
      'button, [href], input, select, textarea, [tabindex]'
    ),
    focusable = [].slice.call(list);

  if (ctrl && region) {
    region.className = [
      region.className.replace(/\bflyout-content\b/, ''),
      'flyout-content'
    ].join(' ');
```

```
    ctrl.setAttribute('aria-expanded', !initialState);
    ctrl.addEventListener('click', function () {
      var hidden = region.getAttribute('aria-hidden') === 'true';

      region.setAttribute('aria-hidden', !hidden);
      ctrl.setAttribute('aria-expanded', hidden);
    });

    /* hide the flyout when focus moves out of the region */
    focusable.forEach(function FocusableInterface(el) {
      el.addEventListener('focusout', function (evt) {
        var next = evt.relatedTarget;
        if (next && !region.contains(next)) {
          region.setAttribute('aria-hidden', true);
        }
      });
    });
  }
});
```

# Journey

## HTML for a Linear Manual Journey

```
<ol aria-label="Pay for your items" class="journey">
  <li aria-current="step">
    <span>Billing Address</span>
  </li>
  <li>
    <span>Shipping Address</span>
  </li>
  <li>
    <span>Payment</span>
  </li>
</ol>
<span role="alert"></span>
```

## HTML for a Nonlinear Manual Journey

```
<nav aria-label="Pay for your items">
  <ol class="journey">
    <li class="completed">
      <a href="/billing">Billing Address</a>
    </li>
    <li aria-current="step">
      <a href="/shipping">Shipping Address</a>
    </li>
    <li>
      <a href="/payment">Payment</a>
    </li>
  </ol>
</nav>
```

# HTML for a Nonlinear Automatic Journey

```html
<ol aria-label="Pay for your items" class="journey">
  <li class="completed">
    <span>Billing Address</span>
  </li>
  <li>
    <span>Shipping Address</span>
  </li>
  <li aria-current="step">
    <span>Payment</span>
  </li>
</ol>
<span role="alert"></span>
```

# CSS

```css
.journey {
  counter-reset: journey;
  display: flex;
  list-style-type: none;
}
.journey > li {
  align-items: center;
  counter-increment: journey;
  cursor: default;
  display: flex;
  line-height: 1.2em;
}
.journey > li > :first-child::after {
  content: '\202f';
  display: block;
  width: 0.5em;
}
.journey > li > :first-child::before {
  background-color: hsla(0, 0%, 100%, 1);
  border-radius: 0.25em;
  border: 0.125em solid currentColor;
  color: hsla(204, 100%, 30%, 1);
  content: counter(journey);
  display: block;
  font-size: inherit;
  margin: 0 0.125em;
  padding: 0 0.125em;
  text-align: center;
  width: 1em;
}
.journey > li[aria-current] a,
.journey > li[aria-current] span {
  background-color: hsla(204, 100%, 90%, 1);
  color: hsla(0, 0%, 0%, 1);
}
```

```css
.journey > li[aria-current] > :first-child::before {
  color: hsla(0, 0%, 0%, 1);
}
.journey > li[aria-current] + li:not(:first-of-type)::before {
  border-left-color: hsla(204, 100%, 90%, 1);
}
.journey > li.completed,
.journey > li.completed a {
  background-color: hsla(204, 100%, 30%, 1);
  color: hsla(0, 0%, 100%, 1);
}
.journey > li.completed > :first-child::before {
  color: hsla(204, 100%, 30%, 1);
  content: '\2713';
}
.journey > li:last-of-type {
  margin-right: 0;
}
.journey > li:not(:first-of-type)::before {
  border-bottom: 0.7em solid transparent;
  border-left: 1em solid hsla(204, 100%, 30%, 1);
  border-top: 0.7em solid transparent;
  content: "\202f";
  display: inline-block;
  font-size: inherit;
  height: 0;
  margin-right: 0.25em;
  width: 0;
}
.journey > li:not(:first-of-type).completed:before {
  border-color: hsla(204, 100%, 30%, 1);
}
.journey > li > :first-child {
  align-items: center;
  display: flex;
  font-size: inherit;
}

.journey + [role="alert"] {
  border: 0;
  clip: rect(0, 0, 0, 0);
  clip-path: polygon(0 0, 0 0, 0 0, 0 0);
  left: -200%;
  outline: none;
  overflow: hidden;
  position: absolute;
}
```

# Menu ⚠

## HTML

```html
<section class="menu"
  aria-label="Text Formatting"
  aria-controls="tools-affect-me"
>
```

```html
<div role="group">
  <button
    aria-label="bold"
    aria-pressed="false"
    value="bold"
  ></button>
  <button
    aria-label="Italic"
    aria-pressed="false"
    value="italic"
  ></button>
  <button
    aria-label="Underline"
    aria-pressed="false"
    value="underline"
  ></button>
</div>
<div role="group">
  <button
    aria-label="Text align left"
    aria-pressed="true"
    value="align-left"
  ></button>
  <button
    aria-label="Text align center"
    aria-pressed="false"
    value="align-center"
  ></button>
  <button
    aria-label="Text align right"
    aria-pressed="false"
    value="align-right"
  ></button>
  <button
    aria-label="Justify text"
    aria-pressed="false"
    value="align-justify"
  ></button>
</div>
<div role="group">
  <button
    aria-disabled="true"
    aria-label="Copy selected text from textarea"
  >
    Copy
  </button>
  <button
    aria-disabled="true"
    aria-label="Paste last copied or cut text to textarea"
  >
    Paste
  </button>
  <button
    aria-disabled="true"
    aria-label="Cut selected text from textarea"
  >
    Cut
  </button>
</div>
```

```html
<div class="font-menu" role="group">
  <div>
    <select
      aria-label="Font family"
      name="font-family"
    >
      <option>
        Sans-serif
      </option>
      <option>
        Serif
      </option>
      <option>
        Monospace
      </option>
      <option>
        Fantasy
      </option>
      <option>
        Cursive
      </option>
    </select>
  </div>
  <div>
    <label for="font-size">Font Size</label>
    <select id="font-size">
      <option>0.5</option>
      <option selected="true">1</option>
      <option>1.5</option>
      <option>2</option>
      <option>2.5</option>
      <option>3</option>
    </select>
  </div>
</div>
</section>
```

# CSS

```css
.menu {
  display: flex;
}
.menu > :not(:first-child):not(:last-child) {
  padding: 0 1em;
}
.menu > :last-child {
  padding-left: 1em;
}
.menu button,
.menu select {
  border-radius: 0.25em;
  font-size: 1em;
  line-height: 0;
  min-height: 1.5em;
  min-width: 1.5em;
  position: relative;
}
```

```css
.menu button[aria-pressed="true"] {
  background-color: hsl(0, 0%, 90%);
}
.menu ol,
.menu ul {
  list-style-type: none;
  margin: 0;
  padding: 0 0.25em;
}
.menu [aria-pressed] + .submenu {
  cursor: pointer;
  position: absolute;
  visibility: hidden;
}
.menu [aria-pressed="true"] + .submenu {
  visibility: visible;
}
.menu {
  background-color: hsl(204, 100%, 90%);
  padding: 0.25em;
}
.menu > :not(:last-child) {
  border-right: 0.125em solid hsl(0, 0%, 75%);
  padding-right: 1em;
}
.menu button:not(.clicked):active::after,
.menu button:not(.clicked):hover::after {
  background-color: hsl(0, 0%, 95%);
  border: 1px solid currentColor;
  border-radius: 0.25em;
  content: attr(aria-label) attr(title);
  display: block;
  font-size: 0.7em;
  line-height: 1.5em;
  margin: 10% 0 0 50%;
  padding: 0.125em 0.25em;
  position: absolute;
  z-index: 1;
}
[value="align-center"]::before {
  content: '┿';
  font-weight: bold;
}
[value="align-justify"]::before {
  content: '≡';
  font-weight: bold;
}
[value="align-left"]::before {
  content: '├';
  font-weight: bold;
  margin-left: -0.5em;
}
[value="align-right"]::before {
  content: '┤';
  font-weight: bold;
  margin-right: -0.5em;
}
```

```css
[value="bold"]::before {
  content: 'B';
  font-weight: bold;
}
[value="cut"]::after {
  content: attr(aria-label);
  display: block;
}
[value="italic"]::before {
  content: 'i';
  font-family: serif;
  font-style: italic;
  font-weight: bold;
}
[value="underline"]::before {
  content: 'U';
  font-weight: bold;
  text-decoration: underline;
}
.font-menu {
  display: flex;
}
.font-menu input {
  flex-grow: 0;
  height: 1.5em;
  width: 2em;
}
.font-menu label {
  clip: rect(0, 0, 0, 0);
  clip-path: polygon(0 0, 0 0, 0 0, 0 0);
  position: absolute;
}
.font-menu ul {
  border: 0.0625em solid hsl(204, 100%, 60%);
  border-radius: 0.25em;
  margin-top: 0.5em;
}
.font-menu ul::before {
  border-bottom: 0.5em solid hsl(204, 100%, 60%);
  border-left: 0.3em solid transparent;
  border-right: 0.3em solid transparent;
  content: ' ';
  display: inline-block;
  position: absolute;
  margin-top: -0.5em;
}
.font-menu > :last-child {
  margin-left: 0.5em;
}
```

# JavaScript

```javascript
[].slice.call(document.getElementsByClassName('menu'))
.forEach(function MenuInterface(bar) {
  [].slice.call(bar.getElementsByTagName('*'))
  .forEach(function (tag) {
    if (tag.getAttribute('aria-pressed')) {
      tag.addEventListener('click', function (e) {
        var aria = 'aria-pressed',
          ctrl = e.target,
          pressed = ctrl.getAttribute(aria) === 'true';

        function onBlur() {
          var cls = ctrl.className;

          ctrl.className = cls
            .replace(/\bclicked\b/, ' ')
            .trim();

          ctrl
              .removeEventListener('blur', onBlur);
        }

        while (
          ctrl &&
          ctrl.nodeName !== 'BUTTON' &&
          ctrl.nodeName !== 'INPUT'
        ) {
          ctrl = ctrl.parentNode;
          pressed = ctrl.getAttribute(aria) === 'true';
        }

        ctrl.setAttribute(aria, !pressed);
        ctrl.className = [
          ctrl.className,
          'clicked'
        ].join(' ').trim();

        ctrl.addEventListener('blur', onBlur);
      });
    }
  });
});

[].slice.call(document.getElementsByClassName('popup'))
.forEach(function PopupInterface(btn) {
  var popupId = btn.getAttribute('aria-controls'),
    popup,
    opts;

  if (popupId) {
    popup = document.getElementById(popupId);
    opts = popup.getElementsByTagName('li');

    function selectOpt(evt) {
      var selected,
        target = (evt || {}).target;
```

```javascript
      switch (evt.key || evt.keyCode) {
        case 'Enter':
        case 13:
        case ' ':
        case 32:
          selected = true;
          break;
        default:
      }
      [].slice.call(opts)
      .forEach(function (opt) {
        opt.setAttribute(
          'aria-current',
          opt === target
        );
      });

      if (target && selected) {
        btn.innerHTML = target.innerHTML;
        btn.setAttribute('aria-pressed', false);
      }
    }

    [].slice.call(opts)
    .forEach(function (opt) {
      opt.setAttribute('tabindex', 0);
      opt.addEventListener('click', selectOpt);
      opt.addEventListener('keydown', selectOpt);
    });
  }
});
```

# Meter 🔋

## HTML

```html
<h2 id="last-payment-age">
  <span id="period">Days</span> since last payment
</h2>
<ol aria-labelledby="last-payment-age" class="meter">
  <li data-max="30"></li>
  <li data-max="60" data-min="31">
    <span aria-describedby="period">45</span>
  </li>
  <li data-max="90" data-min="61"></li>
  <li data-min="91"></li>
</ol>
```

## CSS

```css
.meter {
  display: flex;
  font-size: 2rem;
  margin: 0;
  padding: 0;
}
.meter li {
  align-items: center;
  border: 1px solid hsl(204, 100%, 30%);
  box-sizing: content-box;
  display: inline-flex;
  list-style-type: none;
  height: 1em;
  justify-content: space-evenly;
  line-height: 1em;
  margin: 0.25em 0.125em;
  min-width: 1.5em;
  position: relative;
}
.meter li::before {
  content: attr(data-min);
  font-size: 0.25em;
  left: 0;
  position: absolute;
  top: -2em;
}
.meter li::after {
  content: attr(data-max);
  font-size: 0.25em;
  right: 0;
  position: absolute;
  top: -2em;
}
.meter li:first-of-type {
  border-radius: 0.25em 0 0 0.25em;
  width: 1.5em;
}
.meter li:last-of-type {
  border-radius: 0 0.25em 0.25em 0;
  width: 1.5em;
}

/* color the segments of the meter */
.meter li {
  background-color: green;
}
.meter li:nth-of-type(2),
.meter li:nth-of-type(2) ~ li {
  background-color: yellow;
}
.meter li:nth-of-type(3),
.meter li:nth-of-type(3) ~ li {
  background-color: red;
}
```

```css
/* show the current value inside a circle with a pointer */
.meter li > span {
  background-color: inherit;
  border: 1px solid black;
  border-radius: 100%;
  bottom: -2em;
  display: block;
  font-size: 0.5em;
  left: -30%;
  line-height: 1.5em;
  position: absolute;
  text-align: center;
  width: 1.5em;
  z-index: 1;
}
.meter li > span::before {
  border-bottom: 0.3em solid black;
  border-left: 0.3em solid transparent;
  border-right: 0.3em solid transparent;
  content: '';
  position: absolute;
  left: 30%;
  top: -0.3em;
  width: 0;
}
```

## JavaScript

```javascript
[].slice.call(document.getElementsByClassName('meter'))
.forEach(function MeterInterface(meter) {
  var segments = meter.getElementsByTagName('li'),
    i = segments.length - 1;

  /* calculate the left position of the current value within the range */
  function configSegment(li) {
    if (!li) { return; }

    var min = li.getAttribute('data-min'),
      max = li.getAttribute('data-max'),
      node = li.getElementsByTagName('*').item(0),
      value = node ? node.innerText : '',
      range, offset;

    if (min && max && value) {
      range = Number(max) - Number(min);
      offset = range ?
        ((Number(value) - Number(min)) / range) *
          node.parentNode.offsetWidth :
        0;
      offset += node.offsetLeft;
      node.style.left = `${offset}px`;
    }
  }
```

```
  while (i > -1) {
    configSegment(segments.item(i));
    i -= 1;
  }
});
```

# Number 🔢

## HTML

```html
<span class="field">
  <label for="amt">Payment Amount</label>
  <input class="number" id="amt" inputmode="numeric" type="text" />
  <span class="status"></span>
</span>
```

## JavaScript

```javascript
[].slice.call(document.getElementsByClassName('number'))
.forEach(function NumberInterface(el) {
  if (el.nodeName.toLowerCase() === 'input') {
    el.addEventListener('input', function () {
      /* convert the value string to a value */
      var value = el.value,
        invalid = /[^\d\s,.+-]/.test(value),
        seps = /[\s,.]/g,
        neg = value.indexOf('-') > -1 ? -1 : 1,
        num = value.toString().replace(/[-+]/, ''),
        comma = num.lastIndexOf(','),
        dot = num.lastIndexOf('.'),
        sp = num.lastIndexOf(' '),
        rightmost = Math.max(comma, dot, sp),
        grps = num.split(seps).length,
        normalized = num;

      if (el.value && !invalid) {
        /* if there is a group separator and a decimal separator */
        if ((comma > -1 && dot > -1) ||
            (comma > -1 && sp > -1) ||
            (dot > -1 && sp > -1)) {
          normalized = [num.substr(0, rightmost), num.substr(rightmost)];
          normalized.forEach((v, i, a) => {
            const ref = a;
            ref[i] = v.replace(seps, '');
          });
          normalized = normalized.join('.');
        /* if there are only group separators */
        } else if (grps > 2) {
          normalized = num.replace(seps, '');
        /* if only one separator, assume it's a decimal */
        } else if (grps === 2) {
          normalized = num.replace(seps, '.');
        }
```

```
        normalized *= neg;
        invalid = Number.isNaN(Number(normalized));
        /* if num cannot be converted to a number, return undefined */
      }

      if (!el.value) {
        el.setAttribute('aria-invalid', '');
      } else {
        if (!invalid) {
          el.number = normalized;
        }
        el.setAttribute('aria-invalid', invalid);
      }
    });
    el.addEventListener('keydown', function (e) {
      if (/^[a-z]$/i.test(e.key)) {
        e.preventDefault();
      }
    });
  }
});
```

# Pagination 🔗

## HTML for a Navigational List

```
<ol aria-label="pages" class="pagination" role="navigation">
  <li><a href="/page1">1</a></li>
  <li aria-current="page"><a href="/page2">2</a></li>
  <li><a href="/page3">3</a></li>
  <li><a href="/page4">4</a></li>
  <li><a href="/page5">5</a></li>
</ol>
```

## HTML for a Button Group

```
<ol aria-label="pages" class="pagination" role="group">
  <li><button type="button">1</button></li>
  <li aria-current="page"><button type="button">2</button></li>
  <li><button type="button">3</button></li>
  <li><button type="button">4</button></li>
  <li><button type="button">5</button></li>
</ol>
```

## CSS

```css
ol.pagination {
  list-style-type: none;
}
ol.pagination li {
  align-content: center;
  align-items: middle;
  display: inline-flex;
  flex: 0;
}
ol.pagination li > a,
ol.pagination li > button {
  border: 0.0625rem solid hsl(204, 100%, 30%);
  border-radius: 0.25rem;
  box-sizing: border-box;
  color: currentColor;
  display: inline-block;
  font-size: 1rem;
  line-height: 2rem;
  margin: 0.0625rem;
  padding: 0;
  text-align: center;
  text-decoration: none;
  width: 2rem;
}
ol.pagination li[aria-current="page"] > a,
ol.pagination li[aria-current="page"] > button {
  background-color: hsl(204, 100%, 50%);
  color: hsl(204, 100%, 95%);
}
ol.pagination li > a:hover,
ol.pagination li > button:hover {
  background-color: hsl(204, 0%, 90%);
  color: hsl(204, 0%, 10%);
}
```

# Password 🔒

## HTML

```html
<span class="field password">
  <label for="pwd">Password</label>
  <input aria-describedby="pwd-desc" id="pwd" type="text" />
  <span role="status"></span>
</span>
<ul aria-label="Password requirements" id="pwd-desc">
  <li data-pattern="[A-Z]">
    An uppercase letter is required
  </li>
  <li data-pattern="[a-z]">
    A lowercase letter is required
  </li>
```

```
  <li data-pattern="[0-9]">
    A number is required
  </li>
  <li data-pattern="[!@#$%^&*]">
    One of the following special characters,
    !, @, #, $, %, ^, &amp; or *, is required
  </li>
  <li data-pattern="^[\w\W]{6,8}$">
    The value provided must be 6 to 8 characters long
  </li>
</ul>
```

## CSS

```
.password input[type="text"] ~ button::before {
  color: hsl(0, 100%, 30%);
  content: '|';
  display: inline-block;
  font-size: 2em;
  height: 0;
  line-height: 0;
  position: absolute;
  top: 45%;
  transform: rotate(45deg);
  width: 0;
}
.password input ~ button[aria-label]:focus::after,
.password input ~ button[aria-label]:hover::after {
  background-color: hsl(204, 100%, 100%);
  border: 0.0625em solid hsl(204, 100%, 30%);
  content: attr(aria-label);
  display: inline-block;
  padding: 0.125em;
  position: absolute;
  top: 0.25em;
}
.password + ul {
  list-style-type: none;
  padding: 0 0 0 0.5em;
}
.password + ul > li::before {
  content: '⚠';
  display: inline-block;
  width: 1em;
}
.password + ul > li.completed::before {
  content: '✓';
}
```

# JavaScript

```
[].slice.call(document.getElementsByClassName('password'))
.forEach(function PasswordInterface(field) {
  var button = document.createElement('button'),
    input = field.getElementsByTagName('input').item(0),
    labels = {
      password: {
        label: 'show',
        type: 'text'
      },
      text: {
        label: 'hide',
        type: 'password'
      }
    },
    listId = input.getAttribute('aria-describedby'),
    list = document.querySelectorAll('[id="' + listId + '"] > li'),
    itemStatus = function (item) {
      var pattern = item.getAttribute('data-pattern'),
        regex = new RegExp(pattern);

      if (pattern) {
        item.className = [
          item.className.replace(/(^| )completed( |$)/, ''),
          regex.test(input.value) ? 'completed' : ''
        ].join(' ').trim();
      }
    },
    status = field.querySelector('[role="status"]'),
    valid = input.getAttribute('aria-invalid') || '';

  input.addEventListener('blur', function () {
    var filtered = [].slice.call(list).filter(function (item) {
        return !/\bcompleted\b/.test(item.className);
      }),
      invalid = input.value ? filtered.length === 0 : '',
      ul = document.createElement('ul');

    if (filtered.length && status) {
      filtered.forEach(function (li) {
        ul.innerHTML += li.outerHTML;
      });
      status.innerHTML = ul.outerHTML;
    }
    input.setAttribute('aria-invalid', invalid);
  })
  input.addEventListener('focus', function () {
    input.setAttribute('aria-invalid', '');
  })
  input.addEventListener('input', function () {
    [].slice.call(list).forEach(itemStatus);
  });
  input.setAttribute('aria-invalid', valid);

  button.innerHTML = '👁';
  button.setAttribute('aria-label', labels[input.type].label);
```

```
button.addEventListener('click', function() {
    input.type = labels[input.type].type;
    button.setAttribute('aria-label', labels[input.type].label);
  });

  field.appendChild(button);
});
```

# Progress Bar 📟⚠

## HTML for a ProgressBar

```
<div
  class="progressbar"
  aria-valuemax="200"
  aria-valuemin="0"
  aria-valuetext="14%"
  id="progress"
  role="progressbar"
>
  <div class="indicator"></div>
</div>
```

## HTML for a ProgressBar as a circle

```
<svg
  class="progressbar circle"
  aria-valuemax="200"
  aria-valuemin="0"
  aria-valuenow="14%"
  id="progresscircle"
  role="progressbar"
  viewBox="0 0 36 36"
>
  <path
    d="M18 2.0845
      a 15.9155 15.9155 0 0 1 0 31.831
      a 15.9155 15.9155 0 0 1 0 -31.831"
    stroke-dasharray="100, 100"
  >
  </path>
  <path
    class="indicator"
    d="M18 2.0845
      a 15.9155 15.9155 0 0 1 0 31.831
      a 15.9155 15.9155 0 0 1 0 -31.831"
    stroke-dasharray="14, 100"
    stroke="hsl(204, 100%, 60%)"
  >
  </path>
</svg>
```

# CSS

```css
:not(svg).progressbar {
  border: 0.0625em solid hsl(204, 100%, 30%);
  border-radius: 1em;
  display: inline-flex;
  height: 1em;
  min-width: 10em;
  overflow: hidden;
  position: relative;
  vertical-align: 0.0625em;
}
:not(svg).progressbar::after {
  border: 0.0625em solid transparent;
  content: attr(aria-valuenow);
  color: hsl(204, 0%, 0%);
  line-height: 100%;
  position: absolute;
  text-align: center;
  width: 100%;
}
:not(svg).progressbar > div {
  background-color: hsl(204, 100%, 60%);
}
.progressbar.circle {
  fill: none;
  stroke: hsl(204, 0%, 90%);
}
```

# JavaScript

```javascript
[].slice.call(document.getElementsByClassName('progressbar'))
.forEach(function ProgressBarInterface(bar) {
  var indicator = bar.getElementsByClassName('indicator').item(0);

  Object.defineProperty(bar, 'max', {
    enumerable: true,
    get: function () {
      var value = this.getAttribute('aria-valuemax');

      if (value) {
        return Number(value);
      }
    },
    set: function (value) {
      var num = Number(value);

      if (!Number.isNaN(num)) {
        this.setAttribute('aria-valuemax', num);
      }
    }
  });
```

```
Object.defineProperty(bar, 'min', {
  enumerable: true,
  get: function () {
    var value = this.getAttribute('aria-valuemin');

    if (value) {
      return Number(value);
    }
  },
  set: function (value) {
    var num = Number(value);

    if (!Number.isNaN(num)) {
      this.setAttribute('aria-valuemin', num);
    }
  }
});
Object.defineProperty(bar, 'range', {
  enumerable: true,
  get: function () {
    return this.max - this.min;
  }
});
Object.defineProperty(bar, 'text', {
  enumerable: true,
  get: function () {
    var value = this.getAttribute('aria-valuetext'),
      p = /^(\d+)%$/.exec(value),
      percent,
      num;

    if (p) {
      percent = Number(p[1]) / 100;
      return (this.range * percent) + this.min;
    } else {
      return Number(value);
    }
  },
  set: function (value) {
    this.value = value;
  }
});
Object.defineProperty(bar, 'value', {
  enumerable: true,
  get: function () {
    return this.getAttribute('aria-valuenow');
  },
  set: function (value) {
    var p = /^(\d+)%$/.exec(value),
      percent,
      num,
      valuenow;

    if (p) {
      percent = Number(p[1]) / 100;
      num = (this.range * percent) + this.min;
    } else {
      num = Number(value);
      percent = (num - this.min) / (this.max || 1);
    }
```

```
      valuenow = Math.round(percent * 100);
      if (!Number.isNaN(num)) {
        this.setAttribute('aria-valuetext', num);
      }
      if (!Number.isNaN(percent)) {
        this.setAttribute('aria-valuenow', valuenow + '%');
        if (/^path$/i.test(indicator.nodeName)) {
          indicator.setAttribute('stroke-dasharray', valuenow + ', 100');
        } else {
          indicator.style.width = this.value;
        }
      }
    }
  });

  if (!indicator) {
    indicator = document.createElement('div');
    indicator.setAttribute('class', 'indicator');
    bar.appendChild(indicator);
  }
  bar.setAttribute('role', 'progressbar');
  if (!bar.max) {
    bar.max = 100;
  }
  if (!bar.min) {
    bar.min = 0;
  }
  if (bar.value || bar.text) {
    bar.value = (bar.value || bar.text);
  }
  return bar;
});
```

# Radio Button

## HTML

```
<fieldset class="radio">
  <legend id="group-label">The fruit I like to eat</legend>
  <p>
    Please select the fruit you like to eat.
  </p>
  <span class="field">
    <input aria-describedby="group-label" id="group-apple" name="fruit"
      type="radio" />
    <span>
      <label for="group-apple">Apple</label>
    </span>
  </span>
  <span class="field">
    <input aria-describedby="group-label" id="group-banana" name="fruit"
      type="radio" />
    <span>
      <label for="group-banana">Banana</label>
    </span>
  </span>
```

```html
    <span class="field">
      <input aria-describedby="group-label" id="group-cherry" name="fruit"
        type="radio" />
      <span>
        <label for="group-cherry">Cherry</label>
      </span>
    </span>
    <span class="field">
      <input aria-describedby="group-label" id="group-date" name="fruit"
        type="radio" />
      <span>
        <label for="group-date">Date</label>
      </span>
    </span>
  </fieldset>
```

## CSS

```css
fieldset.radio {
  align-items: baseline;
  border: 0;
  display: flex;
  flex-direction: column;
  margin: 0;
  padding: 0;
}
fieldset.radio > legend {
  font-size: 1.5rem;
  font-weight: bold;
}
fieldset.radio > .field {
  margin-left: 0;
}

.field:not(:last-of-type) {
  margin-bottom: 1em;
}

[type="radio"] {
  border: 0;
  clip: rect(0, 0, 0, 0);
  clip-path: polygon(0 0, 0 0, 0 0, 0 0);
  left: -200%;
  outline: none;
  overflow: hidden;
  position: absolute;
}
[type="radio"] + span {
  align-items: center;
  display: inline-flex;
}
[type="radio"] + span.trailing::after,
[type="radio"] + span:not(.trailing)::before {
  background-color: hsl(0, 0%, 99%);
  border: 0.0625rem solid hsl(0, 0%, 60%);
  border-radius: 50%;
  color: hsl(0, 0%, 1%);
```

```css
  content: '\202F';
  display: inline-block;
  height: 1.2rem;
  line-height: 1.2rem;
  margin: 0 0.5rem;
  text-align: center;
  width: 1.2rem;
}
[type="radio"]:checked + span.trailing::after,
[type="radio"]:checked + span:not(.trailing)::before {
  background-color: hsl(204, 100%, 40%);
  border-color: transparent;
  color: hsl(204, 100%, 99%);
}
[type="radio"]:checked + span.trailing::after,
[type="radio"]:checked + span:not(.trailing)::before {
  content: '•';
}
[type="radio"]:focus + span:before {
  border-color: hsl(204, 100%, 40%);
}
[type="radio"]:focus + span > label {
  text-shadow: 0 0 0.5em hsl(204, 100%, 75%);
}
```

# Search ⚠

## HTML

```html
<section class="search" data-url="">
  <span class="field">
    <label for="search">
      Search Terms
    </label>
    <span role="group">
      <input id="search" type="text" />
      <button class="icon" type="button">
        <svg viewBox="0 0 490 490" xmlns="http://www.w3.org/2000/svg">
          <title>Search</title>
          <path
            stroke-width="36"
            stroke-linecap="round"
            d="m280,278a153,153 0 1,0-2,2l170,170m-91-117
              110,110-26,26-110-110"
          />
        </svg>
      </button>
    </span>
  </span>
  <section aria-live="assertive" class="results"></section>
</section>
```

## CSS

```css
.search [role="group"] input[type="text"] {
  border-bottom-right-radius: 0;
  border-top-right-radius: 0;
}
.search [role="group"] button {
  border-bottom-left-radius: 0;
  border-top-left-radius: 0;
  border-left: 0;
  text-align: center;
}
.search [role="group"] button > svg {
  display: block;
  fill: transparent;
  stroke: currentColor;
  min-width: 1.2em;
}
.search .results:not(:empty) {
  border-top: 0.125em solid hsl(204, 100%, 60%);
  padding: 1em;
}
```

## JavaScript

```javascript
[].slice.call(document.getElementsByClassName('search'))
.forEach(function SearchInterface(el) {
  var button = el.getElementsByClassName('icon').item(0),
    input = el.getElementsByTagName('input').item(0),
    results = el.getElementsByClassName('results').item(0);

  el.search = function () {
    var data = input.value,
      url = el.getAttribute('data-url'),
      good = Number(el.getAttribute('data-returned')),
      failed = Number(el.getAttribute('data-failed'));

    fetch(url, { method: 'post', body: data })
      .then(function (response) {
        el.setAttribute('data-returned', good + 1);

        /* the results should be placed in the _results_ element */
        results.innerHTML = response.status;
      })
      .catch(function (reason) {
        el.setAttribute('data-failed', failed + 1);

        /*
         * the reason the search failed should be communicated,
         * by placing the _reason_ in the _results_ element
         */
        results.innerHTML = reason;
      });
  };
  button.addEventListener('click', el.search);
});
```

# Skip-To 📟

## HTML

```
<a class="skip-to" href="#shipping">Skip to Shipping Methods</a>
```

## CSS

```css
a.skip-to[href^="#"] {
  clip: rect(0, 0, 0, 0);
  clip-path: polygon(0 0, 0 0, 0 0, 0 0);
  left: -200%;
  position: absolute;
}
a.skip-to[href^="#"]:focus {
  clip-path: none;
  position: static;
}
```

## JavaScript

```javascript
[].slice.call(document.getElementsByClassName('skip-to'))
.forEach(function SkipToInterface(anchor) {
  var id = (/^#([^"']+)/i.exec(anchor.href) || [])[1],
    node;

  if (id) {
    node = document.getElementById(id);
    if (node) {
      function blur() {
        node.removeAttribute('tabindex');
        node.removeEventListener('blur', blur);
      }
      function click() {
        node.setAttribute('tabindex', -1);
      }

      anchor.addEventListener('click', click);
      node.addEventListener('blur', blur);
    }
  }
});
```

# Slider ⚒⚠

## HTML

```
<div class="field">
  <label for="payment">Payment Amount</label>
    <div
      class="slider"
      tabindex="-1"
    >
    <input id="payment" type="text"/>
    <div class="value"></div>
    <div class="thumb"
      aria-valuemax="100"
      aria-valuemin="0"
      data-step="10"
      tabindex="-1"
    ></div>
  </div>
</div>
```

## CSS

```
.slider {
  align-items: center;
  background-color: hsl(204, 0%, 99%);
  border: 0.125em solid hsl(204, 100%, 30%);
  border-radius: 0.25em;
  display: inline-flex;
  overflow: visible;
  margin: 0 0.5em;
  min-height: 0.5em;
  min-width: 20em;
  position: relative;
  z-index: 2;
}
.slider input {
  clip: rect(0, 0, 0, 0);
  clip-path: polygon(0 0, 0 0, 0 0, 0 0);
  margin: 0 0 0 -0.5em;
  position: absolute;
  width: 100%;
}
.slider.vertical {
  transform: rotate(270deg);
  position: absolute;
}
.slider.focus {
  outline: hsla(204, 100%, 60%, .8) auto 5px;
}
```

```css
.slider > .value {
  background-color: hsla(204, 100%, 75%, 1);
  color: transparent;
  height: 100%;
  position: absolute;
  width: auto; /* this will be set by js */
  z-index: 1;
}
.slider > .thumb {
  background: radial-gradient(hsla(204, 100%, 30%, 1),
    hsla(204, 100%, 60%, 1));
  border-radius: 50%;
  color: transparent;
  height: 1em;
  margin-left: -0.5em;
  position: absolute;
  width: 1em;
  z-index: 3;
}
```

## JavaScript

```javascript
[].slice.call(document.getElementsByClassName('slider'))
.forEach(function SliderInterface(slider) {
  var container = {
      left: slider.getBoundingClientRect().left,
      top: slider.getBoundingClientRect().top,
      height: slider.offsetHeight || 1,
      width: slider.offsetWidth || 1,
    },
    controls = {
      input: slider.getElementsByTagName('input').item(0),
      thumb: slider.getElementsByClassName('thumb').item(0),
      value: slider.getElementsByClassName('value').item(0)
    },
    evtChange = new CustomEvent('change'),
    onblur = function (e) {
      slider.hasFocus = false;
    },
    onfocus = function (e) {
      slider.hasFocus = true;
    },
    isDragging,
    dragStart,
    dragValue;

  Object.defineProperty(slider, 'hasFocus', {
    enumerable: true,
    set: function (bool) {
      var cls = /\bfocus\b/;

      slider.className = slider.className
        .replace(cls, ' ')
        .trim();
```

```javascript
      if (bool) {
        slider.className = [slider.className,
          'focus'].join(' ').trim();
      }
    }
  });
  Object.defineProperty(slider, 'isVertical', {
    enumerable: true,
    get: function () {
      return /\bvertical\b/i.test(slider.className);
    }
  });
  Object.defineProperty(slider, 'max', {
    enumerable: true,
    get: function () {
      return Number(controls.thumb.getAttribute('aria-valuemax'));
    },
    set: function (n) {
      if (!Number.isNaN(n)) {
        controls.thumb.setAttribute('aria-valuemax', n);
      }
    }
  });
  Object.defineProperty(slider, 'min', {
    enumerable: true,
    get: function () {
      return Number(controls.thumb.getAttribute('aria-valuemin'));
    },
    set: function (n) {
      if (!Number.isNaN(n)) {
        controls.thumb.setAttribute('aria-valuemin', n);
      }
    }
  });
  Object.defineProperty(slider, 'percent', {
    enumerable: true,
    get: function () {
      return Math.max(
        Math.min(
          Math.round((this.value / this.range) * 100),
          100
        ),
        0
      );
    },
    set: function (percent) {
      if (!Number.isNaN(percent)) {
        var n = (percent * this.range) + this.min;
        n = Math.max(n, this.min);
        n = Math.min(n, this.max);
        n = Math.round(n / this.step) * this.step;

        this.value = n;
      }
    }
  });
```

```
Object.defineProperty(slider, 'range', {
  enumerable: true,
  get: function() {
    var lg = Math.max(slider.max, slider.min),
      sm = Math.min(slider.max, slider.min);

    return lg - sm || 1;
  }
});
Object.defineProperty(slider, 'step', {
  enumerable: true,
  get: function () {
    return Number(controls.thumb.getAttribute('data-step')) || 1;
  },
  set: function (n) {
    if (!Number.isNaN(n)) {
      controls.thumb.setAttribute('data-step', n);
    }
  }
});
Object.defineProperty(slider, 'value', {
  enumerable: true,
  get: function () {
    return Number(controls.thumb.getAttribute('aria-valuenow'));
  },
  set: function (n) {
    if (!Number.isNaN(n)) {
      controls.input.value = n;
      controls.thumb.setAttribute('aria-valuenow', n);

      /* set the width of the interface */
      var percent = Math.max(
        Math.min(
          Math.round((n / this.range) * 100),
          100
        ),
        0
      );

      controls.value.style.width = percent + '%';
      controls.thumb.style.left = percent + '%';
      this.dispatchEvent(evtChange);
    }
  }
});
Object.defineProperty(slider, 'decrement', {
  enumerable: true,
  value: function () {
    this.value = Math.max(this.value - this.step, this.min);
  }
});
Object.defineProperty(slider, 'increment', {
  enumerable: true,
  value: function () {
    this.value = Math.min(this.value + this.step, this.max);
  }
});
```

```
function onMouseMoveX (e) {
  if (isDragging) {
    var distance = e.clientX - dragStart,
      percent = (distance / width) + (dragValue / range),
      size = Math.max(
        Math.min(Math.round(percent * 100), 100),
        0
      );

    if (distance) {
      controls.value.style.width = size + '%';
      controls.thumb.style.left = size + '%';
    }
  }
  e.stopPropagation();
}
function onMouseUpX (e) {
  if (isDragging) {
    var distance = Math.abs(e.clientX - container.left),
      percent = distance / width;

    if (distance > 44) {
      slider.percent = percent;
    }
    dragStart = 0;
    dragValue = 0;

    slider.removeEventListener('mousemove', onMouseMoveX);
    slider.removeEventListener('mouseup', onMouseUpX);
    isDragging = false;
  }
  e.stopPropagation();
}
function onMouseDownX (e) {
  width = slider.offsetWidth;
  isDragging = true;
  dragStart = e.clientX;
  dragValue = controls.input.value;

  slider.addEventListener('mousemove', onMouseMoveX);
  slider.addEventListener('mouseup', onMouseUpX);
  e.stopPropagation();
}

function onMouseMoveY (e) {
  if (isDragging) {
    var bottom = controls.value.getBoundingClientRect().bottom,
      dragged = Math.abs(e.clientY - dragStart),
      distance = Math.abs(bottom - e.clientY),
      percent = distance / height,
      size = Math.max(
        Math.min(Math.round(percent * 100), 100),
        0
      );

    if (dragged) {
      controls.value.style.height = size + '%';
      controls.thumb.style.bottom = size + '%';
    }
  }
}
```

```
    e.stopPropagation();
  }
  function onMouseUpY (e) {
    if (isDragging) {
      var bottom = controls.value.getBoundingClientRect().bottom,
          distance = Math.abs(bottom - e.clientY),
        percent = distance / height;

      if (distance > 44) {
        slider.percent = percent;
      }

      dragStart = 0;
      dragValue = 0;

      slider.removeEventListener('mousemove', onMouseMoveY);
      slider.removeEventListener('mouseup', onMouseUpY);
      isDragging = false;
    }
    e.stopPropagation();
  }
  function onMouseDownY (e) {
    height = slider.offsetHeight;
    isDragging = true;
    dragStart = e.clientY;
    dragValue = controls.input.value;
    slider.addEventListener('mousemove', onMouseMoveY);
    slider.addEventListener('mouseup', onMouseUpY);
    e.stopPropagation();
  }

  controls.input.addEventListener('blur', onblur);
  controls.input.addEventListener('focus', onfocus);
  controls.thumb.addEventListener('blur', onblur);
  controls.thumb.addEventListener('focus', onfocus);

  slider.addEventListener('keydown', function (e) {
    switch (e.key) {
      case '-': /* prevent default and fall thru */
      case 'ArrowDown':
      case 'ArrowLeft':
        e.preventDefault();
        slider.decrement();
        break;
      case '+': /* prevent default and fall thru */
      case 'ArrowRight':
      case 'ArrowUp':
        e.preventDefault();
        slider.increment();
        break;
      default:
    }
  });
  slider.addEventListener('mousedown', !slider.isVertical ?
    onMouseDownX :
    onMouseDownY
  );

  return slider;
});
```

# Stars

## HTML

```html
<fieldset class="stars">
  <legend id="grp-label">How would you rate the fruit</legend>

  <!-- this allows the user to 'unset' the number of stars -->
  <input aria-describedby="grp-label" id="star0" name="star"
    type="radio" checked>
  <label for="star0">0</label>
  <input aria-describedby="grp-label" id="star1" name="star"
    type="radio" value="1" />
  <label for="star1">1</label>
  <input aria-describedby="grp-label" id="star2" name="star"
    type="radio" value="2" />
  <label for="star2">2</label>
  <input aria-describedby="grp-label" id="star3" name="star"
    type="radio" value="3" />
  <label for="star3">3</label>
  <input aria-describedby="grp-label" id="star4" name="star"
    type="radio" value="4" />
  <label for="star4">4</label>
  <input aria-describedby="grp-label" id="star5" name="star"
    type="radio" value="5" />
  <label for="star5">5</label>
</fieldset>
```

## CSS

```css
fieldset.stars {
  border: 0;
  margin: 0;
  padding: 0;
}
fieldset.stars > legend {
  font-size: 1.5rem;
  font-weight: bold;
}

input[type="radio"] {
  border: 0;
  clip: rect(0, 0, 0, 0);
  clip-path: polygon(0 0, 0 0, 0 0, 0 0);
  left: -200%;
  overflow: hidden;
  position: absolute;
}
```

```css
fieldset.stars label {
  align-items: center;
  color: transparent;
  display: inline-block;
  font-family: monospace;
  font-size: 44px;
  height: 1em;
  line-height: 1em;
  position: relative;
  text-align: center;
  width: 1em;
}
fieldset.stars input + label::after {
  content: '★';
  color: hsl(204, 100%, 40%);
  left: 0;
  position: absolute;
  top: 0;
}
fieldset.stars input:focus + label:after {
  color: hsl(204, 100%, 40%);
  text-shadow: 0 0 0.5em hsl(204, 100%, 75%);
}
fieldset.stars input:checked ~ label::after {
  content: '☆';
  color: hsl(0, 0%, 60%);
}
fieldset.stars input:checked + label::after {
  color: hsl(204, 100%, 40%);
  content: '★';
}
fieldset.stars label:first-of-type::after {
  content: '↺' !important;
  font-size: 0.7em;
  font-weight: bold;
  padding: 0 0.3em;
}
```

# Stepper ⚠

## HTML

```html
<span class="field stepper">
  <label for="amt">Payment Amount</label>
  <input class="number" data-min="0" data-max="50" data-step="10"
    id="amt" type="text" />
  <span class="status"></span>
  <span class="controls">
    <button aria-label="subtract 10" class="decrement">-</button>
    <button aria-label="add 10" class="increment">+</button>
    <span role="alert"></span>
  </span>
</span>
```

# CSS

```css
.stepper .controls {
  display: inline-flex;
}
.stepper .controls button {
  display: inline-block;
  margin: 0;
  width: 2em;
}
.stepper .controls button:first-of-type {
  border-bottom-right-radius: 0;
  border-top-right-radius: 0;
  border-right: 0;
}
.stepper .controls button:last-of-type {
  border-bottom-left-radius: 0;
  border-top-left-radius: 0;
}
.stepper .controls [role="alert"] {
  border: 0;
  clip: rect(0, 0, 0, 0);
  clip-path: polygon(0 0, 0 0, 0 0, 0 0);
  left: -200%;
  overflow: hidden;
  position: absolute;
}
```

# JavaScript

```javascript
[].slice.call(document.getElementsByClassName('stepper'))
.forEach(function StepperInterface(stepper) {
  var controls = stepper.getElementsByClassName('controls').item(0),
    input = stepper.getElementsByClassName('number').item('0'),
    dec = controls.getElementsByClassName('decrement').item(0),
    inc = controls.getElementsByClassName('increment').item(0),
    aria = controls.getElementsByTagName('span').item(0),
    max = input.getAttribute('data-max'),
    min = input.getAttribute('data-min'),
    step = input.getAttribute('data-step'),
    precision = ([].slice.call(/[,.]([^,.]+)$/g.exec(step) || [])).pop() ||
      '').length,
    clear = function () {
      if (aria) {
        aria.innerHTML = '';
      }
    },
    update = function (n) {
      var fixed = n.toFixed(precision);

      if (fixed !== input.value) {
        input.value = fixed;
        if (aria) {
          aria.innerHTML = fixed;
        }
      }
    },
```

```
  decrease = function () {
    var n = Number(input.value);

    update(Math.max(n - step, min));
  },
  increase = function () {
    var n = Number(input.value);

    update(Math.min(n + step, max));
  };

/* normalize */
max = max ? Number(max) : Number.MAX_SAFE_INTEGER;
min = min ? Number(min) : Number.MIN_SAFE_INTEGER;
step = Number(step) || 1;

dec.addEventListener('blur', clear);
dec.addEventListener('click', decrease);
inc.addEventListener('blur', clear);
inc.addEventListener('click', increase);
input.addEventListener('keydown', function (e) {
  if (e.key === 'ArrowUp') {
    e.preventDefault();
    e.stopPropagation();
    increase();
  } else if (e.key === 'ArrowDown') {
    e.preventDefault();
    e.stopPropagation();
    decrease();
  }
})
});
```

# Switch 🔦

## HTML for Visible Labels

```
<label class="toggle">
  <span class="label" id="tgl-label">Push Notifications</span>
  <span aria-hidden="true" class="switch-label"
    id="tgl-false">Off</span>
  <input aria-labelledby="tgl-label" type="checkbox" />
  <span class="switch">
    <span class="switch-button"></span>
  </span>
  <span aria-hidden="true" class="switch-label" id="tgl-true">On</span>
</label>
```

## HTML for Invisible Labels

```
<label class="toggle no-labels">
  <span class="label" id="tgl-nolabel">Push Notifications</span>
  <span aria-hidden="true" class="switch-label"
```

```
      id="tgl-nolabel-false">Off</span>
    <input aria-labelledby="tgl-nolabel" type="checkbox" />
    <span class="switch">
      <span class="switch-button"></span>
    </span>
    <span aria-hidden="true" class="switch-label"
      id="tgl-nolabel-true">On</span>
</label>
```

## CSS

```
.toggle {
  align-items: center;
  display: flex;
  cursor: pointer;
}
.toggle .label + .switch,
.toggle .label + .switch-label {
  margin-left: 1em;
}
.toggle .switch + .label,
.toggle .switch-label + .label {
  margin-right: 1em;
}
.toggle .switch {
  align-items: center;
  background-color: hsl(204, 0%, 100%);
  border: 0.0625em solid hsl(204, 0%, 0%);
  border-radius: 0.25em;
  box-shadow: 0 0 0.1em 0.1em hsl(204, 0%, 75%) inset;
  cursor: pointer;
  display: inline-flex;
  flex-shrink: 0;
  height: 1.2em;
  margin: 0 1em;
  min-width: 2em;
  padding: 0.0625em;
  position: relative;
}
.toggle .switch-label + .switch {
  margin: 0 1em;
}
.toggle input {
  border: 0;
  clip: rect(0, 0, 0, 0);
  clip-path: polygon(0 0, 0 0, 0 0, 0 0);
  left: -200%;
  outline: none;
  overflow: hidden;
  position: absolute;
}
.toggle input:focus + .switch {
  box-shadow: 0 0 0.1em 0.1em hsl(204, 0%, 100%),
  0 0 0.2em 0.3em hsl(207, 80%, 70%);
}
```

```css
.toggle .switch > .switch-label:first-of-type {
  display: inline-block;
  margin-right: 0.5em;
  padding-left: 0.5em;
}
.toggle .switch > .switch-label:last-of-type {
  display: inline-block;
  margin-left: 0.5em;
  padding-right: 0.5em;
}
.toggle .switch > .switch-button {
  background-color: hsl(204, 0%, 60%);
  border: 1px solid hsl(204, 0%, 30%);
  border-radius: 0.2em;
  box-shadow: 0.125em 0.25rem 1rem 0.1em hsl(204, 0%, 100%) inset;
  display: inline-block;
  height: 90%;
  min-width: 1em;
  position: absolute;
  transition: left 1s;
  width: 49%;
}
.toggle .switch > .switch-button::before {
  content: unset;
}
.toggle input:not(:checked) + .switch > .switch-button {
  left: 0;
}
.toggle input:checked + .switch > .switch-button {
  left: 48%;
}
.toggle.no-labels .switch {
  margin-right: 0;
}
.toggle.no-labels .switch-label {
  clip: rect(0, 0, 0, 0);
  clip-path: polygon(0 0, 0 0, 0 0, 0 0);
  height: 1px;
  left: -200%;
  position: absolute;
  width: 1px;
}
```

# JavaScript

```
/*
Although JavaScript is not necessary for this design to work as expected,
the example script will enhance the accessibility features for the Toggle
by updating the described state using the existing position labels and
switching the aria-describedby attribute to the base id plus the checked
status of the input. As noted earlier, this script requires the input
label to use the naming convention that specifies an input identifier
followed by -label and the labeling element for the "off" or "false"
position to be identified by the input identifer followed by -false and
the labeling element for the "on" or "true" position to be identified by
the input identifier followed by -true. For example, the "Push
Notifications" element uses "mytoggle" as the input identifer, as do the
"Off" and "On" labels with mytoggle-false and mytoggle-true, respectively.
*/

[].slice.call(document.getElementsByClassName('switch'))
.forEach(function SwitchInterface(toggle) {
  var onChange = function onChange(e) {
      var target = e.target,
        checked = target.checked,
        label = target.getAttribute('aria-labelledby') || '',
        description = label.replace(/-label$/, '-' + checked);

      if (description && document.getElementById(description)) {
        target.setAttribute('aria-describedby', description);
      }
    };

  [].slice.call(toggle.getElementsByTagName('input'))
  .forEach(function handle(input) {
    if (input.type === 'checkbox') {
      input.addEventListener('change', onChange);
    }
  });
});
```

# Tabs ⚠

## HTML

```
<section class="tabs">
  <ol>
    <li>
      <a href="#mypanel-1" id="mytab-1" aria-selected="true">Accordion</a>
    </li>
    <li>
      <a href="#mypanel-2" id="mytab-2" aria-selected="false">Alert</a>
    </li>
    <li>
      <a href="#mypanel-3" id="mytab-3" aria-selected="false">Carousel</a>
    </li>
  </ol>
```

```html
<section aria-hidden="false" aria-labelledby="mytab-1" id="mypanel-1">
  <p>
    An <code>Accordion</code> is a widget that expands and collapses
    when the <em>twistie</em> (control) is activated. In some browsers,
    this widget can be built using the <code>summary</code> and
    <code>details</code> elements; however, not all browsers implement
    the expand and collapse feature - notably, Microsoft's Internet
    Explorer and Edge browsers are in this category.
  </p>
</section>

<section aria-hidden="true" aria-labelledby="mytab-2" id="mypanel-2">
  <p>
    There are two types of <code>Alert</code>. One, a simple
    <code>Alert</code>, is a message
    displayed (and announced) to the user within a browser window. The
    other, an <code>AlertDialog</code>, is a message displayed (and
    announced) to the user within a modal (<code>Dialog</code>) window.
    Where an <code>Alert</code> is straightforward and requires little
    in the way of markup and no special styling, an
    <code>AlertDialog</code> - because it is an implementation of a <a
    href="Dialog.md"><code>Dialog</code></a> - requires more markup,
    special styling, and JavaScript as well.
  </p>
</section>

<section aria-hidden="true" aria-labelledby="mytab-3" id="mypanel-3">
  <p>
    A <code>Carousel</code> is a component used to show a series of
    content blocks and allow either animation of the transition or user
    control of the transition. Although there is plenty of debate about
    whether or not they are useful or desireable, they are relatively
    popular for a number of implementations. A large part of the reason
    most haters hate them is because they're seldom built with
    accessibility in mind. The fact remains, however, they are a
    consistent design pattern, so it behooves us to make them
    accessible.
  </p>
  <p>
    In order to be accessible, there are a few requirements we must keep
    in mind.
  </p>
  <ul>
    <li>
      The user is able to start, stop, and pause the animation.
    </li>
    <li>
      The control of the displayed panel is indicated both visually and
      programmatically.
    </li>
    <li>
      All controls have text labels, not just an icon that we hope
      will be understood.
    </li>
    <li>
      All controls have ample <em>target area</em>
    .</li>
  </ul>
```

```
    <p>
      Semantically, a <code>Carousel</code> is a collection of
      <code>Tab</code> components, even though the design is a little
      different.
    </p>
  </section>
</section>
```

# CSS

```
.tabs > ol {
  align-items: flex-end;
  display: flex;
  list-style-type: none;
  margin: 0;
  padding: 0;
}
.tabs > ol > li {
  border: 0.0625rem solid hsla(204, 0%, 60%, 1);
  border-bottom: 0;
  margin-right: 0.0625rem;
  overflow: hidden;
}
.tabs > ol > li > :first-child {
  border-bottom: 0.25rem solid hsla(204, 0%, 90%, 0.5);
  border-top: 0.25rem solid hsla(204, 0%, 90%, 0.5);
  color: hsla(204, 0%, 70%, 1);
  display: block;
  padding: 0.5rem;
  text-decoration: none;
}
.tabs > ol > li > :first-child:focus {
  border-bottom: 0.25rem solid hsla(204, 0%, 80%, 0.5);
  border-top: 0.25rem solid hsla(204, 0%, 80%, 0.5);
  color: hsla(204, 0%, 35%, 1);
}
.tabs > ol > li > :first-child[aria-selected="true"] {
  background-color: hsla(204, 100%, 95%, 1);
  border-bottom-color: transparent;
  border-top-color: hsla(204, 100%, 35%, 0.7);
  color: hsla(204, 100%, 35%, 1);
}
.tabs > ol > li > :first-child[aria-selected="true"]:focus {
  background-color: unset;
}
.tabs > :not(ol) {
  border: 0.0625rem solid hsla(204, 0%, 60%, 1);
  padding: 0.5rem;
}
.tabs > :not(ol) > :first-child {
  margin-top: 0.25rem;
  padding-top: 0;
}
.tabs > [aria-hidden="true"] {
  display: none;
}
```

# JavaScript

```javascript
[].slice.call(document.getElementsByClassName('tabs'))
.forEach(function TabsInterface(tabs) {
  var activePanel, activeTab, anchors = [],
    list = tabs ? tabs.getElementsByTagName('ol').item(0) : null,
    items = list ? [].slice.call(list.getElementsByTagName('li')) : [];

  function activateTab(anchor) {
    if (anchor) {
      if (activeTab) {
        activeTab.setAttribute('aria-selected', false);
      }
      anchor.setAttribute('aria-selected', true);
      activatePanel(anchor);
      activeTab = anchor;
    }
  }
  function activatePanel(anchor) {
    var href = anchor ? anchor.getAttribute('href') : '',
      panel = document.getElementById(href.substr(1));

    if (panel) {
      if (activePanel) {
        activePanel.setAttribute('aria-hidden', true);
      }
      panel.setAttribute('aria-hidden', false);
      activePanel = panel;
    }
  }
  function first() {
    move(items[0]);
  }
  function last() {
    move(items[items.length - 1]);
  }
  function move(item) {
    var anchor = item.getElementsByTagName('a').item(0);
    if (anchor) {
      anchor.focus();
    }
  }
  function next(anchor) {
    var index = Number(anchor.getAttribute('data-index')) + 1;
    if (index > items.length - 1) {
      index = 0;
    }
    move(items[index]);
  }
  function prev(anchor) {
    var index = Number(anchor.getAttribute('data-index')) - 1;
    if (index < 0) {
      index = items.length - 1;
    }
    move(items[index]);
  }
  function onClick(e) {
    activateTab(e.target);
  }
```

```
function onKeyDown(e) {
  var key = (e.key || e.keyCode).toString();
  switch (key) {
    case 'ArrowDown':  case '40':
    case 'ArrowRight': case '39':
      return next(e.target);
    case 'ArrowLeft':  case '37':
    case 'ArrowUp':    case '38':
      return prev(e.target);
    case 'End':        case '35':
      return last();
    case 'Home':       case '36':
      return first();
    default:
  }
}

items.forEach(function initTab(li, c) {
  var a = li.getElementsByTagName('a').item(0);
  if (a) {
    a.setAttribute('data-index', c);
    a.addEventListener('click', onClick);
    a.addEventListener('keydown', onKeyDown);

    if (a.getAttribute('aria-selected') === 'true') {
      activateTab(a);
    }
  }
});
});
```

# Tabs Widget ⚠

## HTML

```
<section class="tabs-widget" id="mytabs">
  <ul div aria-label="Components" role="tablist">
    <li role="presentation">
      <button aria-controls="mc-panel1" id="mc-tab1"
        role="tab" type="button"
      >Accordion</button>
    </li>
    <li role="presentation">
      <button id="mc-tab2"
        role="tab" type="button"
      >Alert</button>
    </li>
    <li role="presentation">
      <button aria-controls="mc-panel3" id="mc-tab3"
        role="tab" type="button"
      >Carousel</button>
    </li>
  </ul>
```

```
<ul class="panels">
  <li aria-labelledby="mc-tab1" id="mc-panel1" role="tabpanel">
    <p>
      An <code>Accordion</code> is a widget that expands and collapses
      when the <em>twistie</em> (control) is activated. In some
      browsers, this widget can be built using the <code>summary</code>
      and <code>details</code> elements; however, not all browsers
      implement the expand and collapse feature - notably, Microsoft's
      Internet Explorer and Edge browsers are in this category.
    </p>
  </li>
  <li aria-labelledby="mc-tab2" id="mc-panel2" role="tabpanel">
    <p>
      There are two types of <code>Alert</code>. One, a simple
      <code>Alert</code>, is a message displayed (and announced) to the
      user within a browser window. The other, an
      <code>AlertDialog</code>, is a message displayed (and announced)
      to the user within a modal (<code>Dialog</code>) window. Where an
      <code>Alert</code> is straightforward and requires little in the
      way of markup and no special styling, an <code>AlertDialog</code>
      - because it is an implementation of a <a
      href="Dialog.md"><code>Dialog</code></a> - requires more markup,
      special styling, and JavaScript as well.
    </p>
  </li>
  <li aria-labelledby="mc-tab3" id="mc-panel3" role="tabpanel">
    <p>
      A <code>Carousel</code> is a component used to show a series of
      content blocks and allow either animation of the transition or
      user control of the transition. Although there is plenty of debate
      about whether or not they are useful or desireable, they are
      relatively popular for a number of implementations. A large part
      of the reason most haters hate them is because they're seldom
      built with accessibility in mind. The fact remains, however, they
      are a consistent design pattern, so it behooves us to make them
      accessible.
    </p>
    <p>
      In order to be accessible, there are a few requirements we must
      keep in mind.
    </p>
    <ul>
      <li>
        The user is able to start, stop, and pause the animation.
      </li>
      <li>
        The contol of the displayed panel is indicated both visually
        and programmatically.
      </li>
      <li>
        All controls have text labels, not just an icon that we hope
        will be understood.
      </li>
      <li>
        All controls have ample <em>target area</em>.
      </li>
    </ul>
```

```html
    <p>
      Semantically, a <code>Carousel</code> is a collection of
      <code>Tab</code> components, even though the design is a little
      different.
    </p>
  </li>
  </ul>
</section>
```

## CSS

```css
.tabs-widget [role="tablist"] {
  align-items: flex-end;
  display: flex;
  list-style-type: none;
  margin: 0;
  padding: 0;
}
.tabs-widget [role="tablist"] > li {
  border: 0.0625rem solid hsla(204, 0%, 60%, 1);
  border-bottom: 0;
  margin-right: 0.0625rem;
  overflow: hidden;
}
.tabs-widget [role="tab"] {
  border-bottom: 0.25rem solid hsla(204, 0%, 90%, 0.5);
  border-top: 0.25rem solid hsla(204, 0%, 90%, 0.5);
  color: hsla(204, 0%, 70%, 1);
  display: block;
  font-size: 1rem;
  padding: 0.5rem;
}
.tabs-widget [role="tab"]:first-of-type {
  margin-right: 0;
}
.tabs-widget [role="tab"]:focus {
  border-bottom: 0.25rem solid hsla(204, 0%, 75%, 0.5);
  border-top: 0.25rem solid hsla(204, 0%, 75%, 0.5);
  color: hsla(204, 0%, 35%, 1);
}
.tabs-widget [role="tab"][aria-selected="true"] {
  background-color: hsla(204, 100%, 90%, 1);
  border-bottom-color: transparent;
  border-top-color: hsla(204, 100%, 30%, 0.7);
  color: hsla(204, 100%, 30%, 1);
}
.tabs-widget [role="tab"][aria-selected="true"]:focus {
  border-bottom-color: hsla(204, 0%, 75%, 0.5);
}
.tabs-widget .panels {
  border: 0.0625rem solid hsla(204, 0%, 60%, 1);
  list-style: none;
  margin: 0;
  padding: 0 0.5rem;
}
```

```css
.tabs-widget [role="tabpanel"] {
  margin: 0;
}
.tabs-widget [role="tabpanel"][tabindex="-1"] {
  display: none;
}
```

# JavaScript

```javascript
[].slice.call(document.getElementsByClassName('tabs-widget'))
.forEach(function TabsWidgetInterface(widget) {
  var SELF = this,
    onkeydown = function keydown(e) {
      var key = (e.key || e.keyCode).toString();

      switch (key) {
        case 'ArrowDown':  case '40':
        case 'ArrowRight': case '39':
          return SELF.tabs.next();
        case 'ArrowLeft':  case '37':
        case 'ArrowUp':    case '38':
          return SELF.tabs.previous();
        case 'End':        case '35':
          return SELF.tabs.last();
        case 'Home':       case '36':
          return SELF.tabs.first();
        default:
      }
    },
    list = widget.querySelector('[role="tablist"]'),
    panels = [].slice.call(widget.querySelectorAll('[role="tabpanel"]')),
    tabs = [].slice.call(list.querySelectorAll('[role="tab"]')),
    onblur = function (e) {
      var target = e.target,
        blurTo = e.relatedTarget,
        role = target && target.getAttribute ?
          target.getAttribute('role') :
          '';

      if (role === 'tab' && list.contains(blurTo)) {
        e.target.setAttribute('tabindex', -1);
      }
    }
    onclick = function (e) {
      var target = e.target,
        role = target && target.getAttribute ?
          target.getAttribute('role') :
          '';

      if (role === 'tab') {
        list.select(target.id);
      }
    },
```

```javascript
    onfocus = function (e) {
      var target = e.target,
        role = target && target.getAttribute ?
          target.getAttribute('role') :
          '';

      if (role === 'tab') {
        e.target.setAttribute('tabindex', 0);
      }
    },
    onkeydown = function (e) {
      switch (e.key) {
        case 'ArrowDown':
        case 'ArrowRight':
          e.preventDefault();
          return list.next();
        case 'ArrowLeft':
        case 'ArrowUp':
          e.preventDefault();
          return list.previous();
        case 'End':
          e.preventDefault();
          return list.last();
        case 'Home':
          e.preventDefault();
          return list.first();
        case 'Enter':
        case ' ':
          e.preventDefault();
          return list.select();
      }
    };

  Object.defineProperty(list, 'first', {
    enumerable: true,
    value: function () {
      tabs[0].focus();
      return list;
    }
  });
  Object.defineProperty(list, 'last', {
    enumerable: true,
    value: function () {
      tabs[tabs.length - 1].focus();
      return list;
    }
  });
  Object.defineProperty(list, 'next', {
    enumerable: true,
    value: function () {
      var next = list.selectedIndex + 1;

      next = next > tabs.length - 1 ? 0 : next;
      tabs[next].focus();
      return list;
    }
  });
```

```
Object.defineProperty(list, 'previous', {
  enumerable: true,
  value: function () {
    var next = list.selectedIndex - 1;

    next = next < 0 ? tabs.length - 1: next;
    tabs[next].focus();
    return list;
  }
});
Object.defineProperty(list, 'select', {
  enumerable: true,
  value: function (id) {
    var item = typeof id !== 'undefined' ?
        id :
          tabs[list.selectedIndex].id,
      num = Number(item);

    if (!Number.isNaN(num)) {
      item = (tabs[num] || {}).id;
    }

    tabs.forEach(function (tab) {
      tab.selected = tab.id === item;
    });
    panels.forEach(function (panel) {
      panel.shown = panel.controller.id === item;
    });
  }
});
Object.defineProperty(list, 'selectedIndex', {
  enumerable: true,
  get: function () {
    return tabs.findIndex(function (tab) {
      return tab.focused;
    });
  },
  set: function (value) {
    var val = Number(value),
      last = tabs.length - 1;

    if (!Number.isNaN(val)) {
      val = val < 0 ? last : val;
      val = val > last ? 0 : val;
      val = tabs[val].id;
      list.select(val);
    }
  }
});

panels.forEach(function (tabpanel, i) {
  var d = new Date().getTime(),
    name = widget.id || 'tabs-widget-' + d,
    panel = tabpanel,
    controller;

  panel.id = panel.id || name + '-panel' + i;
```

```
      controller = tabs.find(function (tab) {
        return tab.getAttribute('aria-controls') === panel.id ||
          panel.getAttribute('aria-labelledby').indexOf(tab.id) > -1;
      }) ||
      tabs[i] ||
      document.createElement('button');
    controller.id = controller.id || name + '-tab' + i;

    controller.setAttribute('aria-controls', panel.id);
    panel.setAttribute('aria-labelledby', controller.id);

    Object.defineProperty(controller, 'focused', {
      enumerable: true,
      get: function () {
        return this.getAttribute('tabindex') === '0';
      }
    });
    Object.defineProperty(controller, 'panel', {
      enumerable: true,
      get: function () {
        return panel;
      }
    });
    Object.defineProperty(controller, 'selected', {
      enumerable: true,
      get: function () {
        return this.getAttribute('aria-selected') === 'true';
      },
      set: function (value) {
        var val = Boolean(JSON.parse(value));
        this.setAttribute('aria-selected', val);
      }
    });
    Object.defineProperty(panel, 'controller', {
      enumerable: true,
      get: function () {
        return controller;
      }
    });
    Object.defineProperty(panel, 'shown', {
      enumerable: true,
      get: function () {
        return this.getAttribute('tabindex') === '0';
      },
      set: function (value) {
        var val = Boolean(JSON.parse(value));
        this.setAttribute('tabindex', val ? 0 : -1);
      }
    });

    controller.addEventListener('blur', onblur);
    controller.addEventListener('click', onclick);
    controller.addEventListener('focus', onfocus);
    controller.addEventListener('keydown', onkeydown);
  });

  if (list.selectedIndex < 0) {
    list.selectedIndex = 0;
  }
});
```

# Table 🗒

## HTML for a Simple Table

```
<table
  aria-describedby="table-status"
  aria-labelledby="table-caption"
  class="banded borderless"
>
  <caption id="table-caption">10 Busiest Airports</caption>
  <thead>
    <tr role="row">
      <th aria-sort="none" role="columnheader" scope="col">
        Airport Name
      </th>
      <th aria-sort="none" role="columnheader" scope="col">
        Airport Code
      </th>
      <th aria-sort="none" role="columnheader" scope="col">
        Country
      </th>
      <th aria-sort="none" role="columnheader" scope="col">
        Passengers
      </th>
    </tr>
  </thead>
  <tbody>
    <tr role="row">
      <td>Hartsfield-Jackson Atlanta International Airport</td>
      <td>ATL</td>
      <td>US</td>
      <td class="num">104,000,000</td>
    </tr>
    <tr role="row">
      <td>Beijing Capital International Airport</td>
      <td>PEK</td>
      <td>CN</td>
      <td class="num">96,000,000</td>
    </tr>
    <tr role="row">
      <td>Dubai International Airport</td>
      <td>DXB</td>
      <td>AE</td>
      <td class="num">88,000,000</td>
    </tr>
    <tr role="row">
      <td>Los Angeles International Airport</td>
      <td>LAX</td>
      <td>US</td>
      <td class="num">84,600,000</td>
    </tr>
    <tr role="row">
      <td>Tokyo Haneda International Airport</td>
      <td>HND</td>
      <td>JP</td>
      <td class="num">85,000,000</td>
    </tr>
```

```
      <tr role="row">
        <td>Chicago O'Hare International Airport</td>
        <td>ORD</td>
        <td>US</td>
        <td class="num">80,000,000</td>
      </tr>
      <tr role="row">
        <td>London Heathrow Airport</td>
        <td>LHR</td>
        <td>GB</td>
        <td class="num">78,000,000</td>
      </tr>
      <tr role="row">
        <td>Hong Kong International Airport</td>
        <td>HKG</td>
        <td>CN</td>
        <td class="num">73,000,000</td>
      </tr>
      <tr role="row">
        <td>Shanghai Pudong International Airport</td>
        <td>PVG</td>
        <td>CN</td>
        <td class="num">70,000,000</td>
      </tr>
      <tr role="row">
        <td>Aéroport de Paris-Charles de Gaulle</td>
        <td>CDG</td>
        <td>FR</td>
        <td class="num">69,000,000</td>
      </tr>
    </tbody>
</table>
<div aria-live="polite" id="table-status" role="status">
<!-- this section is required as the table uses the Sortable interface -->
</div>
```

## HTML for a Table with Complex Multi-level Headers

```
<table
  aria-describedby="table-rg-status"
  aria-labelledby="table-rg-caption"
>
  <caption id="table-rg-caption">10 Busiest Airports</caption>
  <thead>
    <tr role="row">
      <th id="name" role="columnheader" scope="col">
        Airport Name
      </th>
      <th id="code" role="columnheader" scope="col">
        Airport Code
      </th>
      <th id="country" role="columnheader" scope="col">
        Country
      </th>
```

```
      <th id="passengers" role="columnheader" scope="col">
        Passengers
      </th>
    </tr>
  </thead>
  <tbody>
    <tr role="row">
      <th class="rowgroup" colspan="4" id="tbl-rg-grp-d" scope="colgroup">
        Domestic
      </th>
    </tr>
    <tr role="row">
      <th id="ATL" role="rowheader" scope="row">
        Hartsfield-Jackson Atlanta International Airport
      </th>
      <td headers="tbl-rg-grp-d ATL code">ATL</td>
      <td headers="tbl-rg-grp-d ATL country">US</td>
      <td headers="tbl-rg-grp-d ATL passengers">104,000,000</td>
    </tr>
    <tr role="row">
      <th id="LAX" role="rowheader" scope="row">
        Los Angeles International Airport
      </th>
      <td headers="tbl-rg-grp-d code">LAX</td>
      <td headers="tbl-rg-grp-d country">US</td>
      <td headers="tbl-rg-grp-d passengers">84,600,000</td>
    </tr>
    <tr role="row">
      <th id="ORD" role="rowheader" scope="row">
        Chicago O'Hare International Airport
      </th>
      <td headers="tbl-rg-grp-d code">ORD</td>
      <td headers="tbl-rg-grp-d country">US</td>
      <td headers="tbl-rg-grp-d passengers">80,000,000</td>
    </tr>
    <tr role="row">
      <th
        class="rowgroup"
        colspan="4"
        id="tbl-rg-grp-i"
        scope="colgroup"
      >
        International
      </th>
    </tr>
    <tr role="row">
      <th id="PEK" role="rowheader" scope="row">
        Beijing Capital International Airport
      </th>
      <td headers="tbl-rg-grp-i PEK code">PEK </td>
      <td headers="tbl-rg-grp-i PEK country">CN</td>
      <td headers="tbl-rg-grp-i PEK passengers">96,000,000</td>
    </tr>
```

```html
    <tr role="row">
      <th id="DXB" role="rowheader" scope="row">
        Dubai International Airport
      </th>
      <td headers="tbl-rg-grp-i DXB code">DXB</td>
      <td headers="tbl-rg-grp-i DXB country">AE</td>
      <td headers="tbl-rg-grp-i DXB passengers">88,000,000</td>
    </tr>
    <tr role="row">
      <th id="HND" role="rowheader" scope="row">
        Tokyo Haneda International Airport
      </th>
      <td headers="tbl-rg-grp-i HND code">HND</td>
      <td headers="tbl-rg-grp-i HND country">JP</td>
      <td headers="tbl-rg-grp-i HND passengers">85,000,000</td>
    </tr>
    <tr role="row">
      <th id="LHR" role="rowheader" scope="row">
        London Heathrow Airport
      </th>
      <td headers="tbl-rg-grp-i LHR code">LHR</td>
      <td headers="tbl-rg-grp-i LHR country">GB</td>
      <td headers="tbl-rg-grp-i LHR passengers">78,000,000</td>
    </tr>
    <tr role="row">
      <th id="HKG" role="rowheader" scope="row">
        Hong Kong International Airport
      </th>
      <td headers="tbl-rg-grp-i HKG code">HKG</td>
      <td headers="tbl-rg-grp-i HKG country">CN</td>
      <td headers="tbl-rg-grp-i HKG passengers">73,000,000</td>
    </tr>
    <tr role="row">
      <th id="PVG" role="rowheader" scope="row">
        Shanghai Pudong International Airport
      </th>
      <td headers="tbl-rg-grp-i PVG code">PVG</td>
      <td headers="tbl-rg-grp-i PVG country">CN</td>
      <td headers="tbl-rg-grp-i PVG passengers">70,000,000</td>
    </tr>
    <tr role="row">
      <th id="CDG" role="rowheader" scope="row">
        Aéroport de Paris-Charles de Gaulle
      </th>
      <td headers="tbl-rg-grp-i CDG code">CDG</td>
      <td headers="tbl-rg-grp-i CDG country">FR</td>
      <td headers="tbl-rg-grp-i CDG passengers">69,000,000</td>
    </tr>
  </tbody>
</table>
```

# HTML for a Table with Complex Groups

```
<h2>Table with multi-level headers and column groups</h2>
<table
  aria-describedby="table-rg-cg-status"
  aria-labelledby="table-rg-cg-caption"
  style="width: 60%"
>
  <caption id="table-rg-cg-caption">Sales</caption>
  <col><!-- region -->
  <colgroup span="3"></colgroup><!-- q1 -->
  <colgroup span="3"></colgroup><!-- q2 -->
  <thead>
    <tr role="row">
      <th id="region" role="columnheader" rowspan="2" scope="col"
        style="width: 30%"
      >
        Region
      </th>
      <th colspan="3" id="q1" scope="colgroup">
        Q1
      </th>
      <th colspan="3" id="q2" scope="colgroup">
        Q2
      </th>
    </tr>
    <tr role="row">
      <th id="jan" role="columnheader" scope="col">
        January
      </th>
      <th id="feb" role="columnheader" scope="col">
        February
      </th>
      <th id="mar" role="columnheader" scope="col">
        March
      </th>
      <th id="apr" role="columnheader" scope="col">
        April
      </th>
      <th id="may" role="columnheader" scope="col">
        May
      </th>
      <th id="jun" role="columnheader" scope="col">
        June
      </th>
    </tr>
  </thead>
  <tbody>
    <tr role="row">
      <th class="rowgroup" colspan="7" id="tbl-rg-grp-a" scope="colgroup">
        Product A
      </th>
    </tr>
    <tr role="row">
      <th id="pda-north" role="rowheader" scope="row">
        North
      </th>
      <td class="num" headers="tbl-rg-grp-a pda-north q1 jan">345</td>
      <td class="num" headers="tbl-rg-grp-a pda-north q1 feb">370</td>
```

```html
      <td class="num" headers="tbl-rg-grp-a pda-north q1 mar">370</td>
      <td class="num" headers="tbl-rg-grp-a pda-north q2 apr">345</td>
      <td class="num" headers="tbl-rg-grp-a pda-north q2 may">370</td>
      <td class="num" headers="tbl-rg-grp-a pda-north q2 jun">354</td>
    </tr>
    <tr role="row">
      <th id="pda-east" role="rowheader" scope="row">
        East
      </th>
      <td class="num" headers="tbl-rg-grp-a pda-east q1 jan">245</td>
      <td class="num" headers="tbl-rg-grp-a pda-east q1 feb">320</td>
      <td class="num" headers="tbl-rg-grp-a pda-east q1 mar">270</td>
      <td class="num" headers="tbl-rg-grp-a pda-east q2 apr">288</td>
      <td class="num" headers="tbl-rg-grp-a pda-east q2 may">325</td>
      <td class="num" headers="tbl-rg-grp-a pda-east q2 jun">204</td>
    </tr>
    <tr role="row">
      <th id="pda-south" role="rowheader" scope="row">
        South
      </th>
      <td class="num" headers="tbl-rg-grp-a pda-south q1 jan">222</td>
      <td class="num" headers="tbl-rg-grp-a pda-south q1 feb">297</td>
      <td class="num" headers="tbl-rg-grp-a pda-south q1 mar">255</td>
      <td class="num" headers="tbl-rg-grp-a pda-south q2 apr">325</td>
      <td class="num" headers="tbl-rg-grp-a pda-south q2 may">226</td>
      <td class="num" headers="tbl-rg-grp-a pda-south q2 jun">250</td>
    </tr>
    <tr role="row">
      <th id="pda-west" role="rowheader" scope="row">
        West
      </th>
      <td class="num" headers="tbl-rg-grp-a pda-west q1 jan">145</td>
      <td class="num" headers="tbl-rg-grp-a pda-west q1 feb">220</td>
      <td class="num" headers="tbl-rg-grp-a pda-west q1 mar">170</td>
      <td class="num" headers="tbl-rg-grp-a pda-west q2 apr">188</td>
      <td class="num" headers="tbl-rg-grp-a pda-west q2 may">225</td>
      <td class="num" headers="tbl-rg-grp-a pda-west q2 jun">114</td>
    </tr>
    <tr role="row">
      <th class="rowgroup" colspan="7" id="tbl-rg-grp-b" scope="colgroup">
        Product B
      </th>
    </tr>
    <tr role="row">
      <th id="pdb-north" role="rowheader" scope="row">
        North
      </th>
      <td class="num" headers="tbl-rg-grp-b pdb-north q1 jan">145</td>
      <td class="num" headers="tbl-rg-grp-b pdb-north q1 feb">170</td>
      <td class="num" headers="tbl-rg-grp-b pdb-north q1 mar">170</td>
      <td class="num" headers="tbl-rg-grp-b pdb-north q2 apr">145</td>
      <td class="num" headers="tbl-rg-grp-b pdb-north q2 may">170</td>
      <td class="num" headers="tbl-rg-grp-b pdb-north q2 jun">154</td>
    </tr>
    <tr role="row">
      <th id="pdb-east" role="rowheader" scope="row">
        East
      </th>
      <td class="num" headers="tbl-rg-grp-b pdb-east q1 jan">145</td>
      <td class="num" headers="tbl-rg-grp-b pdb-east q1 feb">120</td>
```

```
      <td class="num" headers="tbl-rg-grp-b pdb-east q1 mar">170</td>
      <td class="num" headers="tbl-rg-grp-b pdb-east q2 apr">188</td>
      <td class="num" headers="tbl-rg-grp-b pdb-east q2 may">125</td>
      <td class="num" headers="tbl-rg-grp-b pdb-east q2 jun">104</td>
    </tr>
    <tr role="row">
      <th id="pdb-south" role="rowheader" scope="row">
        South
      </th>
      <td class="num" headers="tbl-rg-grp-b pdb-south q1 jan">122</td>
      <td class="num" headers="tbl-rg-grp-b pdb-south q1 feb">197</td>
      <td class="num" headers="tbl-rg-grp-b pdb-south q1 mar">155</td>
      <td class="num" headers="tbl-rg-grp-b pdb-south q2 apr">125</td>
      <td class="num" headers="tbl-rg-grp-b pdb-south q2 may">126</td>
      <td class="num" headers="tbl-rg-grp-b pdb-south q2 jun">150</td>
    </tr>
    <tr role="row">
      <th id="pdb-west" role="rowheader" scope="row">
        West
      </th>
      <td class="num" headers="tbl-rg-grp-b pdb-west q1 jan">145</td>
      <td class="num" headers="tbl-rg-grp-b pdb-west q1 feb">120</td>
      <td class="num" headers="tbl-rg-grp-b pdb-west q1 mar">170</td>
      <td class="num" headers="tbl-rg-grp-b pdb-west q2 apr">188</td>
      <td class="num" headers="tbl-rg-grp-b pdb-west q2 may">125</td>
      <td class="num" headers="tbl-rg-grp-b pdb-west q2 jun">114</td>
    </tr>
  </tbody>
</table>
```

# HTML for a Table with Complex Groups and Inputs

```
<table
  aria-describedby="table-rg-cg-status"
  aria-labelledby="table-rg-cg-caption"
  style="width: 60%"
>
  <caption id="table-rg-cg-caption">Sales</caption>
  <col> <!-- region -->
  <colgroup span="3"></colgroup> <!-- q1 -->
  <colgroup span="3"></colgroup> <!-- q2 -->
  <thead>
    <tr role="row">
      <th id="region" role="columnheader" rowspan="2"scope="col"
        style="width: 30%"
      >
        Region
      </th>
      <th colspan="3" id="q1" scope="colgroup">
        Q1
      </th>
      <th colspan="3" id="q2" scope="colgroup">
        Q2
      </th>
    </tr>
```

```html
    <tr role="row">
      <th id="jan" role="columnheader" scope="col">
        January
      </th>
      <th id="feb" role="columnheader" scope="col">
        February
      </th>
      <th id="mar" role="columnheader" scope="col">
        March
      </th>
      <th id="apr" role="columnheader" scope="col">
        April
      </th>
      <th id="may" role="columnheader" scope="col">
        May
      </th>
      <th id="jun" role="columnheader" scope="col">
        June
      </th>
    </tr>
  </thead>
  <tbody>
    <tr role="row">
      <th class="rowgroup" colspan="7" id="tbl-cgi-A" scope="colgroup">
        Product A
      </th>
    </tr>
    <tr role="row">
      <th id="pda-N" role="rowheader" scope="row">
        North
      </th>
      <td class="num" headers="tbl-cgi-A pda-N q1 jan">345</td>
      <td class="num" headers="tbl-cgi-A pda-N q1 feb">370</td>
      <td class="num" headers="tbl-cgi-A pda-N q1 mar">370</td>
      <td class="num" headers="tbl-cgi-A pda-N q2 apr">345</td>
      <td class="num" headers="tbl-cgi-A pda-N q2 may">370</td>
      <td class="input">
        <input aria-labelledby="tbl-cgi-A pda-N q2 jun" name="pda-N-jun"/>
      </td>
    </tr>
    <tr role="row">
      <th id="pda-east" role="rowheader" scope="row">
        East
      </th>
      <td class="num" headers="tbl-cgi-A pda-E q1 jan">245</td>
      <td class="num" headers="tbl-cgi-A pda-E q1 feb">320</td>
      <td class="num" headers="tbl-cgi-A pda-E q1 mar">270</td>
      <td class="num" headers="tbl-cgi-A pda-E q2 apr">288</td>
      <td class="num" headers="tbl-cgi-A pda-E q2 may">325</td>
      <td class="input">
        <input aria-labelledby="tbl-cgi-A pda-E q2 jun" name="pda-E-jun">
      </td>
    </tr>
```

```html
<tr role="row">
  <th id="pda-south" role="rowheader" scope="row">
    South
  </th>
  <td class="num" headers="tbl-cgi-A pda-S q1 jan">222</td>
  <td class="num" headers="tbl-cgi-A pda-S q1 feb">297</td>
  <td class="num" headers="tbl-cgi-A pda-S q1 mar">255</td>
  <td class="num" headers="tbl-cgi-A pda-S q2 apr">325</td>
  <td class="num" headers="tbl-cgi-A pda-S q2 may">226</td>
  <td class="input">
    <input aria-labelledby="tbl-cgi-A pda-S q2 jun" name="pda-S-jun">
  </td>
</tr>
<tr role="row">
  <th id="pda-west" role="rowheader" scope="row">
    West
  </th>
  <td class="num" headers="tbl-cgi-A pda-W q1 jan">145</td>
  <td class="num" headers="tbl-cgi-A pda-W q1 feb">220</td>
  <td class="num" headers="tbl-cgi-A pda-W q1 mar">170</td>
  <td class="num" headers="tbl-cgi-A pda-W q2 apr">188</td>
  <td class="num" headers="tbl-cgi-A pda-W q2 may">225</td>
  <td class="input">
    <input aria-labelledby="tbl-cgi-A pda-W q2 jun" name="pda-W-jun">
  </td>
</tr>
<tr role="row">
  <th class="rowgroup" colspan="7" id="tbl-cgi-b" scope="colgroup">
    Product B
  </th>
</tr>
<tr role="row">
  <th id="pdb-north" role="rowheader" scope="row">
    North
  </th>
  <td class="num" headers="tbl-cgi-B pdb-N q1 jan">145</td>
  <td class="num" headers="tbl-cgi-B pdb-N q1 feb">170</td>
  <td class="num" headers="tbl-cgi-B pdb-N q1 mar">170</td>
  <td class="num" headers="tbl-cgi-B pdb-N q2 apr">145</td>
  <td class="num" headers="tbl-cgi-B pdb-N q2 may">170</td>
  <td class="input">
    <input aria-labelledby="tbl-cgi-B pdb-N q2 jun" name="pdb-N-jun">
  </td>
</tr>
<tr role="row">
  <th id="pdb-east" role="rowheader" scope="row">
    East
  </th>
  <td class="num" headers="tbl-cgi-B pdb-E q1 jan">145</td>
  <td class="num" headers="tbl-cgi-B pdb-E q1 feb">120</td>
  <td class="num" headers="tbl-cgi-B pdb-E q1 mar">170</td>
  <td class="num" headers="tbl-cgi-B pdb-E q2 apr">188</td>
  <td class="num" headers="tbl-cgi-B pdb-E q2 may">125</td>
  <td class="input">
    <input aria-labelledby="tbl-cgi-B pdb-E q2 jun" name="pdb-E-jun">
  </td>
</tr>
```

```html
<tr role="row">
  <th id="pdb-south" role="rowheader" scope="row">
    South
  </th>
  <td class="num" headers="tbl-cgi-B pdb-S q1 jan">122</td>
  <td class="num" headers="tbl-cgi-B pdb-S q1 feb">197</td>
  <td class="num" headers="tbl-cgi-B pdb-S q1 mar">155</td>
  <td class="num" headers="tbl-cgi-B pdb-S q2 apr">125</td>
  <td class="num" headers="tbl-cgi-B pdb-S q2 may">126</td>
  <td class="input">
    <input aria-labelledby="tbl-cgi-B pdb-S q2 jun" name="pdb-S-jun">
  </td>
</tr>
<tr role="row">
  <th id="pdb-west" role="rowheader" scope="row">
    West
  </th>
  <td class="num" headers="tbl-cgi-B pdb-W q1 jan">145</td>
  <td class="num" headers="tbl-cgi-B pdb-W q1 feb">120</td>
  <td class="num" headers="tbl-cgi-B pdb-W q1 mar">170</td>
  <td class="num" headers="tbl-cgi-B pdb-W q2 apr">188</td>
  <td class="num" headers="tbl-cgi-B pdb-W q2 may">125</td>
  <td class="input">
    <input aria-labelledby="tbl-cgi-B pdb-W q2 jun" name="pdb-W-jun">
  </td>
</tr>
</tbody>
</table>
```

## CSS

```css
/*
 * columns are distributed evenly by the table-layout; however, a width
 * set on a _specific_ column will override the default width
 */
table {
  border: 1px solid hsl(204, 100%, 60%);
  border-collapse: collapse;
  table-layout: fixed;
  width: 100%;
}
table caption {
  background-color: hsl(204, 100%, 90%);
  border: 1px solid hsl(204, 100%, 60%);
  color: hsl(0, 0%, 5%);
  font-size: 1.5em;
}
table td,
table th {
  border: 1px solid hsl(204, 100%, 60%);
  padding: 0.25em;
}

table.banded tbody > tr:nth-child(even) {
  background-color: hsl(204, 100%, 97%);
}
```

```css
table.borderless td,
table.borderless th {
  border: 0;
}
table:not(.borderless) caption {
  border-bottom: 0;
}
table thead [rowspan],
table thead [scope="colgroup"],
table thead tr:not(:first-of-type) > td,
table thead tr:not(:first-of-type) > th {
  border: 0;
}
table thead [scope="colgroup"]::after {
  border-top: 1px solid hsl(204, 100%, 30%);
  content: '\00A0';
  display: block;
  font-size: 0.1em;
  line-height: 0;
  margin: auto;
  width: 90%;
}

table .input {
  text-align: center;
}
table .input button,
table .input input,
table .input select {
  font-size: 1em;
  max-width: 90%;
}
table .input input[type="number"] {
  text-align: right;
}
table .num {
  text-align: right;
}
table .rowgroup {
  background-color: hsl(204, 100%, 95%);
}

table th[aria-sort="ascending"]::after {
  content: '↑';
  display: inline-block;
}
table th[aria-sort="descending"]::after {
  content: '↓';
  display: inline-block;
}
table th[aria-sort="none"]::after {
  content: '↕';
  display: inline-block;
}
table tr {
  line-height: 1.5em;
}
```

```css
table + [role="status"] {
  display: none;
  margin: 1em 0;
}
table + [role="status"].updated {
  display: block;
}
tbody th {
  text-align: left;
}
[rowspan] {
  vertical-align: bottom;
}
```

## JavaScript

```javascript
[].slice.call(document.getElementsByTagName('table'))
.forEach(function SortableTableInterface(table) {
  var description = document.getElementById(
      table.getAttribute('aria-describedby')
    ) || document.createElement('div'),
    sort = function (e) {
      var target = e.target,
        ordering = {
          ascending: 1,
          descending: -1,
          none: 0
        },
        transition = ['none', 'ascending', 'descending'],
        currentSort = target.getAttribute('aria-sort'),
        nextSort = transition.indexOf(currentSort) + 1,
        sortOrder = transition[nextSort] || transition[0],
        order = ordering[sortOrder],
        col = target ? target.cellIndex : null,
        body = table.tBodies.item(0),
        tbody = document.createElement('tbody'),
        sortAfter = 1 * order,
        sortBefore = -1 * order,
        rows = [].slice.call(body.rows).sort(function (a, b) {
          function toNum(str) {
            if (str.indexOf('.') > -1 && str.split('.').length === 1) {
              return Number(str.replace(/[,\s]/g, ''));
            } else if (
                str.indexOf(',') > -1 &&
                str.split(',').length === 1
              ) {
              return Number(str.replace(/[.\s]/g, '').replace(',', '.'));
            } else {
              return Number(str.replace(/[.,\s]/g, ''));
            }
          }

          var strA = a.cells[col].innerText,
            numA = toNum(strA),
            strB = b.cells[col].innerText,
            numB = toNum(strB);
```

```
          if (!Number.isNaN(numA) && !Number.isNaN(numB)) {
            if (numA > numB) {
              return sortAfter;
            } else if (numA < numB) {
              return sortBefore;
            }
          } else {
            if (strA > strB) {
              return sortAfter;
            } else if (strA < strB) {
              return sortBefore;
            }
          }
          return 0;
        });

      rows.forEach(function (row) {
        tbody.appendChild(row);
      });
      table.replaceChild(tbody, body);
      target.setAttribute('aria-sort', sortOrder);
      description.text = 'Sorted by ' +
        target.innerText + ': ' + sortOrder;
    };
  Object.defineProperty(description, 'text', {
    set: function (message) {
      function removeClass() {
        description.className = (description.className || '')
          .replace(/\bupdated\b/, ' ').trim();
      }

      this.innerHTML = message;
      this.className = [
        this.className,
        'updated'
      ].join(' ').trim();

      window.setTimeout(removeClass, 3000);
    }
  });

  [].slice.call(table.getElementsByTagName('th'))
  .forEach(function (th) {
    if (th.getAttribute(`aria-sort`) !== '') {
      th.addEventListener('click', sort);
    }
  })
});
```

# Timer ⚠

## HTML for a Counting Timer

```
<h3 id="elapsed">Elapsed Time</h3>
<div aria-labelledby="elapsed" class="timer" id="elapsed">
  <time class="elapsed">01:00</time>
  <time class="remaining">00:00</time>
</div>
<button type="button" onclick="window['elapsed'].start();">Start</button>
<button type="button" onclick="window['elapsed'].stop();">Stop</button>
```

## HTML for a Countdown Timer

```
<h3 id="countdown-label">Countdown Clock</h3>
<div aria-labelledby="countdown-label" class="timer" id="remain">
  <time class="elapsed" data-format="00:00:00">00:00</time>
  <time class="remaining" data-format="00:00:00">1:00:00</time>
</div>
<button type="button" onclick="window['remain'].start();">Start</button>
<button type="button" onclick="window['remain'].stop();">Stop</button>
```

## HTML for a Dual-purpose Timer

```
<h3 id="dpt">Elapsed Time</h3>
<div aria-labelledby="dpt" class="timer" id="dual">
  <time class="elapsed">00:00</time>
  <time class="remaining">01:30</time>
</div>
<button type="button" onclick="window['dual'].start();">Start</button>
<button type="button" onclick="window['dual'].stop();">Stop</button>
```

## CSS

```
.timer {
  align-items: center;
  border: 0.25rem solid hsl(204, 100%, 60%);
  border-radius: 50%;
  display: inline-flex;
}
.timer::after {
  content: '';
  display: block;
  padding-bottom: 100%;
}
.timer > time {
  display: block;
  font-family: monospace;
  padding: 0.2em;
}
```

```css
.timer .audio {
  clip: rect(0, 0, 0, 0);
  clip-path: polygon(0 0, 0 0, 0 0, 0 0);
  left: -200%;
  overflow: hidden;
  position: absolute;
}
```

## JavaScript

```javascript
[].slice.call(document.getElementsByClassName('timer'))
.forEach(function TimerInterface(timer) {
  var blnExpire = false,
    evtExpired = new CustomEvent('expired'),
    evtTick = new CustomEvent('tick'),
    intInterval,
    intElapsed, // milliseconds
    intRemaining, // milliseconds
    intSpoken, // milliseconds
    intTicked, // milliseconds from getTime
    elAudio = timer.getElementsByClassName('audio'),
    elElapsed = timer.getElementsByClassName('elapsed').item(0),
    elRemaining = timer.getElementsByClassName('remaining').item(0),
    elAudioElapsed,
    elAudioRemaining;

  function FixedArray(length) {
    return Array.apply(null, new Array(length));
  }

  // value is milliseconds
  function Time(value) {
    return {
      value: value || 0,
      toDuration: function () {
        var ts = Math.round(this.value/1000),
          prefix = ['P', '', 'T', '', ''],
          suffix = ['Y', 'D', 'H', 'M', 'S'],
          mods = [31536000, 86400, 3600, 60, 1],
          c = 0,
          amt,
          to = '';

        while (ts > 0 && c < mods.length) {
          amt = Math.floor(ts / mods[c]);
          to += prefix[c] + (amt > 0 ? amt + suffix[c] : '');
          ts -= (amt * mods[c]);
          c += 1;
        }

        return to;
      },
```

```javascript
        toString: function (format) {
          var amt,
            c = 0,
            d = (format || '').split(':').map(function (p) {
              return p.length;
            }),
            l = [0, 0, 0, 2, 2],
            missing = FixedArray(l.length - d.length),
            mods = [31536000, 86400, 3600, 60, 1],
            to = [],
            ts = Math.round(this.value/1000);

          if (format) {
            l = missing.concat(d).map(function (v) {
              return v || 0;
            });
          }
          if (ts) {
            while (c < mods.length) {
              amt = Math.floor(ts / mods[c]);
              to.push(amt);
              ts -= (amt * mods[c]);
              c += 1;
            }
          }
          return to.map(function (val, i) {
            var str = (val || l[i] ? val : '') + '',
              len = l[i] - str.length,
              fill = len > 0 ?
                FixedArray(l[i] - str.length).reduce(function (ttl) {
                    return ttl + '0';
                  }, '') :
                  '';
            return fill + str;
          }).filter(function (val, idx) {
            return !!val.length;
          }).join(':') || l.map(function (l) {
            return FixedArray(l).map(function () {
                return '0';
              }).join('');
          }).filter(function (s) {
            return !!s;
          }).join(':');
        }
    };
}

Object.defineProperty(timer, 'elapsed', {
  enumerable: true,
  get: function () {
    return new Time(intElapsed);
  },
  set: function (value) {
    var ms = Number(value || '0');

    if (!Number.isNaN(ms)) {
      intElapsed = ms;
    }
  }
});
```

```javascript
Object.defineProperty(timer, 'remaining', {
  enumerable: true,
  get: function () {
    return new Time(intRemaining);
  },
  set: function (value) {
    var ms = Number(value || '0');

    if (!Number.isNaN(ms)) {
      blnExpire = ms > 0;
      intRemaining = ms;
    }
  }
});
Object.defineProperty(timer, 'start', {
  enumerable: true,
  value: function (ts) {
    intElapsed = intElapsed || 0;
    intInterval = setInterval(tick, 1000);
    intRemaining = intRemaining || 0;
    intSpoken = new Date().getTime();
    intTicked = new Date().getTime();
  }
});
Object.defineProperty(timer, 'stop', {
  enumerable: true,
  value: function () {
    intSpoken = 0;
    clearInterval(intInterval);
  }
});

function audioCreate(elapsed, remaining) {
  if (!elapsed) {
    elAudioElapsed = document.createElement('span');
    elAudioElapsed.setAttribute('class', 'audio elapsed');
    timer.appendChild(elAudioElapsed);
  }
  if (!remaining) {
    elAudioRemaining = document.createElement('span');
    elAudioRemaining.setAttribute('class', 'audio remaining');
    timer.appendChild(elAudioRemaining);
  }
}
function audioMap() {
  var c = elAudio.length - 1;

  while (c > -1) {
    if (/\belapsed\b/.test(elAudio.item(c).className)) {
      elAudioElapsed = elAudio.item(c);
    }
    if (/\bremaining\b/.test(elAudio.item(c).className)) {
      elAudioRemaining = elAudio.item(c);
    }
    c -= 1;
  }
```

```
      if (!elAudioElapsed || !elAudioRemaining) {
        audioCreate(elAudioElapsed, elAudioRemaining);
      }
    }
    function tick() {
      var since = new Date().getTime() - (intTicked || 0),
        elapsedFormat = elElapsed.getAttribute('data-format'),
        remainingFormat = elRemaining.getAttribute('data-format');

      intTicked = new Date().getTime();
      timer.dispatchEvent(evtTick);

      intElapsed += since;
      intElapsed = Math.max(intElapsed, 0);
      elElapsed.innerHTML = timer.elapsed.toString(elapsedFormat);

      if (intRemaining) {
        intRemaining -= since;
        intRemaining = Math.max(intRemaining, 0);
        elRemaining.innerHTML = timer.remaining.toString(remainingFormat);
      } else if (blnExpire) {
        elAudioRemaining.innerHTML = timer.remaining.toString();
        blnExpire = false;
        timer.dispatchEvent(evtExpired);
      }

      if (intTicked - intSpoken > 19999) {
        if (intElapsed) {
          elAudioElapsed.innerHTML = timer.elapsed.toString();
        }
        if (intRemaining) {
          elAudioRemaining.innerHTML = timer.remaining.toString();
        }
        intSpoken = intTicked;
      }
    }
    function toMilliseconds(value) {
      var mods = [1000, 60, 60, 24],
        time = (value || '').split(':')
          .reverse()
          .reduce(function (ttl, val, idx) {
            var mod = mods.slice(0, idx + 1)
              .reduce(function (acc, cur) {
                acc *= cur;
                return acc;
              }, 1);

            ttl += Number(val) * mod;
            return ttl;
          }, 0);

      return time;
    }

    // configure the display nodes
    if (!elElapsed) {
      elElapsed = document.createElement('time');
      elElapsed.setAttribute('class', 'elapsed');
      timer.appendChild(elElapsed);
    }
```

```
  if (!elRemaining) {
    elRemaining = document.createElement('time');
    elRemaining.setAttribute('class', 'remaining');
    timer.appendChild(elRemaining);
  }

  // configure the speaking nodes
  if (!elAudio) {
    audioCreate();
  } else {
    audioMap();
  }

  elAudioElapsed && elAudioElapsed.setAttribute('role', 'alert');
  elAudioRemaining && elAudioRemaining.setAttribute('role', 'alert');

  // configure the elapsed and remaining time from the attributes
  timer.elapsed = toMilliseconds(elElapsed.innerText);
  timer.remaining = toMilliseconds(elRemaining.innerText);

  return timer;
});
```

# Toolbar ⚠

## HTML

```
<section class="toolbar"
  aria-label="Text Formatting"
  aria-controls="tools-affect-me">
  <div role="group">
    <button
      aria-label="bold"
      aria-pressed="false"
      value="bold">
    </button>
    <button
      aria-label="Italic"
      aria-pressed="false"
      value="italic"
    >
    </button>
    <button
      aria-label="Underline"
      aria-pressed="false"
      value="underline"
    >
    </button>
  </div>
  <div role="group">
    <button
      aria-label="Text align left"
      aria-pressed="true"
      value="align-left"
    >
    </button>
```

```
<button
  aria-label="Text align center"
  aria-pressed="false"
  value="align-center"
>
</button>
<button
  aria-label="Text align right"
  aria-pressed="false"
  value="align-right"
>
</button>
<button
  aria-label="Justify text"
  aria-pressed="false"
  value="align-justify"
>
</button>
</div>
<div role="group">
  <button
    aria-disabled="true"
    title="Copy selected text from textarea"
  >
    Copy
  </button>
  <button
    aria-disabled="true"
    title="Paste last copied or cut text to textarea"
  >
    Paste
  </button>
  <button
    aria-disabled="true"
    title="Cut selected text from textarea"
  >
    Cut
  </button>
</div>
<div class="font-menu" role="group">
  <div>
    <button
      aria-haspopup="true"
      aria-controls="font-list"
      aria-label="Font family"
      aria-pressed="false"
      id="font-family"
    >
      <span style="font-family: sans-serif">
        Sans-serif
      </span>
    </button>
    <ul
      aria-labelledby="font-family"
      class="submenu"
      id="font-list"
      role="listbox"
      tabindex="-1"
    >
```

```html
        <li role="option">
          <span style="font-family: sans-serif">
            Sans-serif
          </span>
        </li>
        <li role="option">
          <span style="font-family: serif">
            Serif
          </span>
        </li>
        <li role="option">
          <span style="font-family: monspace">
            Monospace
          </span>
        </li>
        <li role="option">
          <span style="font-family: fantasy">
            Fantasy
          </span>
        </li>
        <li role="option">
          <span style="font-family: cursive">
            Cursive
          </span>
        </li>
      </ul>
    </div>
    <div>
      <label for="font-size">Font Size</label>
      <select id="font-size">
        <option>0.5</option>
        <option selected="true">1</option>
        <option>1.5</option>
        <option>2</option>
        <option>2.5</option>
        <option>3</option>
      </select>
    </div>
  </div>
</section>
```

# CSS

```css
.toolbar {
  display: flex;
}
.toolbar > :not(:first-child):not(:last-child) {
  padding: 0 1em;
}
.toolbar > :last-child {
  padding-left: 1em;
}
.toolbar button,
.toolbar select {
  border-radius: 0.25em;
  font-size: 1em;
  line-height: 0;
  min-height: 1.5em;
  min-width: 1.5em;
  position: relative;
}
```

```css
.toolbar button[aria-pressed="true"] {
  background-color: hsl(0, 0%, 90%);
}

.toolbar ol,
.toolbar ul {
  list-style-type: none;
  margin: 0;
  padding: 0 0.25em;
}
.toolbar [aria-pressed] + .submenu {
  cursor: pointer;
  position: absolute;
  visibility: hidden;
}
.toolbar [aria-pressed="true"] + .submenu {
  visibility: visible;
}

/* implementation specific */
.toolbar {
  background-color: hsl(204, 100%, 90%);
  padding: 0.25em;
}
.toolbar > :not(:last-child) {
  border-right: 0.125em solid hsl(0, 0%, 75%);
  padding-right: 1em;
}
.toolbar button:not(.clicked):active::after,
.toolbar button:not(.clicked):hover::after {
  background-color: hsl(0, 0%, 95%);
  border: 1px solid currentColor;
  border-radius: 0.25em;
  content: attr(aria-label) attr(title);
  display: block;
  font-size: 0.7em;
  line-height: 1.5em;
  margin: 10% 0 0 50%;
  padding: 0.125em 0.25em;
  position: absolute;
  z-index: 1;
}
[value="align-center"]::before {
  content: '┼';
  font-weight: bold;
}
[value="align-justify"]::before {
  content: '☰';
  font-weight: bold;
}
[value="align-left"]::before {
  content: '├';
  font-weight: bold;
  margin-left: -0.5em;
}
[value="align-right"]::before {
  content: '┤';
  font-weight: bold;
  margin-right: -0.5em;
}
```

```css
[value="bold"]::before {
  content: 'B';
  font-weight: bold;
}
[value="cut"]::after {
  content: attr(aria-label);
  display: block;
}
[value="italic"]::before {
  content: 'i';
  font-family: serif;
  font-style: italic;
  font-weight: bold;
}
[value="underline"]::before {
  content: 'U';
  font-weight: bold;
  text-decoration: underline;
}
.font-menu {
  display: flex;
}
.font-menu input {
  flex-grow: 0;
  height: 1.5em;
  width: 2em;
}
.font-menu label {
  clip: rect(0, 0, 0, 0);
  clip-path: polygon(0 0, 0 0, 0 0, 0 0);
  position: absolute;
}
.font-menu ul {
  border: 0.0625em solid hsl(204, 100%, 60%);
  border-radius: 0.25em;
  margin-top: 0.5em;
}
.font-menu ul::before {
  border-bottom: 0.5em solid hsl(204, 100%, 60%);
  border-left: 0.3em solid transparent;
  border-right: 0.3em solid transparent;
  content: ' ';
  display: inline-block;
  position: absolute;
  margin-top: -0.5em;
}
.font-menu > :last-child {
  margin-left: 0.5em;
}
.toolbar [id="font-family"] li > span {
  font-size: 1rem;
  line-height: 1rem;
}
```

## JavaScript

```javascript
[].slice.call(document.getElementsByClassName('toolbar'))
.forEach(function ToolbarInterface(bar) {
  [].slice.call(bar.getElementsByTagName('*'))
  .forEach(function (tag) {
    var ctrlId = tag.getAttribute('aria-controls'),
      controls = document.getElementById(ctrlId);

    if (controls) {
      tag.controls = controls;

      // if the tag is an input, update value, else use innerHTML
      controls.addEventListener('change', function () {
        if (tag.nodeName.toLowerCase() === 'input') {
          tag.value = controls.value;
        } else {
          tag.innerHTML = controls.value;
        }
        tag.pressed = false;
      });
    }
    if (tag.getAttribute('aria-pressed')) {
      Object.defineProperty(tag, 'pressed', {
        enumerable: true,
        get: function () {
          return Boolean(JSON.parse(this.getAttribute('aria-pressed')));
        },
        set: function (value) {
          this.setAttribute('aria-pressed', Boolean(JSON.parse(value)));
        }
      });

      tag.addEventListener('click', function (e) {
        tag.pressed = !tag.pressed;
        tag.pressed && tag.controls.focus();
      });
    }
  });
});
```

# Tooltip 🔧

## HTML

```html
<span class="field">
  <label for="tid">
    Tax ID Number (required)
    <span role="tooltip" tabindex="0">
      <svg alt="" aria-hidden="true" role="presentation"
        xmlns="http://www.w3.org/2000/svg" version="1.1"
        viewBox="0 0 1024 1024"
      >
```

```
            <path d="m640.8 12.64c40.68-5.326 85.35 9.973 106.5 47.33 28.91
              51.11 12.97 122.6-40.87 156.7-41.97 26.63-98.75 28.74-137.6
              0.9018-33.6-23.9-45.5-73.5-33.7-115.1 13.7-48 56.6-83.33
              105.7-89.76zm23.7 330.9c22.1 55.7-5.4 119.8-25.3 174.7-35.6
              97.2-104.8 279-116.7 315.4-13.7 41.6-0.4 59.4 26.3 48.8
              45.6-18.5 96-98.6 131.2-124 14.4-10.4 30
              13.6 23.1 29.6-27.9 64.8-138.5 161.5-225.5 199.2-48 20.8-111.2
              35.8-157.3 14.8-38.9-17.5-45.9-60.9-40.4-97.4 16.3-107.1
              64.7-205.3 102.8-305.6 22.03-58 64.68-156.2 68-173.3
              6.1-31.3-16.2-39.1-41.1-25.7-50.4 27.2-98.4 106-125.6
              123.2-15.3 9.7-31.3-7.1-28-20.8 8-33.6 84-106.4 112-129.6
              74.4-61.6 140.7-75.3 187.3-79.51 41.41-3.781 92.42 7.921 109.2
              50.21z"
            />
          </svg>
          <span id="tid-tooltip" role="alert">
            We are required by law to collect this information; however, it
            will not be shared.
          </span>
        </span>
      </label>
      <input aria-describedby="tid-description tid-tooltip" aria-invalid=""
        id="tid" type="text"
      />
      <span role="status"></span>
      <span class="hint" id="tid-description">999-99-9999</span>
</span>
```

# CSS

```css
[role="group"] [role="tooltip"] {
  margin-left: 100%;
  top: 0;
}
[role="tooltip"] {
  align-items: center;
  clip-path: polygon(0 0, 0 1.5em, 1.5em 1.5em, 1.5em 0);
  cursor: pointer;
  display: inline-flex;
  position: absolute;
  z-index: 1;
}
[role="tooltip"] [role="presentation"] {
  align-self: flex-start;
  background: hsl(204, 100%, 90%);
  border: 0.1em solid transparent;
  border-radius: 50%;
  fill: currentColor;
  flex-grow: 0;
  flex-shrink: 0;
  line-height: 1.3em;
  height: 1em;
  padding: 0.0625em;
  width: 1em;
}
```

```css
[role="tooltip"] [role="alert"] {
  background-color: hsl(0, 100%, 100%);
  border: 0.1em solid hsl(204, 100%, 30%);
  border-radius: 0.25em;
  display: none;
  font-size: 0.8em;
  margin: 0 0.3em;
  max-width: 10em; /* change this to the max width of the tooltip text */
  padding: 0.25em;
}
[role="tooltip"] [role="alert"]::before {
  border: 0.3em solid hsl(204, 100%, 30%);
  border-bottom-color: transparent;
  border-left: 0;
  border-top-color: transparent;
  border-radius: 0;
  content: '';
  display: inline-block;
  height: 0;
  margin: 0.1em 0.6em 0.1em -0.6em;
  position: relative;
  width: 0;
}
[role="tooltip"]:active [role="presentation"],
[role="tooltip"]:focus [role="presentation"],
[role="tooltip"]:hover [role="presentation"] {
  border-color: hsl(204, 100%, 30%);
}
label [role="tooltip"] {
  margin-left: 0.25em;
}
label [role="tooltip"] [role="presentation"] {
  height: .8em;
  width: .8em;
}

/* tooltip shows on focus */
[role="tooltip"]:not(.dismissed):active,
[role="tooltip"]:not(.dismissed):focus,
[role="tooltip"]:not(.dsimissed):hover {
  clip-path: none;
  outline: none;
}
[role="tooltip"]:not(.dismissed):active [role="alert"],
[role="tooltip"]:not(.dismissed):focus [role="alert"],
[role="tooltip"]:not(.dsimissed):hover [role="alert"] {
  display: inline-flex;
}

/* tooltip shows on adjacent form element focus */
.field button:focus ~ [role="tooltip"],
.field input:focus ~ [role="tooltip"],
.field select:focus ~ [role="tooltip"],
.field textarea:focus ~ [role="tooltip"] {
  clip-path: none;
  outline: none;
}
```

```css
.field button:focus ~ [role="tooltip"] [role="alert"],
.field input:focus ~ [role="tooltip"] [role="alert"],
.field select:focus ~ [role="tooltip"] [role="alert"],
.field textarea:focus ~ [role="tooltip"] [role="alert"] {
  display: inline-flex;
}
```

## JavaScript

```javascript
[].slice.call(document.getElementsByTagName('input'))
.forEach(function DismissbleTooltipInterface(el) {
  /* loop through siblings to see if there is a tooltip */
  var sibling = el.nextElementSibling,
    dismissed = function (evt) {
      if (evt.key === 'Escape' || evt.keyCode === 27) {
        evt.className = [
          (evt.className || '').replace(/\bdismissed\b/, ' ').trim(),
          'dismissed'
        ].join(' ');
      }
    };

  while (sibling) {
    if (sibling.getAttribute('role') === 'tooltip') {
      el.addEventListener('keydown', dismissed);
      sibling.addEventListener('keydown', dismissed);
      break;
    }
    sibling = sibling.nextElementSibling;
  }
});
```

# Tree ⚠

## HTML

```html
<ul class="tree" role="tree">
  <li id="account profile" role="treeitem">
    <span>Account Profile</span>
    <ul role="group">
      <li id="contact information" role="treeitem">
        <span id="contact-info">Contact Information</span>
        <ul role="group">
          <li id="addresses" role="treeitem">
            <span id="addresses">Addresses</span>
            <ul aria-labelledby="addresses" role="group">
              <li class="p-adr" id="addresses-work" role="treeitem">
                <span>Work</span>
```

```html
        <div>
          <div class="p-org">My Company</div>
          <div class="p-street-address">123 Any St</div>
          <span class="p-locality">Anytown</span>
          <span class="p-region">AZ</span>
          <span class="p-postal-code">85999</span>
        </div>
      </li>
      <li class="p-adr" id="addresses-home" role="treeitem">
        <span>Home</span>
        <div>
          <div class="p-street-address">999 E Notalane Rd</div>
          <span class="p-locality">Anytown</span>
          <span class="p-region">AZ</span>
          <span class="p-postal-code">85999</span>
        </div>
      </li>
    </ul>
  </li>
  <li id="email" role="treeitem">
    <span id="emailaddresses">Email</span>
    <ul aria-labelledby="emailaddresses" role="group">
      <li id="email-work" role="treeitem">
        <span>Work</span>
        <div>
          noname-work@mailinator.com
        </div>
      </li>
      <li id="email-personal" role="treeitem">
        <span>Personal</span>
        <div>
          noname-personal@mailinator.com
        </div>
      </li>
    </ul>
  </li>
  <li id="telephone" role="treeitem">
    <span id="phones">Telephone</span>
    <ul aria-labelledby="phones" role="group">
      <li id="telephone-work" role="treeitem">
        <span>Work</span>
        <div>
          (999) 555-1212
        </div>
      </li>
      <li id="telephone-personal" role="treeitem">
        <span>Personal</span>
        <div>
          (602) 555-1212
        </div>
      </li>
    </ul>
  </li>
  </ul>
</li>
```

```html
      <li id="balances" role="treeitem">
        <span id="balances">Balances</span>
        <table>
          <thead>
            <tr>
              <th>Account</th>
              <th>Description</th>
              <th>Balance</th>
            </tr>
          </thead>
          <tbody>
            <tr>
              <td>PayPal</td>
              <td>USD</td>
              <td>100.00</td>
            </tr>
            <tr>
              <td>PayPal</td>
              <td>EUR</td>
              <td>999.99</td>
            </tr>
          </tbody>
        </table>
      </li>
    </ul>
  </li>
</ul>
```

## CSS

```css
.tree [tabindex] {
  border: 0.0625em solid transparent;
  box-shadow: 0 0 0.5em 0.25em transparent;
  outline: none;
}
.tree :focus {
  border: 0.0625em solid hsl(204, 100%, 30%);
  box-shadow: 0 0 0.5em 0.25em hsl(204, 100%, 30%);
  outline: none;
}
.tree ul {
  margin: 0;
}
.tree li {
  list-style-type: none;
}
[role="treeitem"][aria-expanded]::before {
  display: inline-block;
  height: 1em;
  padding: 0.125em;
  width: 1em;
}
[role="treeitem"][aria-expanded="false"]:before {
  content: '+';
}
```

```css
[role="treeitem"][aria-expanded="true"]:before {
  content: '-';
}
[role="treeitem"][aria-expanded="false"] :not(:first-child) {
  display: none;
}
```

## JavaScript

```javascript
[].slice.call(document.getElementsByClassName('tree'))
.forEach(function TreeInterface(tree) {
  var treeItems = [].slice.call(tree.getElementsByTagName('li'))
      .filter(function (li) {
        return li.getAttribute('role') === 'treeitem';
      }),
    actions = {
      close: function (e) {
        var item = e.target;

        if (item) {
          item.open = false;
        }
        return item;
      },
      end: function (e) {
        var item = treeItems[treeItems.length - 1];

        if (item) {
          item.focus();
        }
        return item;
      },
      home: function (e) {
        var item = treeItems[0];

        if (item) {
          item.focus();
        }
        return item;
      },
      moveChild: function (e) {
        var group = e.target.group,
          item = group && group.items.shift();

        if (item) {
          item.focus();
        }
        return item;
      },
```

```javascript
  moveParent: function (e) {
    var target = e.target,
      item = target.parent;

    if (item) {
      item.focus();
    }
    return item;
  },
  next: function (e) {
    var item = e.target;

    while (item && !item.next) {
      item = item.parent;
    }

    item = item && item.next;
    item.focus();
    return item;
  },
  open: function (e) {
    var item = e.target;

    if (item) {
      item.open = true;
    }
    return item;
  },
  openSiblings: function (e) {
    var siblings = e.target.siblings || [];

    siblings.filter(function (item) {
        return !item.open;
      }).forEach(function (item) {
        item.open = true;
      });
  },
  previous: function (e) {
    var item = e.target;

    while (item && !item.previous) {
      item = item.parent.group.items.pop();
    }

    item = item && item.previous;
    item.focus();
    return item;
  },
  select: function (e) {
    // update item selected
    var item = e.target;

    if (item) {
      item.selected = true;
    }
    return item;
  }
},
```

```
keys = {
  '*': actions.openSiblings,
  'ArrowDown': actions.next,
  'ArrowLeft': function (e) {
    var target = e.target;

    if (target.open) {
      actions.close(e);
    } else {
      actions.moveParent(e);
    }
  },
  'ArrowRight': function (e) {
    var target = e.target;

    if (!target.open) {
      actions.open(e);
    } else {
      actions.moveChild(e);
    }
  },
  'ArrowUp': actions.previous,
  'End': actions.end,
  'Enter': actions.select,
  'Home': actions.home,
  ' ': actions.select
},
onblur = function (e) {
  e.target.setAttribute('tabindex', -1);

  if (!tree.contains(e.relatedTarget)) {
    treeItems[0].setAttribute('tabindex', 0);
  }
},
onclick = function (e) {
  var item = e.target;

  e.stopPropagation();
  while (item &&
    item.getAttribute &&
    item.getAttribute('role') !== 'treeitem') {
    item = item.parentNode;
  }

  if (item.getAttribute('role') === 'treeitem') {
    item.open = !item.open;
  }
},
onfocus = function (e) {
  e.target.setAttribute('tabindex', 0);
},
```

```javascript
  onkeydown = function (e) {
    var handler = keys[e.key];

    if (handler) {
      e.stopPropagation();
      return handler(e);
    } else if (e.key.length === 1) {
      e.stopPropagation();
      return tree.search(e.key);
    }
  };

treeItems.forEach(function (li, c) {
  Object.defineProperty(li, 'group', {
    enumerable: true,
    get: function () {
      return [].slice.call(this.getElementsByTagName('ul'))
        .filter(function (ul) {
          return [].slice.call(ul.getElementsByTagName('li'))
            .some(function (li) {
              return li.getAttribute('role') === 'treeitem';
            });
        }).shift();
    }
  });
  Object.defineProperty(li, 'name', {
    enumerable: true,
    get: function () {
      return this.firstElementChild.innerText;
    }
  });
  Object.defineProperty(li, 'next', {
    enumerable: true,
    get: function () {
      var item = !this.open || !this.group ?
        this.nextElementSibling || this.parent.nextElementSibling :
        this.group.items[0];

      while (item &&
        item.getAttribute &&
        item.getAttribute('role') !== 'treeitem') {
        item = item.nextElementSibling;
      }
      return item;
    }
  });
  Object.defineProperty(li, 'open', {
    enumerable: true,
    get: function () {
      return this.getAttribute('aria-expanded') === 'true';
    },
    set: function (value) {
      this.setAttribute('aria-expanded', Boolean(JSON.parse(value)));
    }
  });
```

```
Object.defineProperty(li, 'parent', {
  enumerable: true,
  get: function () {
    var item = this.parentNode;

    while (item &&
      item.getAttribute &&
      item.getAttribute('role') !== 'treeitem') {
      item = item.parentNode;
    }
    return item;
  }
});
Object.defineProperty(li, 'previous', {
  enumerable: true,
  get: function () {
    var item = this.previousElementSibling || this.parent;

    while (item &&
      item.getAttribute &&
      item.getAttribute('role') !== 'treeitem') {
      item = item.previousElementSibling || item.parent;
    }
    return item;
  }
});
Object.defineProperty(li, 'selected', {
  enumerable: true,
  get: function () {
    return this.getAttribute('aria-selected') === 'true';
  },
  set: function (value) {
    this.setAttribute('aria-selected', Boolean(JSON.parse(value)));
    this.open = true;
  }
});
Object.defineProperty(li, 'siblings', {
  enumerable: true,
  get: function () {
    return this.parentNode.getElementsByTagName('li');
  }
});

[].slice.call(li.getElementsByTagName('ul'))
.filter(function (ul) {
  if (!ul.hasOwnProperty('items')) {
    Object.defineProperty(ul, 'items', {
      enumerable: true,
      get: function () {
        return [].slice.call(ul.getElementsByTagName('li'))
          .filter(function (li) {
            return li.getAttribute('role') === 'treeitem';
          });
      }
    });
  }
});
```

```javascript
      li.setAttribute('aria-expanded', false);
      li.setAttribute('tabindex', c ? -1 : 0);
      li.addEventListener('blur', onblur);
      li.addEventListener('click', onclick);
      li.addEventListener('focus', onfocus);
      li.addEventListener('keydown', onkeydown);
    });

  Object.defineProperty(tree, 'selected', {
    enumerable: true,
    get: function () {
      return treeitems.filter(function (item) {
        return item.selected;
      });
    }
  });
  Object.defineProperty(tree, 'selectedIndex', {
    enumerable: true,
    get: function () {
      return treeitems.findIndex(function (item) {
        return item.selected;
      });
    }
  });
  Object.defineProperty(tree, 'search', {
    enumerable: true,
    value: function (key) {
      var from = treeitems.findIndex(function (item) {
          return item.getAttribute('tabindex') === 0;
        }),
        match = items.slice(from)
          .find(function (item) {
            return item.name.substr(0, 1) === key;
          });

      if (match) {
        match.focus();
      }
      return match;
    }
  });
});
```

# Video ⚠

## HTML

```
<div class="video-player">
  <video aria-describedby="video-synopsis">
    <source

src="http://publicdomainmovie.net/movie.php?id=BigBuckBunny_310&type=.mp4"
      type="video/mp4"
    />
    <track

src="https://amara.org/en/subtitles/sbpf8fMnSckL/fr/3/download/Big%20Buck%
20Bunny.fr.vtt"
      kind="subtitles"
      srclang="en"
      label="English"
    />
    <p>
      Message to display when video is not supported.
    </p>
  </video>
  <div aria-hidden="true" class="captioning" role="status"></div>
  <div class="controls" role="group">
    <button
      aria-label="Play"
      aria-pressed="false"
      class="play"
      type="button"
    >
      <svg alt="" viewBox='0 0 90 90' role='presentation'>
        <path class="off" d="M 20 10 L 70 45 L 20 80 Z"/>
        <g class="on">
          <rect height="70" width="20" x="20" y="10"></rect>
          <rect height="70" width="20" x="50" y="10"></rect>
        </g>
      </svg>
    </button>
    <button
      aria-label="Stop"
      class="stop"
      type="button"
    >
      <svg alt="" viewBox="0 0 90 90" role="presentation">
        <rect height="40" width="40" x="25" y="25"></rect>
      </svg>
    </button>
    <button
      aria-label="Rewind"
      class="rewind"
      type="button"
    >
      <svg alt="" viewBox="0 0 90 90" role="presentation">
        <path d="M 80 80 L 60 65 L 60 25 L 80 10 Z"/>
        <path d="M 60 80 L 10 45 L 60 10 Z"/>
      </svg>
    </button>
```

```
<button
  aria-label="Forward"
  class="forward"
  type="button"
>
  <svg alt="" viewBox="0 0 90 90" role="presentation">
    <path d="M 10 10 L 30 25 L 30 65 L 10 80 Z"/>
    <path d="M 30 10 L 80 45 L 30 80 Z"/>
  </svg>
</button>
<button
  aria-controls="volume"
  aria-expanded="false"
  aria-label="Volume"
  class="volume"
  type="button"
>
  <div class="slider vertical" id="volume" tabindex="-1">
    <input id="vid-volume" type="hidden"/>
    <div class="value"></div>
    <div class="thumb"
      aria-valuemax="10"
      aria-valuemin="0"
      aria-valuenow="0"
      tabindex="-1"
    ></div>
  </div>
  <svg alt="" viewBox="0 0 90 90" role="presentation">
    <path d="M 9 25 L 25 25 L 41 13 L 41 69 L 25 57 L 9 57 Z"/>
    <g class="on">
      <path class="soft"
        d="M 49 33 C 52 38 52 44 49 49"
        style="fill: none; stroke-width: 0.5em;"/>
      <path class="medium"
        d="M 57 25 C 65 34 65 48 57 57"
        style="fill: none; stroke-width: 0.5em;"/>
      <path class="loud"
        d="M 65 17 C 72 23 76 32 76 41 C 76 50 72 59 65 65"
        style="fill: none; stroke-width: 0.5em;"/>
    </g>
    <path class="off"
      d="M 81 26 L 51 56 M 51 26 L 81 56"
      style="stroke-width: 0.5em;"/>
  </svg>
</button>
```

```
<button
  aria-label="Captions"
  aria-pressed="false"
  class="captions"
  type="button"
>
  <svg alt="" viewBox="0 0 90 90" role="presentation">
    <path
      d="M 10 10 L 80 10 L 80 50 L 60 50 L 35 80 L 40 50 L 10 50 Z"/>
    <line
      class="off"
      x1="10" x2="80" y1="80" y2="10"
      style="stroke-width: 0.5em;"
    />
  </svg>
</button>
<button
  aria-label="Size"
  aria-pressed="false"
  class="screen"
  type="button"
>
  <svg alt="" viewBox="0 0 90 90" role="presentation">
    <path
      class="off"
      d="M 55 35 L 65 35 L 65 30 L 80 45 L 65 60 L 65 55 L 55 55 L 55
         65 L 60 65 L 45 80 L 30 65 L 35 65 L 35 55 L 25 55 L 25 60 L
         10 45 L 25 30 L 25 35 L 35 35 L 35 25 L 30 25 L 45 10 L 60 25
         L 55 25 Z"
    />
      <g class="on">
        <path
          d="M 15 80 L 7 73 L 23 56 L 15 49 L 40 46 L 37 71 L 30 63
             Z"/>
        <path
          d="M 63 30 L 71 37 L 46 40 L 49 15 L 56 23 L 73 7 L 80 15
             Z"/>
      </g>
  </svg>
</button>
</div>
<div class="clock">
  <div class="elapsed"></div>
  <div class="field">
    <div class="slider" id="time" tabindex="0">
      <input id="vid-timestepper" type="hidden"/>
      <div class="value"></div>
      <div class="thumb"
        aria-valuemax="10"
        aria-valuemin="0"
        aria-valuenow="0"
        tabindex="-1"
      ></div>
    </div>
  </div>
  <div class="duration"></div>
</div>
</div>
</div>
```

# CSS

```css
.video-player {
  bottom: 0.5em;
  display: flex;
  flex-direction: column;
  justify-content: stretch;
  left: 0.5em;
  right: 0.5em;
  text-align: center;
  top: 0.5em;
}
.video-player.fullscreen {
  position: absolute;
}
.video-player video {
  flex-basis: 100%;
  flex: 1;
}
.video-player .captioning {
  background: hsl(0, 0%, 95%);
  color: hsl(0, 0%, 5%);
  flex-grow: 0;
  flex-shrink: 0;
  min-height: 3em;
}
.video-player .captioning[aria-hidden="true"] {
  display: none;
}
.video-player .captioning[aria-hidden="true"] + .controls .captions .off {
  display: block;
}
.video-player .controls {
  align-self: center;
  display: flex;
  flex-grow: 0;
  flex-shrink: 0;
  justify-content: center;
}
.video-player .controls > button {
  align-items: center;
  border-radius: 0.25em;
  color: hsl(204, 100%, 30%);
  display: inline-flex;
  flex-direction: column;
  min-height: 44px;
  min-width: 44px;
  position: relative;
}
.video-player .controls > button > svg {
  fill: hsl(204, 100%, 60%);
  height: 44px;
  stroke: currentColor;
  stroke-width: 2px;
  width: 44px;
}
```

```css
.video-player .controls > button:disabled {
  background-color: hsl(0, 0%, 90%);
}
.video-player .controls button .off {
  stroke: currentColor;
}
.video-player .controls button:disabled .off {
  stroke: currentColor;
}
.video-player .controls > button::after {
  content: attr(aria-label);
}
.video-player .controls [aria-pressed] .off,
.video-player .controls [aria-pressed] .on {
  display: none;
}
.video-player .controls [aria-pressed="false"] .off {
  display: block;
}
.video-player .controls [aria-pressed="true"] .on {
  display: block;
}
.video-player .controls [data-level] .off,
.video-player .controls [data-level] .on,
.video-player .controls [data-level] .on path {
  display: none;
}
.video-player .controls [data-level="off"] .off {
  display: block;
}
.video-player .controls [data-level="soft"] .on,
.video-player .controls [data-level="medium"] .on,
.video-player .controls [data-level="loud"] .on {
  display: block;
}
.video-player .controls [data-level="soft"] .on :not(.medium):not(.loud) {
  display: block;
}
.video-player .controls [data-level="medium"] .on :not(.loud) {
  display: block;
}
.video-player .controls [data-level="loud"] .on path {
  display: block;
}
.video-player .controls .forward,
.video-player .controls .rewind {
  stroke: hsl(204, 100%, 30%);
}
.video-player .controls .volume:not([data-level]) .off,
.video-player .controls .volume:not([data-level]) .on {
  display: none;
}
```

```css
.video-player .controls .slider {
  align-items: center;
  background-color: hsl(0, 0%, 99%);
  border: 0.125em solid hsl(204, 100%, 30%);
  border-radius: 0.25em;
  display: inline-flex;
  overflow: visible;
  min-height: 0.5em;
  min-width: 20em;
  position: relative;
  z-index: 2;
}
.video-player .controls .slider.vertical {
  bottom: 90%;
  display: inline-block;
  left: 50%;
  min-height: 20em;
  min-width: 0.5em;
  position: absolute;
}
.video-player .controls .slider.focus {
  outline: hsla(204, 100%, 60%, .8) auto 5px;
}
.video-player .controls .slider > .value {
  background-color: hsla(204, 100%, 75%, 1);
  color: transparent;
  height: 100%;
  position: absolute;
  width: auto; /* this will be set by js */
  z-index: 1;
}
.video-player .controls .slider > .thumb {
  background: radial-gradient(hsl(204, 100%, 30%), hsl(204, 100%, 60%));
  border-radius: 50%;
  color: transparent;
  height: 1em;
  margin-left: -0.5em;
  position: absolute;
  width: 1em;
  z-index: 3;
}
.video-player .controls .slider.vertical .value {
  bottom: 0;
  height: auto; /* this will be set by js */
  width: 100%;
}
.video-player .controls .slider.vertical .thumb {
  margin-left: -0.25em;
  margin-top: -0.5em;
  margin-bottom: -0.5em;
}
.video-player .controls .screen [class^="size-description"] {
  border: 0;
  clip: rect(0, 0, 0, 0);
  clip-path: polygon(0 0, 0 0, 0 0, 0 0);
  outline: 0;
  overflow: hidden;
  position: absolute;
  z-index: -1;
}
```

```css
.video-player .controls [aria-controls][aria-expanded="false"] > :not(svg)
{
  display: none;
}
.video-player .clock {
  align-items: center;
  align-self: center;
  display: flex;
  flex-grow: 0;
  flex-shrink: 0;
  justify-content: center;
  margin-top: 1em;
}
.video-player .clock .elapsed {
  flex-grow: 0;
  flex-shrink: 0;
  margin: 0 1em 0 0;
}
.video-player .clock .duration {
  flex-grow: 0;
  flex-shrink: 0;
  margin: 0 0 0 1em;
}
```

## JavaScript

```javascript
[].slice.call(document.getElementsByClassName('video-player'))
.forEach(function VideoInterface(player) {
  var video = player.getElementsByTagName('video').item(0),
    sources = player.getElementsByTagName('source'),
    track = player.getElementsByTagName('track').item(0),
    captioning = player.getElementsByClassName('captioning').item(0),
    clock = player.getElementsByClassName('clock').item(0)
      .getElementsByClassName('slider').item(0),
    elapsed = player.getElementsByClassName('elapsed').item(0),
    duration = player.getElementsByClassName('duration').item(0),
    controls = {
      play: player.getElementsByClassName('play').item(0),
      stop: player.getElementsByClassName('stop').item(0),
      rev: player.getElementsByClassName('rewind').item(0),
      ff: player.getElementsByClassName('forward').item(0),
      cc: player.getElementsByClassName('captions').item(0),
      screensize: player.getElementsByClassName('screen').item(0),
      volume: player.getElementsByClassName('volume').item(0)
    },
    rewinding = false,
    Time = {
      get: function () {
        var html = this.innerText || '',
          mods = [1, 60, 60, 24, 365];
```

```
      return html.split(':').reverse().reduce(function (t, v, i) {
        return t += Number(v) * mods.slice(0, i + 1)
          .reduce(function (ttl, val) {
            return ttl *= val;
          }, 1);
      }, 0);
    },
    set: function (secs) {
      var mods = [1, 60, 60, 24, 365],
        ts = mods.reverse().map(function (val, idx) {
          var amt = Math.round(secs),
            c,
            mod,
            len = -2;

          for (c = 0; c < idx; c += 1) {
            mod = mods.slice(c).reduce(function (t, v) {
              return t *= v;
            }, 1);
            amt = amt % mod;
          }
          mod = mods.slice(idx).reduce(function (t, v) {
            return t *= v;
          }, 1);
          amt = Math.floor(amt / mod).toString();
          len = Math.min(-2, amt.length * -1);

          return ('0' + amt).substr(len);
        })
        .join(':')
        .replace(/^00:(00:(00:)?)?/, '');

      this.innerHTML = ts;
    }
  };

Object.defineProperty(controls.cc, 'pressed', {
  enumerable: true,
  get: function () {
    return this.getAttribute('aria-pressed') === 'true';
  },
  set: function (value) {
    var values = ['true', 'false'],
      bool = typeof value === 'boolean' || values.indexOf(value) > -1 ?
      JSON.parse(value) :
      false;

    this.setAttribute('aria-pressed', bool);
    captioning.setAttribute('aria-hidden', !bool)
  },
});
Object.defineProperty(controls.play, 'pressed', {
  enumerable: true,
  get: function () {
    return this.getAttribute('aria-pressed') === 'true';
  },
```

```javascript
    set: function (value) {
      var values = ['true', 'false'],
        bool = typeof value === 'boolean' || values.indexOf(value) > -1 ?
          JSON.parse(value) :
          false;

      this.setAttribute('aria-pressed', bool);
      this.setAttribute('aria-label', bool ? 'Pause' : 'Play');
    },
});
Object.defineProperty(controls.screensize, 'pressed', {
  enumerable: true,
  get: function () {
    return this.getAttribute('aria-pressed') === 'true';
  },
  set: function (value) {
    var values = ['true', 'false'],
      bool = typeof value === 'boolean' || values.indexOf(value) > -1 ?
        JSON.parse(value) :
        false,
      description = [].slice.call(this.childNodes)
      .filter(function (node) {
        var pattern = bool ? /\bon\b/i : /\boff\b/i;

        return pattern.test(node.className) || pattern.test(node.id);
      }).pop(),
      describedBy = description ? description.id : null,
      rand = Math.random().toString().substr(2);

    this.setAttribute('aria-pressed', bool);
    describedBy = describedBy || 'video-volume-' + rand;
    description && this.setAttribute('aria-describedby', describedBy);
  }
});
Object.defineProperty(controls.screensize, 'fullscreen', {
  enumerable: true,
  value: function (value) {
    if (value) {
      player.requestFullscreen();
    } else if (document.fullscreenElement) {
      document.exitFullscreen();
    }
  }
});
Object.defineProperty(controls.volume, 'expanded', {
  enumerable: true,
  get: function () {
    return this.getAttribute('aria-expanded') === 'true';
  },
```

```javascript
      set: function (value) {
        var values = ['true', 'false'],
          bool = typeof value === 'boolean' || values.indexOf(value) > -1 ?
            JSON.parse(value) :
            false,
          onChange = function () {
            controls.volume.value = controls.volume.slider.value;
          };

        this.setAttribute('aria-expanded', bool);
        if (bool) {
          this.value = Math.floor(this.slider.value || video.volume * 10);
          this.slider.addEventListener('change', onChange);
          this.slider.focus();
        } else {
          this.slider.removeEventListener('change', onChange);
        }
      }
    });
    Object.defineProperty(controls.volume, 'slider', {
      enumerable: true,
      get: function () {
        return this.getElementsByClassName('slider').item(0);
      }
    });
    Object.defineProperty(controls.volume, 'value', {
      enumerable: true,
      get: function () {
        return this.slider.value;
      },
      set: function (value) {
        var l = ['off', 'soft', 'medium', 'loud'],
          level = Math.max(0, Math.min(l.length - 1, Math.ceil(value / 3))),
          amount = value / 10;

        this.setAttribute('data-level', l[level]);
        video.volume = amount;
      }
    });

    Object.defineProperty(duration, 'value', Time);
    Object.defineProperty(elapsed, 'value', Time);

    Object.defineProperty(player, 'enabled', {
      enumerable: true,
      get: function () {
        var bool = true;
        Object.keys(controls).forEach(function (name) {
          if (controls[name].disabled) {
            bool = false;
          }
        });
        return bool;
      },
      set: function (value) {
        Object.keys(controls).forEach(function (key) {
          controls[key].disabled = !value;
        })
      }
    });
```

```
player.addEventListener('fullscreenchange', function (e) {
  player.className = [
    player.className.replace(/\bfullscreen\b/, ''),
    !!document.fullscreenElement ? 'fullscreen' : ''
  ].join(' ').trim();
  controls.screensize.pressed = !!document.fullscreenElement;
});

video.addEventListener('canplay', function () {
  controls.volume.value = video.volume * 10;
  duration.value = video.duration || 0;
  clock.setAttribute('data-max', duration.value);
  player.enabled = true;
});
video.addEventListener('durationchange', function() {
  duration.value = video.duration || 0;
  clock.setAttribute('data-max', duration.value);
});
video.addEventListener('timeupdate', function () {
  /* update-progress */
  elapsed.value = video.currentTime;
  clock.value = video.currentTime;
});
track.addEventListener('cuechange', function (cue) {
  captioning.innerHTML = cue;
});

controls.cc.addEventListener('click', function (e) {
  var target = e.target;

  target.pressed = !target.pressed;
  return target.pressed;
});
controls.screensize.addEventListener('click', function (e) {
  var target = e.target,
    on = !target.pressed;

  target.pressed = on;
  controls.screensize.fullscreen(on);
  return on;
});
controls.ff.addEventListener('click', function (e) {
  video.play();
  video.playbackRate = 4;
});
controls.play.addEventListener('click', function () {
  controls.play.pressed = !controls.play.pressed;

  if (rewinding) {
    clearInterval(rewinding);
  }
  if (controls.play.pressed) {
    video.playbackRate = 1;
    video.play();
  } else {
    video.pause();
  }
});
```

```javascript
controls.rev.addEventListener('click', function (e) {
  rewinding = setInterval(function () {
    var timeIndex = Math.max(video.currentTime - .1, 0);

    video.currentTime = timeIndex;
    if (timeIndex === 0) {
      clearInterval(rewinding);
      controls.stop.click();
    }
  }, 0);
});
controls.stop.addEventListener('click', function (e) {
  controls.play.pressed = false;
  video.pause();
  video.currentTime = 0;
});
controls.volume.addEventListener('click', function (e) {
  controls.volume.expanded = true;
});
controls.volume.addEventListener('keydown', function (e) {
  if (e.key === 'Escape') {
    controls.volume.expanded = false;
  }
});
controls.volume.slider.addEventListener('blur', function (e) {
  controls.volume.focus();
  controls.volume.expanded = false;
});

player.enabled = false;
elapsed.value = 0;
duration.value = 0;
})
```

## About the Author

Robert is a philosopher, engineer, and sometimes writer who looks for ways to connect his passions into a cohesive whole.

Frustrated by the lack of comprehensive guides to web accessibility, Robert committed himself to drawing on his vast experience in the design and construction of user interfaces and thinking the problem through from every angle he could, compiling a resource that addresses the business needs, the design and content needs, and the technical coding needs for accessibility, as well as where those areas overlap, and *Thinking About Web Accessibility* was born.

Although Robert left much of his visual design activity behind when he embarked on his career in the tech industry, he has been building human-computer interfaces for nearly three decades, first as a Software Engineer and later as a User Interface engineer. In that time he has been involved with interface design and construction at various levels and covered nearly every engineering role related to development both on and off the web, from system administration and database design to building large-scale customer-facing web applications in both the public and private sectors, working for government agencies, startups, and Fortune

100 companies with US and international operations serving over 100 million active users.

Over the last twenty years, he's worked to ensure the interfaces he has built were accessible, conforming to *Section 508* or the *Web Content Accessibility Guidelines*, and he has developed a particular set of skills along the way.

When not thinking about the next interface to be built, Robert and his wife share responsibility for a small herd of children, both with and without fur, in the southwestern desert of the United States while he tries to find time to share his thoughts on social media and through smaller writing projects on his blog, *Getting Paid to Think*.